Public Education Under Siege

Public Education Under Siege

Edited by

Michael B. Katz

and

Mike Rose

A Dissent Book

PENN

UNIVERSITY OF PENNSYLVANIA PRESS

PHILADELPHIA

Published by
University of Pennsylvania Press
Philadelphia, Pennsylvania 19104-4112
www.upenn.edu/pennpress

Printed in the United States of America
on acid-free paper

2 4 6 8 10 9 7 5 3 1

Library of Congress Cataloging-in-Publication Data

Public education under siege / edited by Michael B. Katz and
Mike Rose. — 1st ed.
    pages   cm
Includes bibliographical references and index.
ISBN 978-0-8122-4527-1 (hardcover : alk. paper)
    1. Educational change—Social aspects—United States. 2.
Public schools—Social aspects—United States. 3. Teachers—
United States—Social conditions. I. Katz, Michael B., 1939– II.
Rose, Mike (Michael Anthony)
LC191.4.P82   2013
371.010973—dc23   2013011632

CONTENTS

Part II. Education, Race, and Poverty

Part III. Alternatives to Technocratic Reform

Part IV. Conclusions

Introduction

In his remarks at the Centennial Conference of the National Urban League on July 29, 2009, President Barack Obama reminded his audience that "from day one of this administration, we've made excellence in American education—excellence for all our students—a top priority." Even Republicans would not have disagreed with this choice. The imperative of educational reform became a national rallying cry issued from the left and right as politicians on both sides of the aisle claimed that a slide in the quality of American public education left the nation behind its competitors, its future prosperity imperiled. Obama backed up his clarion call with his $4 billion Race to the Top Fund and billions more for education embedded in the American Recovery and Reinvestment Act (also referred to as the economic stimulus bill). As educational reform blossomed around the country, a rough consensus emerged about the source of the problem and the direction that change should take. Blame fell heavily on teachers and especially on their unions, which, it was claimed, blocked reform by putting their own self-interest ahead of the well-being of their students. Blame extended backward to the schools of education that had trained legions of ineffective teachers, the lack of rigor that permitted "social promotion," unreliable methods for assessing student progress and teacher quality, and job tenure which protected bad teachers—deficiencies all summed up with the term accountability. Accountability required improved methods of assessment and the injection of competition into a moribund system. Reform, in short, rested on new high-stakes testing regimes and the application of market principles to public education.

High-stakes testing became national education policy with the No Child Left Behind (NCLB) legislation signed into law by president George W. Bush on January 8, 2002. NCLB dramatically expanded the federal role in education by ramping up federal education spending and promising to hold schools accountable for their students' achievement by requiring states to design and administer tests to all students in grades three through eight and assure the presence of qualified teachers in every classroom. NCLB included sanctions and other correctives to schools that failed to make adequate yearly progress. In practice, the law proved difficult to implement and appeared to have little impact on the quality of instruction in American schools. More and more states sought waivers from its provisions, which were granted in large numbers by the administration of President Obama. In 2012, the law appeared headed for major overhaul or revision.

The chapters in *Public Education Under Siege* build on and help to frame a growing reaction against a reform paradigm rooted in a market model and stressing high-stakes testing. The contributors analyze the limitations of current approaches such as the use of standardized tests to define and measure academic achievement and teacher effectiveness and, more generally, the search for technocratic or structural solutions to complex educational problems. The contributors also broaden the discussion, bringing in, for example, concerns about economic inequality, race, language diversity, parent involvement, and leadership. This book's contributions to the debate lie in its range and accessibility of its chapters, offering jargon-free short chapters on topics that should be at the center of school reform discussions, but are typically marginal, if heard at all.

Too often those who are not satisfied with the state of public education but dissent from the test-driven, market-oriented thrust of reform are branded supporters of the status quo. This is inaccurate. In fact, they see both strengths and weaknesses in the current educational reform movement. Its strengths are its refusal to be satisfied with the status quo and its commitment to the idea that all children should receive a quality education and have a capacity to learn and grow, whatever their race or ethnicity or the economic circumstances of their parents. But the reform movement also has significant weaknesses.

One of these is a narrowly economistic view of the purposes of education, or, to put it a little differently, a subordination of the democratic vision of education for citizenship that has been integral to the purposes of American public education since the days of its origins in the nineteenth century. A second problem has been an over-reliance on a particular kind of testing as the technology that will fix American education. If there is one lesson from the history of education, it is that there is no silver bullet. A regime of high-stakes testing, moreover, narrows the content of education and frustrates creative teachers, discouraging the very young people reformers want to attract to the schools. At the same time, the application of market-oriented principles proceeds without careful discussion of the limits as well as the strengths of markets. Followed to their extreme, market models call for privatization of public education. The failure to question market models reflects general inattention to issues of political economy and social justice in today's discussions of school reform. Schools are agents of mobility, but also agents of stratification. The resources available to children in different municipalities vary enormously. Despite the Civil Rights Movement, racial and ethnic segregation remain commonplace.

Public Education Under Siege grows out of articles commissioned for *Dissent* magazine, whose editors asked Michael Katz and Mike Rose to edit a series on public education. The series ran in the magazine's spring, summer, fall 2011, and winter 2012 issues. For this book, the editors commissioned additional articles. The authors are all experts on the issues about which they write, and their contributions rest on research and experience. All of them want to change the status quo, but in ways that challenge or expand the reigning ideology of school reform. They want to encourage both practitioners and students of education to question the thrust of school reform and to give them material that will assist them in broadening the conversation.

Public Education Under Siege is divided into three sections. Part I, The Perils of Technocratic Educational Reform, begins with Mike Rose's use of his observations of classrooms combined with his research to explore the negative effects of current reform initiatives on schooling. This theme is picked up in Joi Spencer's reflection on teaching mathematics to low-income African American students in the current reform environment. David Labaree argues that school reform proposals, notably value-added evaluation, ignore the actual characteristics of teaching as a complex and demanding form of professional practice, and Joanne Barkan investigates the education reform movement's "high profile, well-financed, and seriously misguided campaign to transform the [teaching] profession." Richard Kahlenberg is concerned about the "bipartisan and unfounded" assault on teachers' unions, while Kevin Welner shows how conservative think tanks have influenced the adoption of market-based approaches to school reform by "progressive" reformers. Historians Harvey Kantor and Robert Lowe offer a trenchant overview of the mixed influence of human capital thinking on federal education policy, from the Smith-Hughes Vocational Education Act in 1917 to the No Child Left Behind Act in 2001. In the section's last chapter, Janelle Scott examines the civil rights claims of market-based reformers to argue that such reforms not only are disconnected from the issues that animated historical civil rights organizing, but also fail to tap into existing and vibrant grassroots organizing around educational inequality.

Part II focuses on the intersection of education, race, and poverty. Historian Michael Katz shows why public education is part of the American welfare state and how its recent history exacerbates income inequalities by following the same market-based trajectory as the rest of the welfare state. Pamela Walters, Jean Robinson, and Julia Lamber examine the use of school finance reform to equalize educational opportunities and find that shifts in the meaning of equality have allowed opponents of finance reform to undermine its equalitarian potential. Maia Cucchiara raises uncomfortable questions about public-private relations in school reform. She uses the example of a public school in a gentrifying city neighborhood to examine the equity issues involved in using public funds to increase the school's resources in an effort to draw and hold middle-class families. Ansley Erickson compares the rhetoric of choice in the language of both desegregation and charter schools to obscure the reality of historic and present-day policies that structure inequality. In the section's closing chapter, Heather Thompson examines the impact of the huge rise in incarceration on schools and children, arguing that massive incarceration is a neglected source of the achievement gap between whites and racial and ethnic minorities.

Part III proposes alternatives to technocratic reform. In the opening chapter, prominent education reformer Deborah Meier draws on the material elsewhere in this volume to reflect on recent reforms. Tina Trujillo and Sarah Woulfin profile a principal who exercises strong leadership in creating a successful public school for English-language learners, and Claire Robertson-Kraft highlights the polarized debate on teacher unionism and proposes a model of professional unionism to reconcile opposing positions. Paul Skilton-Sylvester cuts through polarities in the charter school debate with his description of how the environmental mission of a K-8 charter school has helped the faculty hold their ground against pressures to narrow the curriculum to achieve higher test scores. Pedro Noguera connects the achievement gap to broader patterns of inequality in American society and presents lessons learned from schools that successfully educate poor children of color, while Eugene Garcia argues that reductive language policies have restricted learning and contributed to inequality of outcomes for English-language learners. The last two chapters focus on the role of public accountability and low-income parents in school reform. Eva Gold, Jeffrey Henig, and Elaine Simon draw on their research on mayor Michael Bloomberg's assumption of control of the New York City public schools, and Rema Reynolds and Tyrone Howard give examples of the work of low-income parents in reforming their local schools.

In the final section, the editors look at what these chapters collectively tell us about education reform, followed by Mike Rose's advice to young teachers.

PART I

The Perils of Technocratic Educational Reform

Chapter 1

The Mismeasure of Teaching and Learning: How Contemporary School Reform Fails the Test

Mike Rose

The good classroom is rich in small moments of intelligence and care. There is the big stuff of course—the week-long science experiment, the dramalogue, the reporting of one's research—but important as well are the spontaneous question, the inviting gesture, the tone in a voice. They reveal the cognitive and philosophical intimacy of a room.

In the border town of Calexico, California, third-grade teacher Elena Castro is working with a group of students when a boy who is still learning English comes over from a book he's reading to ask what the word "admire" means. She turns and gives him a definition and, as he is walking away, she calls after him to ask if he admires the farmer in a story the class had read that morning.

In a combined middle-school classroom in Chicago, Kim Day and Dianna Shulla begin class by listening to their students' distress about a new bus schedule that is getting some kids home late and missing other stops entirely. The teachers suggest that the class discuss the problem and try to develop some strategies to solve it. Several students raise their hands. Dianna walks close to them, leans in slightly, and says, "Talk to me."

In a one-room schoolhouse in Polaris, Montana, Andy Bayliss is having his students keep a journal on the willows in the creek behind the school. He is working with one of the older students; both are bent over the boy's sketches and measurements. Andy points to one nicely detailed drawing and asks his student why he thinks the willows grow in these dense clusters, rather than long and snaky up a tree. The boy has fished in these creeks for years, Andy later explains, and "I just wanted him to take a little different look at what he already knows."

Back in Chicago, high school mathematics teacher Michelle Smith is calling her class to order and sees that a young man who plays the class clown is sitting way in the back. She calls him by name, then, with a flourish says, "My young gentleman, I'd like you to sit up here where I can see you." The student groans, uncurls himself from his desk, and walks to the front, sauntering for the benefit of his peers. "C'mon darlin'," Smith adds, head tilted, hand on hip, "humor me." She watches; he sits. "Thank you, sir. I feel better." Then, "OK, people. We have work to do today. Let's go!"

Stephanie Terry's first-grade classroom in Baltimore, Maryland, is packed with books, botanical experiments, and children's drawings and writing. There are areas in the room for students to read, to do science, to write and read their writing aloud. On this day, she introduces a visiting writer to the class. "We're going to have an author stay with us." "Ooooo, Miss Terry," one of the students exclaims, waving his hand, "We're authors, too!"

These vignettes are drawn from my book *Possible Lives*, an account of a cross-country journey observing good teachers, and, through their work, trying to capture the meaning of public education in our time. Such episodes are commonplace, available to anyone who would take the time to see them. In the first vignette, a teacher creates a moment of instruction on the fly, leading a student to apply a word he has just learned. In that Chicago middle school, an erratic bus schedule is turned into a problem to solve collaboratively—and what students have to say is invited and taken seriously. In rural Montana, a science experiment leads a boy to see the familiar in a new light. Next, a math teacher, with a mix of humor and direction, deftly allows a young man to save face while bringing order to her classroom. And finally, the embrace of literacy is revealed as a first-grader claims the role of an author.

It might come as a surprise to some that, given the thirty-year drumbeat of public education failure, these scenes are drawn from public schools, and that, except for the one-room schoolhouse, the schools serve low-income communities of color. It is also worth noting that, with the possible exception of the boy learning the word "admire," none of this would be captured by current measures of accountability. Yet most parents would want their children taught and treated this way.

*   *   *

This chapter is about what is missed or distorted in current school reform and the consequences for educational practice. Reform is guided by a technocratic-managerial orientation to education that is not informed by deep knowledge of the classroom, and, in fact, can be dismissive of it. This orientation has already led to some sizable policy blunders and results in a restricted definition of teaching and learning—and therefore a restricted sense of the person. It is telling, I think, that you rarely find portrayals of classroom life in the thousands of pages of school reform documents. Students and teachers are discussed, to be sure, but as abstractions, stick figures on a policy grid.

The purpose of education in this environment is thoroughly economic and, in all fairness, was so for decades before the current reforms, coinciding with our nation's precarious position in the emerging global economy. From the president to the secretary of education to governors and mayors, the purpose of education is "to prepare students for twenty-first century jobs." True, a major goal of American education is to prepare the young to make a living. But in a democracy, we send children to school for many other reasons as well: intellectual, social, civic, ethical, aesthetic. Historically, these justifications for schooling have held more importance. Not today.

The reformers are a varied lot, representing a wide range of ideology and motive—including free-marketers who would like to see public education shrunk or dismantled. But overall, reformers are addressing issues of real importance. Though they tend to downplay disparities in resources between affluent and poor districts or the effects of poverty and discrimination on young people's lives in school, they rightly target the education of low-performing students and low expectations for what these students can achieve. As well, they criticize the recruitment, education, and evaluation of teachers; the structure and the anonymity of schooling, particularly in the large high school; and the state of school governance, especially in big districts, bureaucratic inertia, and seemingly intractable school politics. No wonder that a number of prominent liberals and civil rights groups support the reforms.

But it is with the remedies, the methods of reform, that problems arise, for it is the methods, and the assumptions behind them, that directly affect what happens in the classroom. The federal No Child Left Behind Act (NCLB) provides some unfortunate examples, the features of which are present in more current reforms.

The fundamental mechanism of NCLB has been an accountability system of high-stakes standardized tests of the core subjects, mathematics and reading. How schools and districts perform on the tests has big consequences and can ultimately lead to sanctions, withholding of federal funding, and a change in leadership. The assumptions underlying NCLB are that teachers and administrators hold low expectations for their students, particularly those who are less advantaged, and aren't putting in enough effort to educate them. NCLB, its framers claim, holds administrators' and teachers' feet to the fire.

NCLB did jolt some low-performing schools to evaluate their inadequate curricula and engage in staff development aimed at improving their students' mastery of the basic math and reading skills measured by the tests. But the use of such tests and the high stakes attached to them led to other outcomes as well, and any student of organizational behavior could have predicted them. A number of education officials at various levels reacted to the high stakes by manipulating the system. They lowered the cutoff test scores for proficiency, withheld from testing students who would perform poorly, or, occasionally, flat out fudged the results. So some cases of remarkable improvement in test scores (remember the "Texas Miracle"?) turned out to be unstable or simply fraudulent, not miraculous at all.

Studies of what went on in classrooms were equally troubling—and again predictable. The high-stakes tests led many administrators and teachers to increase math and reading test preparation and reduce time on other subjects: science, history, and geography received less attention, and the arts were, in some cases, drastically reduced or eliminated. (Think here of losing that time-intensive study of the willows in the creek behind the one-room school or not having time to engage those Chicago middle-school students in solving the bus scheduling problem in their community.) Also trimmed were activities involving the core subjects of math and reading that didn't directly map onto the tests even though they could lead to broader understanding and appreciation of these subjects. Group reading, the writing of stories, and children's public reading of their stories (all of which led to the Baltimore first-grader proclaiming an author's identity) were jeopardized in the pedagogical calculus of high-stakes testing.

There is certainly an argument to be made for concentrating on the basics of math and reading, for they are so central to success in school, and an unacceptable number of students don't master them. And a score on a standardized test seems like a straightforward measure of mastery. But in addition to the kinds of manipulation I discussed, there are a host of procedural and technical problems in developing, scoring, and interpreting such tests. "In most cases," writes measurement specialist Robert Linn in the March 2000 issue of *Educational Researcher*, "the instruments and technology have not been up to the demands placed on them by high-stakes accountability." Thus there is debate among testing experts about what, finally, can be deduced from the scores about a student's or a school's achievement. Similar debates surround the currently popular use of "value-added" methods to determine teacher effectiveness (see David Labaree's and Joanne Barkan's chapters in this book for a closer examination of these methods).

There is a related issue. Tests embody definitions of knowledge and learning. A test that would include, say, the writing of an essay or a music recital or the performance of an experiment embodies different notions of instruction and achievement than do the typical tasks on standardized tests: multiple choice items, matching, fill-ins. I have given both kinds of tests. Both have value, but they get at different things, represent knowledge in different ways, and can require different kinds of teaching. When one kind of test is emphasized and the stakes are high, the tests, as we just saw, can drive and compress a curriculum.

This concern about the nature of a school's response to high-stakes pressure is especially pertinent for those students at the center of reform: poor children, immigrants, and racial and ethnic minority students. You can prep kids for a standardized test, get a bump in scores, yet not be providing a very good education. The end result is the replication of a troubling pattern in American schooling: poor kids get an education of skills and routine, a lower-tier education, while students in more affluent districts get a robust course of study.

It's important to remember how far removed standardized tests are from the cognitive give and take of the classroom. That's one reason why there is a debate as to whether a test score—which is, finally, a statistical abstraction—is really an accurate measure of learning. Yet the scores on standardized tests have become the gold standard of excellence—and this is the case for post-NCLB initiatives, most notably the Obama administration's Race to the Top Fund. Though the Department of Education is calling for multiple measures of achievement, to date the standardized tests of math and reading dominate, and because of their ease of use and aura of objectivity, there is good reason to believe they will continue to dominate.

Over the past few years, I've been privy to a lot of classrooms caught in the high-stakes machinery, so let me bring all this down to the level of a particular teacher in a particular school. Priscilla (a pseudonym) is a thirty-year veteran teaching in an elementary school in a working-class community. The school has thirty students in each of its first-, second-, and third-grade classrooms; thirty-six to forty-one children in grades four through six.

The school's test scores were not adequate last year, so the principal, under immense pressure, mandated a "scripted" curriculum, that is, a regimented curriculum focused on basic math and literacy skills followed by all teachers. The principal also directed the teachers not to change or augment this curriculum. So Priscilla cannot draw on her cabinets full of materials collected over the years to enliven, extend, or individualize instruction (although like any experienced teacher, she figures out ways to use what she can when she can). The teachers have also been directed by the principal to increase the time spent on the literacy and math curriculum and to trim back science and social studies. Art and music have been cut entirely. "There is no joy here," she told me, "only admonition." All this led her to do a remarkable thing, right out of a Jimmy Stewart movie. With her own money she flew to Washington, D.C., intent on telling the story of her school to somebody, anybody in authority. At the National Education Association, the nation's largest teachers' union, she met with one of the officers. After that, she went to the Department of Education, but was unable to find anyone there who would talk to her.

*   *   *

Just as learning and achievement get narrowly defined in this reform world, so does teaching. Priscilla's story is emblematic not only of the mechanical and restrictive pedagogy that is frequently laid on teachers in a test-driven environment but also of the attitude toward teachers and the walling off of their participation and on-the-ground knowledge. Teachers today live in a bipolar world. They are praised as central to student achievement and routinely condemned as the cause of low performance. And the overriding measure of competence or (the term used these days) effectiveness is the standardized test score in math and reading. The teacher becomes a knowl-edge-delivery system, and the better the students do, the more effective the teacher is judged to be.

No doubt, a focus on the K-12 teacher is an important feature of cur-rent school reform. Though parental income continues to be the strongest predictor of academic achievement, within the school the teacher is key. And in comparison to countries such as Finland and South Korea, whose educational system our policy makers admire, teachers in the United States are paid less, have less substantial professional development, and enjoy less occupational status. So it could be a good thing to have the teacher's role acknowledged on a national scale. And, as noted, some of the problems the reformers target are important ones. There is wide variation in competence in the teaching profession. How could there not be with a work force of close to four million, the largest profession in the country?

Many of these teachers—but by no means all—work within a poorly exe-cuted evaluation system, and they complain about inadequate assessment of their performance and, therefore, inadequate guidance. One reason for this state of affairs is that principals are so awash in administrative duties that they have neither the time to conduct careful evaluations nor the training to do what their title originally signified: be the principal teacher, able to pro-vide guidance about pedagogy. The current managerial orientation of school reform will do little to remedy that.

*   *   *

Sadly, it is true that some teachers hold low expectations for their students, especially those who are less advantaged. I remember sitting in Elena Castro's warm and stimulating classroom—she's the teacher mentioned at the open-ing of this chapter who asked her student to apply the word "admire"—when a group of teachers from a neighboring district with similar working-class demographics walked through on a visit. I heard one of the visitors whisper to another, "Our students couldn't handle this." Low expectations can come from out-and-out bigotry, jaded weariness, or misguided sympathy—and the reformers are right to assail them.

I want to dwell on this business of low expectations for a moment lon-ger—particularly on NCLB's response to them, for the NCLB approach re-veals a lot about the one-dimensional way teachers are understood in our reform environment. For NCLB, it is lack of effort and low expectations that lead to low student achievement. That's quite a claim, given all the other factors that contribute to student achievement, but let's grant it momentarily. You'll recall that the mechanism that will correct those low expectations is the threat of high-stakes testing. This is a pretty simplified notion of motivation: raise your expectations or you'll be punished, what a friend of mine calls the caveman theory of motivation. And there's an even more simplistic theory of cognitive and behavioral change at work: threat will lead to a change in beliefs, whether these beliefs come from prejudice or pity.

This kind of reductive understanding of teachers and teaching characterizes a good deal of post-NCLB reform as well. I'll select two phenomena in current reform as illustration: the discounting of experience and the attempt to determine effective teaching practices.

For the standardized test score to be locked in as the reigning measure of teacher effectiveness, other indicators of competence need to be discounted. One is seniority—which reformers believe, not without reason, overly constrains an administrator's hiring decisions. Another is post-baccalaureate degrees and certifications in education, a field many reformers hold in contempt. Fortunately for the reformers, there are studies that do report low correlations between experience (defined as years in the profession) and student test scores. There are also studies that report similarly low correlations between student scores and post-baccalaureate degrees and certifications. These studies lead to an absolute claim heard frequently these days that neither experience nor schooling beyond the bachelor's degree make any difference in teacher effectiveness—and that the test score remains our only legitimate measure of competence.

On the face of it, this is a remarkable assertion. Can you think of any other profession—from hair styling to fire fighting to neurosurgery—where we wouldn't value experience and training? If reformers had a more comprehensive understanding of teaching, they would at least consider the possibility that something is amiss with the studies. The problem is that the studies for the most part deal in simple aggregates and define experience or training in crude ways. Experience is defined as years on the job, and it's no surprise that years alone don't mean much. But if you define experience in one of the ways *Webster's New World College Dictionary* suggests—"activity that includes training, observation of practice, and personal participation and knowledge gained from this"—then you would most likely find a connection between experience and competence. What people *do* with their time on the job is crucial and becomes the foundation of expertise. As for the question about post-baccalaureate work, the same principle applies: What kind of training? Where? What was the curriculum? The quality of supervision? I'll be the first to admit that a number of education programs leave a lot to be desired, but to discount experience and training in blanket fashion is not only wrong-headed but also undercuts attempts to create better working conditions for teachers, more robust professional development, and opportunities for career advancement—all things the reformers say they want.

The qualities of good work—study and experimentation, the accumulation of knowledge, and refinement of skill—are thinly represented in descriptions of teacher quality, overshadowed by an often inadequately understood language of testing. In a similar vein, it is telling that the long history of Western thought on education—from Plato to Septima Clark—is rarely if ever mentioned in the reform literature. History, experience, and inquiry are replaced with a technological metric.

The cases of experience and training provide an example of the way many of the reformers' foundational assumptions about teaching and learning are constructed. There is much made about science in current reform, talk of "data-driven decision making" and "evidence-based practice." But some policy decisions (like the expansion of charter schools) are made without much research support, and bedrock claims such as "experience and training don't matter" are based on narrowly conceived and executed analyses.

*   *   *

In March 2010 there was a long article in the *New York Times Magazine* about attempts to pinpoint the techniques that make up good teaching—from standing still when giving directions to ways to pose a math problem and call on students—and teaching those techniques to teachers. The article was titled "Building a Better Teacher," and that title captured for me both the promise and the potential limitations of a powerful strand in current school reform: a technique-and-testing orientation to improving teacher quality.

Teaching is a complex activity that, when done well, requires, among other qualities, subject matter knowledge as well as skill in teaching what you know. Teaching requires knowledge of young people's minds and hearts and, more particularly, knowledge of one's students and the ability to read them, read the dynamics of the room, and react appropriately. A good teacher holds a belief in human ability and a commitment to fostering it—and one manifestation of that belief is the creation of a safe and respectful as well as demanding classroom. Effective techniques are an important part of this mix, and good mentorship includes a close analysis of what a teacher is doing—like a coach and athlete watching a film—and providing corrective feedback. Contrary to the story reformers tell, teachers of teachers have been doing this for a long time. What is new is the strong focus on techniques, the increased role of electronic and testing technology to study them, and the attempt to define "effective" by seeking positive correlations between specific techniques or clusters of techniques and, you guessed it, students' standardized test scores. What is also new is the magnitude of the effort, punched up considerably by a $45 million project funded by the Bill and Melinda Gates Foundation. There is, indeed, a considerable push among some reformers to build a better teacher.

Because teaching does involve a good deal of craft, I'm sympathetic to this attempt to analyze useful techniques and make them available to new and developing teachers. But given the technocratic orientation of contemporary school reform, I worry that other aspects of teaching less easily observed and circumscribed—from bearing and pacing to beliefs about learning—will get short shrift. The *building* of effective teachers will occur through the accumulation of techniques. And given the need in reform-initiated research to find correlations between techniques and test scores, researchers will veer toward those techniques that are most readily definable, leading to a possible narrowing of the repertoire of techniques themselves.

There is a further issue: the use of any technique gains meaning in a particular time and place. Consider the Chicago math teacher Michelle Smith's decision to move her student from the back to the front of the room. She's rearranging seating to ensure order in the room, an activity that could be considered an effective technique for classroom management. Imagine, however, the other unpleasant ways that decision could have played out: the student refusing to move or insulting or threatening her or stirring up his comrades sitting nearby. But Smith's action occurs in the context of a relationship with the class and with that young man, a legacy of care and learning. ("Miss Smith," he later told me, "she's teaching us how to do things we couldn't do before.") Smith knows local culture, understands rituals of masculinity and the huge importance of allowing that student a little space to save face. She has developed a classroom persona that blends sass and seriousness and uses it strategically. Technique is contextual and part of a performative flow of events.

When you focus on technique without regard to context, you can get analyses like the following, taken from a column in the *New York Times*, on the Gates project. Two researchers are rating the videotape of a teacher they don't know. They zero in on a segment where she doesn't see or ignores a boy who is raising his hand repeatedly. The teacher gets a low mark on "respect and rapport." That's a legitimate possible rating. But what if that boy frequently takes up conversational space and the teacher has spoken with him about it, explaining that she can't always call on him? I and other teachers I know have done this. Then that teacher's actions would be seen in a different light—demonstrating a potential error in rating.

A further level of error can occur as we move to the center of this machine, finding what practices correlate with test scores, for the scores themselves are typically not stable. (In value-added measures, for example, a significant number of teachers who are in the top quartile of scores one year will not be in the top the next; the same holds for the bottom quartile.) And finally there is the attempt to correlate practice to test scores, which, precedent for this kind of study suggests, could yield a slew of inconsequential correlations. The research design is mechanistic and reductive—it segments human activity—and is complicated with layers of potential error.

But even if you grant my concerns, isn't it worthwhile to at least call attention to the tricks of the trade that good teachers use and make those widely available? Absolutely. And here is where we run into perhaps the most considerable problem for reformers as they turn their attention to teacher development.

* * *

The entire history of this reform movement has been built not on teacher development but rather on a punitive accountability system of high-stakes testing. (Recall the NCLB feet-to-the-fire approach to motivating teachers.) Lip service was paid to helping teachers use their students' scores to improve instruction, but little broad-scale infrastructure was put in place to enable even that kind of development to happen. In order for the current program to be successful there will need to be a sea change in attitudes toward and understanding of teachers and the teaching profession. Now would be the time to start.

Though I am disheartened by how few reformers express a robust vision of public education, there is no doubt that they are committed to education itself, and particularly for those who have not been well served by our schools. But to get the kind of teaching we saw in the opening vignettes, to make more of our schools the potent democratic institutions they can and should be, the reform movement will have to generate within itself a much richer sense of teaching and learning. We have a strong belief in our country that to find a measure for something is to understand it; we confuse counting with analysis. Education reform needs a conceptual framework that certainly would include testing and technique, but both must be embedded in the cognitive and emotional world of the classroom.

Chapter 2

Views from the Black of the Math Classroom

Joi A. Spencer

It's hard to forget Donovon (a pseudonym). He sat in the far right corner of his sixth-grade math classroom facing the wall. He was quiet and listened to the teacher's class discussions and lectures, even though he could not actually see her or engage with her. He was deemed too far behind to work with the other kids and was assigned computation problems out of an old fourth-grade textbook. Published in 1968, Donovon's tattered textbook was older than I was. On occasion, I would sit next to him and encourage him to work on the problems assigned to his classmates. Like the equation $x + 3 = 7$. I gave him a series of simpler problems, talking about all the ways one could arrive at 7 when adding, and discussed for what seemed to be the entire class period why the letter x was in the problem in the first place. And then the light went on. He realized not only what x meant, but also *why* it must equal 4. Through mathematics instructional practices centered on student thinking and sense-making versus rule-giving and recall, Donovon was able to understand the equation.

Donovon's experience in math class may have been substandard and uninspiring, but he was not missing out on much. Though they worked from a sixth-grade textbook, his classmates often copied long columns of problems from the board, solving them with predetermined steps. On this day they were told to subtract 3 from each side of the equation. No explanation was given for why the method worked, and students spent the entire session completing nearly identical problems by rote. We have all heard the argument that repetition is essential to math success. Yet, only 2 percent of the sixth-graders at Donovon's school were scoring at or above proficiency on their state math exams.

Things were not much different in the Southeast Los Angeles community next to Donovon's. Driving on the freeway, I couldn't help noticing that most of the cars were going in the opposite direction. Happy as I was to drive on a virtually empty freeway, I understood that the lack of cars going my way signaled something disturbing about the nature of life and opportunities in these communities. On the route between my freeway exit and the school, the men (both young and old) standing around on sidewalks, wandering the streets, and sometimes stretched out on bus stop benches told the story all too well. Unemployment in this community was among the highest in the nation, and the often resultant ills of poverty, incarceration, and drug abuse had taken their toll.

In a school similar to Donovon's, students sat in rows, faced with computation problems written on their whiteboard. A column of fractions with like denominators, another column with unlike denominators, a column of triple digit by double digit multiplication, and a column of long division problems— with and without decimals. After the work session, students would be called one by one to give their solutions. When a student gave a correct answer, the teacher moved on. When it was incorrect, the teacher called on a different student until the correct answer came. On occasion, a student was called to the board to write down her solution to a problem. Once the session was over, students were free to work on their homework (a set of problems virtually identical to those solved in class). Some worked. Others just waited for the bell.

In my role as a mathematics education researcher, I have spent time in lovelier places. In one assignment in the affluent Los Angeles Westside, I conducted more than twenty observations of middle school math classrooms. These observations entailed documenting the rigor of the mathematics being taught, and noting the level and depth of teacher questions. In the majority of these, students had a bounty of resources. They worked from individual up-to-date math workbooks instead of wasting time copying problems from the board. They were seated in grouped arrangements, not rows, and they worked to solve problems that pushed them to explore the real world relevance of mathematics. In one classroom, students used math to explore earthquakes and tsunami waves. In another, they investigated and subsequently made arguments about whether there were patterns in the prime numbers between

1 and 100. In still another, they used their understanding of surface area and volume to craft smaller, more economical food packaging.

In each of these classrooms, students were expected to talk with one another, propose solutions and counter-solutions, and provide justification for the solutions they finally offered. Students who receive this kind of instruction learn that mathematics is systematic, that it makes sense, and that it has relevance and application in the world. My time in these classrooms always left me frustrated that there was such a divide between the mathematics education given to some children and that given to others. To be sure, not every classroom on the Westside was exemplary. However, taken as a whole, the mathematics education in Donovon's community was so different from that on the Westside that an outsider would question how two such offerings could exist in the same town, in the same century.

Many Americans are worried about the nation's student performance in mathematics. We are bombarded by editorials, charts, blogs, and nightly CNN news stories about our children's rankings on international assessments such as the Program for International Student Assessment (PISA) and Trends in International Mathematics and Science Study (TIMSS). Charts compare our test scores to those of Japan, Korea, and more recently Finland. As in decades past, we are called on again to address this great national risk. But what do these exam scores actually demonstrate? Rather than a failure of the American system as a whole, they demonstrate a lack of equity within our system. Exam data reveal large differences between racial and ethnic minorities and white students in the United States. For example, on the 2009 PISA administration, black students' scores looked similar to those of the lowest scoring nations (approximately 50 percent of black students in the United States scored as low achieving in math). Alternatively, many students receive a world-class mathematics education in American public schools. These students score on par with many of those whose scores we envy and do well enough on their SAT and Advanced Placement tests to bypass the beginning mathematics courses at their colleges or universities.

*   *   *

Too often, students like Donovon and others in his community receive a mathematics education we should find both embarrassing and shameful. Standing between us and high mathematics PISA scores are thousands of

Donovons attending low-resourced public schools. And although I think that the unending comparisons of our test scores to other nations' don't address the real problem with mathematics education, they have been helpful in at least one regard. They have given us another opportunity to address a persistent reality of the American educational system, which is that two children residing in the same city, even attending school in the same district, can receive wildly different sets of educational opportunities.

The No Child Left Behind Act (NCLB) tied Title I funding (designated for schools serving students in poverty) to student performance on standardized exams. One rationale for this arrangement was that American taxpayers should not reward schools with funds if those schools were not providing all kids with a quality education. Put in these terms, the NCLB sounds logical. Unfortunately, its implementation has not honored the millions of students it professed to support. Arguably, the most devastating impact of the act has been on mathematics instruction and therefore mathematics learning. Because a school's only means of demonstrating growth is through raising its standardized exam scores, many have taken extreme measures to do so.

In one Title I district I visited, math lessons in classroom after classroom were presented in disconnected fashion. Little attention was given to mathematical sense-making, leaving students with the impression that mathematics was a disjointed jumble of facts and formulas. In one classroom, a teacher presented a lesson on what seemed to be equivalent fractions. Students were asked to determine the value of x in the problem $1/2 = x/4$. They were instructed to use the "criss-cross" method to find their solution. They were to multiply the numerator of the first fraction by the denominator of the second fraction (1 multiplied by 4). Likewise, they were told to multiply the denominator of the first fraction by the numerator of the second (2 multiplied by x). After this, they were told to solve for x by dividing 4 by 2. The teacher then assigned the students multiple similar problems instructing them to use the method she had taught them.

During student work time, I had a conversation with two male students who were using the teacher's method fairly successfully. I pointed to one of their answers and asked them whether the solution they found was correct. Both replied yes. I asked whether there was any other way to solve the problem. One student replied by stating that what his teacher had shown them was the way to get an answer. Probing more, I asked, "But why does the criss-cross method work?" "That's just the way you have to do it," said one of the boys.

Methods like the criss-cross may produce correct answers, but they generate little mathematical understanding. Alternative solution methods (of which there are many) could have asked students to consider which fraction over 4 would be equivalent to ½ and why? Not only would this question force students to see the relationship across the equal sign, but it would also prevent numerous computational errors sure to arise from the convoluted criss-cross method. The criss-cross method and others like it are detrimental to student growth and development in mathematics, for students are confined to solving only problems identical to the ones they have already done. Alternatively, students who understand what they are doing will not only be able to solve what is familiar, but have a means by which to attack a range of novel mathematical tasks. No teacher could ever teach his or her students how to solve every possible math problem that they will encounter, but providing students an opportunity to develop mathematical understanding positions them to approach and tackle mathematical tasks with dexterity and competence. Reductive, test-driven policies such as those embedded in NCLB sacrifice real mathematics learning for superficial, fleeting gains.

*   *   *

Implementation of NCLB has also meant a host of rigidly applied laws pertaining to access and equity. For example, teachers are taught that it is illegal not to provide all kids with access to all the mathematical standards prescribed for their grade level. In any given grade, the number of mathematical standards and sub-standards a student is expected to know can be well over seventy-five or one hundred. To protect themselves, many NCLB schools produce a pacing guide that details which standards (including textbook page numbers) teachers ought to be on for any given day in the school year. I have been in schools where principals patrol classrooms to make sure teachers are adhering to the guide. In these schools, standard after standard is presented at breakneck speed so teachers can prove to their principals that they have covered all the information in the textbook. It is little surprise that these lessons produce rote mathematical knowledge instead of rich mathematical understanding. These schools satisfy the law, but forsake the students the law was designed to serve.

NCLB implementation has succeeded in exacerbating our already bifurcated public school system. Schools that do not receive Title I funds (because they do not have substantial numbers of poor and minority children) have greater freedom to provide rigorous, thoughtful, and even creative mathematics instruction to their students. Schools with higher numbers of poor children are chained to an unimaginative, drill-based system. Given a choice of schools to teach in, it is no wonder that teachers prefer the former.

The new graduates from my university's teacher-education program almost always receive their first job placements at Title I schools, as these are the schools most likely to have openings. As teachers gain seniority, they leave the restrictive, test-driven environments of Title I schools and opt for those serving wealthier student populations. These less restrictive environments honor teachers as professionals, allowing them to make thoughtful, often individualized instructional decisions to meet the needs of their students. It is a sad fact of schooling in the United States that there has rarely been a waiting list of teachers hoping to work in schools that serve poor students or students of color. But the current NCLB implementation exacerbates the situation by further pushing seasoned teachers out of the neediest schools.

Whenever I have worked with teachers in Title I schools, there is a good deal of energy and enthusiasm in response to the teaching methods I propose. In one project, our research team conducted a series of professional development sessions over a two-year period. During these sessions, teachers worked on rigorous math problems; examined and discussed classroom videos showing dynamic, learner-based mathematics instruction; and worked on planning similar lessons with the fellow mathematics teachers at their school. Yet, when I visited the classrooms of our participants, I rarely saw teachers implementing what we had discussed.

The same happens with our pre-service math teachers. These students receive several semesters of postgraduate teacher-education instruction geared toward teaching mathematics with understanding. Yet, when I enter their classrooms, I see very few making use of the strategies, principles, and ideas they were taught. When I speak to both practicing and student teachers, I receive the same message. They love the ideas and agree that teaching mathematics for understanding is the best way to deliver instruction. However, because of the restrictions placed on them concerning standardized testing, they cannot use these techniques. They do not have time to help students *understand* the math they are doing. Their work is to introduce students (even if only in superficial ways) to the topics they might encounter on the annual exam.

*   *   *

Much of the math we were required to memorize and drudge through during our own schooling can now be done on the computer. A student can type an equation into a graphing calculator, and the calculator will display the line or curve the equation describes. The calculator can plot particular points along the line or curve as well. Software packages can display geometrical transformations and simplify long, complicated algebraic sentences. Elementary school students can go to popular sites for math homework help. They can input fraction after fraction or triple-digit multiplication problems, and the site will provide a solution and even a set of solution steps. Beginning statistics students can type long strings of numbers into free online sites that will (within moments) display the string's mean, median, mode, and standard deviation.

Perhaps one of the reasons this work is so accessible is that much of the work we were doing in math classrooms in the past did not push us to see the principles and concepts below the surface. Yes, we were computing and figuring, and many students operated at high levels of accuracy. There was a time, in the nineteenth century, in American schools when students were expected to solve long division problems without paper or pencil. Students would be presented with a problem such as 27,852 divided by 325 and asked to stand up and provide a verbal step-by-step solution. We might find this sort of exercise arduous and unnecessary today. However, when there were no calculators, and exact calculations of land or feed were necessary, this type of mental work made sense.

Which kind of mathematical work makes sense today? This question is broader than "Which math skills will graduates need to be successful in today's economy?" Rather it deals with mathematical ideas and problems a student ought to be able to navigate to be a full, functioning, and active global citizen. Undoubtedly, students today ought to have an understanding of energy sources and costs, infrastructure, wealth distribution, financial markets, and environmental issues such as global warming, over-fishing, and deforestation. They should be able to use mathematics to make thoughtful, informed decisions involving these problems. As well, at a time when we are inundated with vast amounts of information, students today ought to be able to understand and make judgments about statistical data. They should be able to ask questions about these data and discern which are important. They should be able to make the connection between their personal finances and financial decisions and those of their governments and other significant institutions. Furthermore, as members of a democracy, they should be able to use mathematics to push for more just and inclusive societies. Our current system emphasizes computational skill almost exclusively. Yet computational skill alone is not enough. Students must be able to define and solve problems, identify and represent mathematical relationships, reason logically, justify their solutions, and persist even in the face of complexity. Likewise, the work of mathematics teachers must center on the development of instructional practices that lead students to these understandings. Test preparation is not mathematics instruction for the twenty-first century.

What TIMSS and PISA have revealed is the increased need for students to have usable, high-level, complex mathematical knowledge. For example, the PISA shows that low percentages of students in the United States reach the highest levels of proficiency (levels five and six). These levels coincide most with the skills of analysis, conceptualization, modeling, and generalizing often termed twenty-first-century skills. Likewise, TIMSS collected data on mathematics curriculum, mathematics teaching, teachers' lives (including their years of experience), and students' lives (including the amount of time they devoted to homework). Researchers found that mathematics courses in the United States required less high-level mathematical thought and were focused more on giving students techniques for solving problems than on helping them understand mathematical concepts. While American teachers report familiarity with reform recommendations, very few applied those reforms in their classrooms. Interestingly, the reform recommendations of American mathematics educators and researchers were widely adopted by Japanese teachers.

*   *   *

In May 2011, I attended a conference organized by one of the leading thinkers on black education—Janice Hale. She referred to the urgency for school integration in the 1950s and 1960s, stating that in those days neither the poor black child nor the wealthy one could attend the schools they wanted. "We were all in the same boat," she said. Then, the entire black community joined together as even Martin Luther King, Jr., who had a Ph.D., couldn't enroll his kids in the elite, all-white schools in Atlanta. There was an urgency—a deep belief in the unfairness of denying a child a high quality education based on a doctrine of racial inferiority. It is possible that many of those who first crafted the accountability policies associated with NCLB had a similar sense of urgency. Their truest intent was to address the educational inequities they saw in American public K-12 education. They, like me, were tired of seeing such disparate outcomes between majority students and their minority peers. The problem, however, comes into plain view when we realize the kind of work it will take to move us from where we are educationally to where we would like to be. It cannot be a test-driven, narrow skills-focused program. Rather, it must be one that encourages a true understanding of mathematics and establishes the kind of teacher development that generates understanding in students and teachers alike.

Chapter 3

Targeting Teachers

David F. Labaree

The mantra of the current school reform movement in the United States is that high-quality teachers produce high-achieving students. As a result, we should hold teachers accountable for student outcomes, offering bonus pay to the most effective teachers and shoving the least effective ones out the door. Of course to implement such a policy needs a valid and reliable measure of teacher quality, and the reformers have zeroed in on one such measure, known as the value-added approach. According to this method the effectiveness of individual teachers is calculated by the increase in test scores students demonstrate after a year in their classroom.

Propelling this trend is a flood of research purporting to show that differences in teacher quality can lead to huge differences in the outcomes of schooling, both for students and for society. For example, in a 2010 study for the National Bureau of Economic Research, Eric Hanushek argues that a teacher judged to be strong by the value-added measure (one standard deviation above the mean) might raise the lifetime earnings of a student by $200,000. From this perspective, improving the quality of teaching promises to increase individual opportunity for the disadvantaged—which will reduce social inequality—and at the same time increase human capital—which will promote economic growth and national competitiveness. Sounds great. Of course, this calculation is based on the assumption that test scores measure the economically useful knowledge of the future worker, which is far from obvious. But arguments like these provide a big incentive to generate usable data on who's a good teacher and who's not.

All this makes the current effort to develop a simple and statistically sound measure for good teaching quite understandable. But it doesn't make the effort justifiable. The problem with this approach is that teaching is an extraordinarily complex and demanding form of professional practice whose quality is impossible to capture accurately in a simple metric. As Mike Rose highlights in his chapter in this volume, the push to develop such a metric threatens to reduce good teaching—and good education—to whatever produces higher scores on a standardized test. As a result, the value-added measure of teacher quality may end up promoting both the wrong kind of teaching and the wrong kind of schooling.

In this chapter, I explore three major questions that arise from this development. Why did the value-added measure of teaching emerge at this point in the history of American education? What are the core characteristics of teaching as a professional practice that make it so hard to perform effectively and so hard to measure accurately? And under these circumstances, what are the likely consequences of using the value-added measure of teaching?

*   *   *

Before the 1980s, Americans had been comfortable measuring the effectiveness of their schools by their broad social outcomes. As long as graduates tended to find jobs at a higher level than the jobs their parents had, then schools were seen to be promoting social opportunity. And as long as the economy grew in size and productivity, then schools were seen to be effectively producing human capital and spurring economic prosperity. Under these circumstances, which lasted from the emergence of the common school in the early nineteenth century until the 1980s, there was little reason to seek out hard data about how much students were actually learning in school.

In the 1980s, however, this began to change with the emergence of a new kind of educational reform movement that focused on raising the standards for student achievement. Starting with the 1983 report "A Nation at Risk," the idea was to set strict curriculum standards and enforce them with high-stakes tests to shore up the American economy with higher achievement. Then came the No Child Left Behind Act of 2001, which required schools to demonstrate they were distributing educational and social opportunity more equally.

This radical shift to measuring learning outcomes in schooling came about in the late twentieth century because of two converging changes in the politics of education: growing fiscal constraints and growing educational inequality. For one thing, the rising cost of financing the expansion of schooling was beginning to run into severe fiscal limits. By the end of the twentieth century, state and local governments were spending about 30 percent of their total budgets on education, at an aggregate cost of about $400 billion. Exacerbating this cost rise was the rise in educational level of the population. From 1900 to 1975 the average education level of a twenty-four-year-old rose from eight years of elementary school to two years of college. The problem is that the per-student cost of education is markedly higher as one moves up the system, from elementary to secondary to college to graduate school. As a result, schools at all levels came under pressure to demonstrate that they were producing learning outcomes that would justify the cost.

At the same time, a parallel concern emerged about radical differences in educational quality and outcomes for different groups in the population, sharply undercutting the hoary fiction that all high school or college diplomas were the same. Middle-class parents have long shown an acute awareness of this distinction and have had the means to pursue the best schools for their children. Parents with more limited resources have been stuck with their local schools, which were too often dirty, dangerous, and dysfunctional.

Under these circumstances, value-added measures of education have obvious value in potentially helping us measure the contribution a school makes to the educational and social outcomes of its students. The value-added approach seeks to take into account the educational achievement of students coming into a school or a classroom in order to measure what added contribution the school or teacher makes to student achievement. By controlling for the selection effect, this technique seeks to focus on the school's socialization effect.

The Bill and Melinda Gates Foundation has plunged $355 million into the effort to measure teacher effectiveness. Grounded in the value-added approach, this effort is using analysis of videos of teaching in individual classrooms to establish which teacher behaviors are most strongly associated with the highest value-added scores for students. And the Brookings Institution published a study in 2010 that provided support for the value-added approach. But, as Kevin G. Welner points out in his chapter in this book, the evidence for the validity of the Gates value-added measures is weak. In a 2011 review titled "Learning About Teaching," economist Jesse Rothstein from the University of

California, Berkeley performed an analysis of the Gates data that shows that 40 percent of teachers whose performance put them in the bottom quartile using the value-added measure scored in the top half by an alternative measure of student achievement. In short, the value-added approach is hardly the gold standard for measuring teacher effectiveness its supporters claim it is.

*   *   *

It's clear where this new measure of teaching effectiveness came from and why it emerged when it did. But why does it fail to capture the elements of good teaching, and why are school reformers so willing to deploy it anyway in formulating school policy?

The answer lies in the structure of the system. The nature of American teaching arose from the school system established before the Civil War, a system whose primary mission was political. Founders wanted these schools to solve the core problem of a liberal democracy: to reconcile the self-interested pursuit of personal advantage demanded by a market economy with the civic commitment to community required by a republic. In the second quarter of the nineteenth century, this problem was particularly acute, because the market was expanding rapidly and the republic was young and fragile. The idea was to create community schools that would instill republican principles in the young while also giving them a shared experience that might ameliorate growing class divisions. To accommodate the huge influx of students, and to provide a setting in which students could be taught as a group and ranked by ability, they established the self-contained classroom, graded by age. And to make sure that the school community was inclusive, they gradually made school attendance compulsory.

From this structure emerge three core characteristics of teaching in the United States: teaching is hard, teaching looks easy, and teachers are an easy target. Let me say a little about each.

Teaching Is Hard

In many ways, teaching is the most difficult of professions. In other occupations, professional success lies in the skills and knowledge of the practitioner, and outcomes are relatively predictable. Not so with teaching. Why?

Teachers depend on students for their success. Teachers can only be successful if students choose to learn. This is the core problem facing every teacher every day in every classroom. Surgeons operate on clients who are unconscious; lawyers represent clients who remain mute; teachers need to find a way to motivate students to learn the curriculum. The teacher's knowledge of the subject and skill at explaining this knowledge amount to nothing if students choose not to learn what they're taught. Student resistance to learning can come from a wide variety of sources. Maybe students don't like the subject or the teacher. Maybe they don't want to be in school at all. Maybe they're distracted by fear of a bully, hunger in the belly, or lust for the student in the next seat. Maybe they're bored to death. The reasons for not learning are endless, and the teacher's job is to find a way to understand these reasons and work around them, one student at a time.

What makes this challenge even more difficult is that the teacher's task extends beyond just getting students to learn the subject. Teaching is a people-changing profession. Education involves more than acquiring knowledge, since we ask it to take students and turn them into something else—law-abiding citizens, productive workers, ambitious achievers. Changing people's behavior, attitude, character, and cultural yearnings is a lot harder than fixing a technical problem in the human body. A surgeon can remove a diseased appendix, and a physician can prescribe a pill to cure an infection. But teaching is less like these highly esteemed and technically advanced arenas of medicine and more like the less prestigious and less certain practice of psychotherapy. For therapists, the problem is getting patients to abandon a set of practices they are unwilling or unable to manage on their own—like countering negative thoughts or calming anxiety. Changing people in these nether realms of medicine is very difficult, but these practitioners do enjoy one advantage: the patient approaches the therapist asking for help in making the change. This is not the case with teachers, where students enter class under duress.

Students are conscripts in the classroom. Students are in the classroom for a variety of reasons that often have nothing to do with wanting to learn. They are compelled by strong pressures from their parents, the job market, cultural norms, and truant officers. Also, all their friends are there, so what would they do if they stayed home? Except for rare cases, one thing that does not bring them to the classroom is a burning desire to learn the formal curriculum. As a result, unlike the clients of nearly all other professionals, they are not volunteers asking for a professional service but conscripts who have little reason to cooperate with, much less actively pursue, the process of learning teachers are trying to facilitate.

The problem is that teachers don't have much ability to impose their will on students or to make them learn. They have weak disciplinary tools, they are vastly outnumbered, and they have to deal with their students behind the doors of the self-contained classroom, without the help of colleagues. In the end, all strict discipline can achieve is maintain classroom order; inducing learning is another thing entirely. The result is that teachers have to develop a complex mechanism for motivating their students to learn.

Teachers need to develop a teaching persona to manage the relationship with their students. Teaching means finding a way to get students to want to learn the curriculum. And this requires the teacher to develop a highly personalized and professionally essential teaching persona. That persona needs to incorporate a judicious and delicately balanced mix of qualities. You want students to like you, so they look forward to seeing you in class and want to please you. You want them to fear you, so they studiously avoid getting on your bad side and can be stopped dead in their tracks with the dreaded "teacher look." You want them to find your enthusiasm for learning the subject matter so infectious that they can't help getting caught up in the process and lured into learning.

Constructing such a persona is a complex task that takes years of development. It's part of why the first years of teaching are so difficult, until the persona falls in place and becomes second nature. The problem is that there is no standard way of doing this. The persona has to be a combination of what the situation demands—grade level, subject matter, cultural and personal characteristics of the students—and what the teacher can pull together from the pieces of his or her own character, personality, and interests. It can't be an obvious disguise, because students have an eye toward the fake and place high value on authenticity, and because it has to be maintained day in and day out over the years of a career. So the persona has to be a mix of who you are as a person and what you need and want to be as a teacher.

When it all comes together, it's a marvel to behold. In his book *Small Victories*, Samuel Freedman provides a vivid portrait of the teaching persona of a New York high school English teacher named Jessica Siegel. She wears eye-catching clothing (one student asks, "Miss Siegel, do you water that dress?") and moves effortlessly between captivating and controlling her students, making wisecracks out of the corner of her mouth ("Gimme a *break*"). He calls this persona The Tough Cookie. It works for her, but successful teachers all need to find their own persona. Think about it: how can you measure this? Measurement is particularly difficult because the criteria for defining a successful professional performance are up in the air.

Teachers need to carry out their practices under conditions of high uncertainty. There is no definitive code for effective teaching practice to parallel the kinds of codes that exist in other professions. In general, professionals can defend themselves against malpractice by demonstrating they were following standard professional practice. The patient died but the physician was doing her job appropriately. Teaching has no guide for optimal professional standards. Instead, there are rules about minimum criteria of acceptable behavior: don't hit kids (in thirty of fifty states) and show up for class.

As I've said, one reason for the absence of such a code of professional practice for teachers is that the task of teaching involves the effort to manage a complex process of motivating learning in your students through the construction of a unique teaching persona. Another is the problem of trying to identify what constitutes a definitive measure of teaching success. The things that are easiest to measure are the most trivial: number of right answers on a Friday quiz, a homework assignment, or—I might add—whatever is represented in value-added test scores. These things may show something about what information students retained at that point, but they don't say anything about the long-term benefits of the class on these students. Did the teacher make students better citizens, productive workers, lifelong learners, innovative entrepreneurs? These are the outcomes we care about, but how can you measure them? Even if you could find a way to measure such outcomes later in life, how could you trace the impact that the student's fourth-grade teacher had on those outcomes?

This suggests another problem that raises the uncertainty of defining good teaching. As a society, we are not of one mind about the individual and social ends we want schools to produce. If we can't agree on ends, how can we determine whether a teacher was effective? Effective at what? One goal running through the history of American schooling is to create good citizens. Another is to create productive workers. A third is to provide individuals with social opportunity. These goals lead schools in conflicting directions, and teachers can't accomplish them all with the same methods.

One final form of uncertainty facing teachers is that we can't even agree on who is the teacher's client. In some ways, the client is the student, the object of education. But students don't contract with teachers to carry out their role; school boards do, as representatives of the community as a whole, which would make them the client. But then there are the parents, a third constituency teachers must deal with and try to please. Are teachers the agents of the child, the society that sets up the school system, or the parents who send their children to school? The answer is yes.

*   *   *

So teaching is very hard, which makes it extraordinarily difficult to construct a good measure of effective teaching. But at the same time, in the eyes of the public, teaching doesn't look that hard at all. And this makes us easy targets for anyone selling a simple mechanism for distinguishing the good teacher from the bad.

One reason teaching looks easy is that it seems to be an extension of child-rearing. You don't need professional training to be a parent, which means that being a teacher doesn't seem like a big thing. Students coming into teacher education programs are often already imbued with this spirit. I care for the kids, so I'll be a good teacher.

Another reason it looks easy is that teaching is extremely familiar. Every prospective teacher—every adult—has done a twelve-year apprenticeship of observation in the elementary and secondary classroom. We have watched teachers, up close and personal, during our formative years, and nothing about the practice of teaching seems obscure or complicated. You keep order, give out and collect assignments, talk, test, and take the summer off. No big deal. Missing from this observation, of course, is all the thinking and planning that go into the process students experience in the classroom, much less the laborious construction of the teaching persona.

A third thing that makes teaching look easy is that the knowledge and skills teachers convey are the knowledge and skills all competent adults have. This isn't the kind of complex and obscure knowledge you find in medical texts or law books; it's ordinary knowledge that doesn't seem to require an advanced degree of skill for the practitioner. Of course, missing from this kind of understanding of teaching is an acknowledgment of the kind of skill required to teach these subjects and motivate students to learn them, which is not obvious at all. But the impression of ordinariness is hard for teaching to shake.

A factor that adds to this problem is that, unlike other professionals, teachers give away their expertise. One test of a successful teacher is that the student no longer needs her. Good teachers make themselves dispensable. Other professions don't give away their expertise; they rent it by the hour. You have to keep going back to the doctor, lawyer, accountant, and even pharmacist. In these arenas, you're rarely on your own. But teachers are supposed to launch you into adult life and then disappear into the background. As a result, it is easy for adults to forget how hard it was for them to acquire the skills and knowledge they now have and therefore easy to discount the critical role that teachers played in getting them to their current state.

*   *   *

It's tough being in a profession that is extraordinarily difficult to practice effectively and that other people consider a walk on the beach. As a group, teachers are too visible to be inscrutable and too numerous to be elite. They don't have the distance, obscurity, and selectivity of the high-status professions. As a result, no one is willing to bow to their authority or yield to their expertise. Teachers, school administrators, and education professors have all had the experience of sitting next to someone on an airplane or at a dinner party who proceeds to tell them the problem with schools and offer a cure. Everyone is an expert on education except the educator.

One consequence is that teachers become an easy target for school reformers. This follows from the nature of teaching as a practice, as I've been describing here, and also from the nature of school reform as a practice. The history of school reform in the United States is a history of efforts to change the education of Other People's Children. The schools reformers' own children attend are generally seen as pretty good; the problem is with the schooling of Others. It's those kids who need more structure, higher standards, more incentives, and more coercion to bring their learning up to a useful level. They are the ones who are dragging down our cities and holding back our economic growth. And public school teachers are the keepers of Other People's Children. Since we don't think those children are getting the kind of schooling they need, teachers must be a major part of the problem. As a result, these teachers, too, are seen as needing more structure, higher standards, more incentives, and more coercion to bring their teaching up to a socially useful level.

We tell ourselves that we're paying more than we can afford for schools that don't work, so we have to intervene. The value-added measure of teacher performance is ideally suited to this task. It's needed because, in the eyes of reformers, teachers are not sufficiently professional, competent, or reliable to be granted the autonomy of a real profession. And what will be the consequences?

As in medicine, the first rule of school reform should be "Do no harm." But the value-added intervention violates this rule, driven by the arrogance of reformers who are convinced teaching is a simple process of delivering content and learning just a matter of exerting the effort to acquire this content. That approach is likely to increase test scores, simply by pressuring teachers to teach to the test. But my concern is that in the process it's also likely to interfere with their ability to lure students into learning. This requires them to develop and nurture an effective teaching persona, so they can in turn develop and nurture in students the motivation to learn and to continue learning over a lifetime.

As usual, the results of this reform are likely to be skewed by social class. Schools for the disadvantaged are going to be under great pressure to teach to the test and raise scores on core skills, while schools for the advantaged will be free to pursue a much richer curriculum. If your children, unlike "Others," are not "At Risk," then the schools they attend will not need to be obsessed with drilling to meet minimum standards. Teachers in these schools will be able to lead their classes in exploring a variety of subjects, experiences, and issues excluded from the classrooms further down the social scale. In the effort to raise standards and close the achievement gap, we will be creating just another form of educational distinction to divide the top from the bottom.

Chapter 4

Firing Line: The Grand Coalition Against Teachers

Joanne Barkan

In a nation as politically and ideologically riven as ours, it's remarkable to see so broad an agreement on what ails public schools: it's the teachers. The consensus includes Democrats from various wings of the party, virtually all Republicans, most think tanks that deal with education, progressive and conservative foundations, a proliferation of nonprofit advocacy organizations, right-wing anti-union groups, hedge fund managers, writers from right leftward, and editorialists in most mainstream media. They all concur that teachers, protected by their unions, deserve primary blame for the failure of 15.6 million poor children to excel academically. Teachers also bear much responsibility for the decline of K-12 education overall (about 85 percent of children attend public schools), to the point that the United States is floundering in the global economy.

Attention to the role of public school teachers in the last few years has escalated into a high-profile, well-financed, seriously misguided campaign to transform the profession based on this reasoning: if we can place an outstanding teacher in every classroom, the achievement gap between middle-class white students and poor and minority students will close; all students will be prepared to earn a four-year college degree, find a "twenty-first-century job" at a good salary, and help restore United States preeminence in the world economy.

Here is Barack Obama speaking at Kenmore Middle School in Arlington, Virginia, on March 14, 2011:

The best economic policy is one that produces more college graduates. And that's why, for the sake of our children and our economy
and America's future, we're going to have to do a better job educating
every single one of our sons and daughters. . . . But when the quality
of a teacher can make or break a child's education, we've got to make
sure our certified teachers are also outstanding teachers—teachers
who can reach every last child.

This chapter will investigate the fix-the-teachers campaign of today's "education reformers." It's not their only project. They also want public schools run
with the top-down, data-driven, accountability methods used in for-profit
businesses; they aim to replace as many regular public schools as possible
with publicly funded, privately managed charter schools; some are trying to
expand voucher programs to allow parents to take their per-child public-
education funding to private and religious schools. All this will reshape who
controls the approximately $525 billion spent on public elementary and sec-
ondary schools every year. It also endangers the democratic nature of public
schooling. But, most immediately, the fix-the-teachers campaign negatively
affects children in the classroom.

Some Necessary Context

Certainly everyone who supports public education believes that only effective
teachers should be in the classroom; ineffective teachers who can't improve
should lose their jobs. Accomplishing this requires a sound method for evaluating teachers and a fair, timely process for firing. School principals have
traditionally been responsible for assessing performance and dismissing inadequate teachers. Making sure that principals do this well has been the district superintendent's job (not the teachers' or the unions'). The system works
only if administrators at all levels and school boards perform competently.

Even with these assumptions stated, a productive discussion can't begin without first addressing two questions: what accounts for variations in
student achievement, and what is the overall state of K-12 education in the
United States?

On the first question, research shows that teachers are the most important *in-school* factor determining students' academic performance. But they

are not the only in-school factor: class size and the quality of the school principal, for example, matter a great deal. Most crucially, out-of-school factors—family characteristics such as income and parents' education, neighborhood environment, health care, housing stability, and so on—count for twice as much as all in-school factors. In 1966, a groundbreaking government study known as the Coleman Report first identified a "one-third in-school factors, two-thirds family characteristics" ratio to explain variations in student achievement. Since then researchers have endlessly tried to refine or refute the findings. Education scholar Richard Rothstein described their results in his 2004 book, *Class and Schools*: "No analyst has been able to attribute less than two-thirds of the variation in achievement among schools to the family characteristics of their students" (14). Factors such as neighborhood environment give still more weight to what goes on outside school.

Education reformers have only one response to this reality: anyone who brings up out-of-school factors such as poverty is defending the status quo of public education and claiming schools can do nothing to overcome the life circumstances of poor children. The response is silly and, by now, tiresome. Some teachers will certainly be able to help compensate for the family backgrounds and out-of-school environments of some students. But the majority of poor children will not get all the help they need: their numbers are too great, circumstances too severe, and resources too limited. Imagine teachers from excellent suburban public schools transferring en masse to low-performing, inner-city public schools. Would these teachers have as much success in the inner city as in the suburbs? Would they be able to overcome the backgrounds of 15.6 million poor children? Even with bonus pay, would they stay with the job for more than a few years? Common sense and experience say no, yet the reformers insist they can fix public schools by fixing the teachers.

On the second question—what is the state of education in the United States?—both critics and advocates of the reform movement agree that some public schools need significant improvement and that improvement is achievable. But in order to mobilize broad support for their program, education reformers from Obama on down have pumped up a sense of crisis about the international standing of the entire education system. In reality, however, students in American *public* schools serving middle-class and affluent children surpass students in other nations in standardized test scores (which reformers use obsessively to define success).

The most recent data come from the 2009 Program for International Student Assessment (PISA), released in December 2010. PISA tested fifteen-year-olds in sixty countries (plus five non-state entities such as Hong Kong) in reading, math, and science. Consider the results in reading, the subject assessed in depth in 2009: U.S. students in public schools with a poverty rate of less than 10 percent (measured by eligibility for free or reduced-price lunches) scored 551, second only to the 556 score of the city of Shanghai, which doesn't release poverty data. American students outperformed students in all eight participating nations whose reported poverty rates fall below 10 percent. Finland, with a poverty rate of just 3.4 percent, came in second with a score of 536. As the level of student poverty in American public schools increased, scores fell. Because of the high overall child-poverty rate (20.7 percent), the average reading score for all students in the United States was 500 (fourteenth place). In short, poverty drags down our international standing.

Find and Fire Bad Teachers the Reform Way

The education reformers have a formula for producing an outstanding teaching force: identify and dismiss all bad teachers, replace them with excellent ones, keep the latter on staff by paying them more, and evaluate everyone regularly to make sure no teacher is slipping. Private schools supposedly have the freedom to do this. But public schools, according to the reform credo, are hamstrung by three protections for teachers, which are written into union contracts and many state laws: due process (imprecisely called tenure), seniority, and set salary scales. (Teachers receive due process after several years of probation; it guarantees they will not be fired without a fair hearing to determine just cause, and they do not have to reapply for their jobs every year. Seniority lists teachers according to how long they've been teaching; when a district imposes layoffs, teachers with less seniority are laid off before those with more. Salary scales set raises according to the number of years of teaching and, in most districts, additional credentials such as a graduate degree.)

Because of due process, the reformers claim, it's too difficult to get rid of bad teachers; because of seniority, they aren't necessarily the first laid off; because of salary scales, they get paid as much as better teachers. The reformers want the quality of teaching alone to determine whether a public school teacher stays employed or gets a raise.

But how do you measure quality accurately? The reformers promote heavy reliance on students' standardized test scores: students who do well on these tests have clearly learned something, the argument goes. Therefore if you track the test scores of each teacher's students every year, you can measure how much students have learned and use that number to evaluate the teacher. The traditional protections can go, the unions will be weaker (a boon to reformers who consider them roadblocks to change), and, voilà, public schools will improve.

Due process, seniority, and salary scales predate unionization: they grew out of state and local civil service reforms in the early twentieth century when political machines thrived in large part by controlling jobs. Civil service laws protected teachers against the graft, cronyism, favoritism, and patronage that plagued public school systems under the thumb of political bosses. The laws benefited children by aiming for a meritocracy: teaching jobs would go to those who had training and skills. Since the 1960s, when public employees in many states won the right to bargain collectively, teachers' contracts have included the same protections.

The traditional protections are just that—protections against corruption and favoritism; they have nothing to do with evaluating teachers. Even if an ideal evaluation system existed, teachers would still need recourse when administrators and politicians ignored regulations. Yet the reformers have misleadingly conflated the two issues: we can't get proper evaluations, they claim, without eliminating protections. Since state laws can be written to take precedence over teachers' contracts, the most effective way to eliminate protections is to get state laws changed. This is what the reform campaign is doing around the country.

A short digression on due process: it doesn't mean that public school teachers cannot be fired. The problem is that the procedures for hearings and rulings can be extremely drawn-out and costly. Unions get the blame for this, but district departments of education (notorious for bureaucratic snafus and foot-dragging) and the lawyers on both sides (also foot-draggers) bear equal responsibility. The solution is straightforward: strict time limits for the process. But, perversely, with the escalation of the reform campaign, "reform superintendents" have a greater interest in showing that due process doesn't work than in repairing it.

Consider what happened in New York City. In 2002 Mayor Michael Bloomberg and his schools' chancellor Joel Klein, both ardent reformers, gave school principals the power to accuse and immediately remove any teacher for alleged misconduct or incompetence. The number of teachers removed from the classroom and waiting for hearings rose. Klein assigned them to seven sites around the city where they sat, under the watch of security guards, for months, some for years. Klein's holding sites, dubbed "rubber rooms," turned into a media bonanza for Bloomberg's reform program after the *New Yorker* ran an article in August 2009 that placed the blame for due process delays on the union. In April 2010, under increased pressure from teachers, Klein finally agreed to a procedure for speeding up the cases. According to the *New York Times* (December 7, 2010), 534 of the total 770 cases were closed by mid-November (keep in mind that New York City employed about 84,000 public school teachers). The saga demonstrates this much: due process can be speeded up and made to work. It's not an impenetrable logjam scuttling the system, as reformers claim.

Forging Ahead with a Dubious Notion

The reformers' plan to improve teaching relies on annual teacher evaluations based heavily on student's standardized test scores. But if this procedure isn't consistently accurate, it will hurt children as well as teachers: it will misidentify good and bad teachers (should "good" be defined as good at test prep in any case?), get the wrong ones fired, demoralize entire staffs, and discourage talented people from entering the profession. So far, the consensus judgment of the research community is not positive. Experts at the National Research Council of the National Academy of Sciences, National Academy of Education, RAND, and Educational Testing Service have repeatedly warned policy makers against using test scores to measure teacher effectiveness. The calculations require carefully calibrated, high-quality tests and "value-added modeling." VAM uses complex mathematical models to compare teachers by trying to control for variations among the in-school and outside factors that influence individual test scores over time. In a 2009 report to the U.S. Department of Education, the Board on Testing and Assessment of the National Research Council wrote, "Even in pilot projects, VAM estimates of teacher effectiveness that are based on data for a single class of students should not be used to make operational decisions because such estimates are far too unstable to be considered fair or reliable" (10).

Yet reformers have not only made this approach the cornerstone of their project, they have also sold the idea to politicians across the country who are rushing to write it into state laws. Most of the media, and therefore the public, are going along without confronting how seriously this "high-stakes testing" distorts teaching and narrows the curriculum. It's doubtful that many of VAM's non-expert promoters could describe the modeling methods accurately, but that doesn't curb their enthusiasm. VAM has the appeal of being mathematical, complex, and data-based. It's the kind of technical fix that sounds convincing; it readily wins hearts, not minds.

John Ewing, president of Math for America (which promotes better math education in public high schools), describes the VAM phenomenon in "Mathematical Intimidation: Driven by the Data" in the May 2011 issue of *Notices of the American Mathematical Society*:

> People recognize that tests are an imperfect measure of educational success, but when sophisticated mathematics is applied, they believe the imperfections go away by some mathematical magic. But this is not magic. What really happens is that the mathematics is used to disguise the problems and intimidate people into ignoring them—a modern, mathematical version of the Emperor's New Clothes. . . . Of course we should hold teachers accountable, but this does not mean we have to pretend that mathematical models can do something they cannot. . . . In any case, we ought to expect more from our teachers than what value-added attempts to measure.

An (Optional) Introduction to VAM

This seems like the right place to offer an introductory description of how VAM is used to estimate teacher effectiveness for readers who are interested. Not everyone will be, and those who aren't should guiltlessly skip over this section. I wrote it because I couldn't find what I needed for my work—a step-by-step explanation for the general reader of "basic VAM" and the problems it raises. As state after state mandates test-based teacher evaluations, pays statisticians to develop value-added models, and narrows how teachers teach and what children learn, the relevance of this abstruse subject to citizens is bound to grow . . . even if it never makes for fun reading.

"Growth models" in education typically compare a student's test score one year to that student's previous scores in the same subject. Value-added models are one type of growth model that statisticians use in education to estimate how much Teacher X added to the learning of her students in subject Y during the school year.

The most commonly used variant of VAM compares the average score of a teacher's students (in, say, fourth-grade math) at the end of the school year to the average score of the same students at the end of the previous year in the same subject. The difference between the two scores is the "actual growth" of the teacher's students. Their actual growth is then compared to what is called their "expected growth," which is the average growth of a comparison group. For example, the actual growth of Teacher X's students in fourth-grade math is compared to the average growth in fourth-grade math of all students in the state who are the same race and income category as Teacher X's students. The difference between the actual growth and expected growth of a teacher's students is the teacher's value-added score. Teachers with scores at the top of the distribution of all value-added scores are considered the best teachers; those at the bottom of the distribution are considered the worst. (In a slight variation, the end-of-the-year average score is compared to the beginning-of-the-year average score in the same subject. This requires testing twice a year.)

VAM has serious flaws. First of all, the tests don't account for the fact that the specific content in a subject changes from year to year. Here's an illustration: a teacher's value-added score is calculated by comparing the scores on this year's test in geometry to last year's test in algebra, or this year's reading test heavy in comprehension skills with last year's test heavy in phonics. Many researchers consider this kind of comparison meaningless. Instead, tests should track one type of content (say, reading comprehension) from year to year. Tests designed this way are "vertically scaled." A briefing paper called "Problems with the Use of Student Test Scores to Evaluate Teachers," authored by ten scholars and published by the Economic Policy Institute (EPI), describes the problem this way:

> Value-added measurement of growth from one grade to the next should ideally utilize vertically scaled tests, which most states (including large states like New York and California) do not use. In order to be vertically scaled, tests must evaluate content that is measured along a continuum from year to year.

Year-to-year scaling is extremely complicated even in a subject like elementary school reading. It's impossible when the skill set changes from something like algebra to an entirely different skill set like geometry. So, in the real world, a teacher's value-added score is usually calculated by comparing the percentage of her students scoring "proficient" on this year's test with the percentage of the same students scoring "proficient" on the earlier test. The change in percentage of proficient students is then compared to the change in the comparison group. But the concept of proficiency has no scientifically valid meaning: it's just a score above an arbitrary cut-off point that separates failing from passing. As Richard Rothstein explains in his 2008 book (co-authored with Rebecca Jacobsen and Tamara Wilder), *Grading Education: Getting Accountability Right*, "There is nothing scientific about defining a standardized test's passing score, and there are several methods for doing so. But all require subjective decisions by panels of judges" (60). This is how the panels (usually made up of teachers, members of the general public, administrators, and specialists) work:

> One common method is to ask each judge to imagine what a barely proficient student can generally do, and then estimate, for each question on a test, the probability that such a student will answer the question correctly. The minimum test score (in percent correct) that a student must achieve to be deemed proficient is determined by averaging the judges' probability estimates for all the questions. (60)

This technique looks appallingly arbitrary and imprecise for deciding which teachers are "failing." Politicians and state officials then make the "proficiency" calculation useless by changing the cut-off point at will—down if they want to show their policies are succeeding, up if they want to create a sense of emergency about the quality of public schools. Think of New York City's mayor declaring that his administration was working wonders in raising proficiency rates (I use examples from New York because it has the largest and most comprehensive education reform program, and it's where I live). It later came to light that the cut-off points for passing grades were embarrassingly low; the bar was raised in 2010, and proficiency rates plunged ("On New York School Tests, Warning Signs Ignored," *New York Times*, October 10, 2010).

In addition, VAM estimates of a teacher's effectiveness are intrinsically unstable: the number of students taught is too small a sample to provide reliable results. Who happens to be absent on test day, how lucky students are at guessing correct answers, how many students are "having a bad day"—chance factors like these can skew the class average significantly. High student mobility in low-income schools and the non-random assignment of students to teachers also skew results. Because VAM requires two tests, the measurement errors of both tests become part of the calculation. A 2010 study commissioned by the federal Department of Education and conducted by Mathematica Policy Research found that "error rates for comparing a teacher's performance to the average are likely to be about 25 percent with three years of data and 35 percent with one year of data."

VAM has still other shortcomings. How do you calculate the value-added score in team teaching? How do you account for the effects of outside tutoring that only some students receive or (depending on when the tests are given) the widely differing gains and losses in learning over the summer? How should students who transfer into a class midyear be counted? The EPI paper also analyzes unintended negative effects: disincentives for teachers to work with the neediest students, even more "teaching to the test," less collaboration among teachers, and demoralization. On top of all this, many standardized tests are of poor quality to begin with. For most subjects, they don't yet exist and will have to be developed on a rushed schedule because of new state laws.

As an accurate and therefore useful tool to measure teacher effectiveness, VAM fails. Yet this gives reformers no pause.

The Political Triumph of VAM

The Bush administration launched the era of federally mandated, high-stakes testing in public schools with its No Child Left Behind Act (NCLB) in 2001. Schools not making Adequate Yearly Progress—the accountability system mandated by NCLB—in raising math and reading scores risked being re-staffed, replaced with charters, or shut down. This quickly produced predictable results: teaching to the test, narrowed curriculum, and incidents of cheating. But the next step—the federal drive to use student test scores to grade teachers—came exclusively from the Obama administration.

Obama chose education reformer Arne Duncan as secretary of education, and Duncan in turn hired John Schnur, another reformer, as an advisor. Schnur came up with the idea of using the reform agenda as the core of a contest for federal grants from the Race to the Top Fund. The contest offered states the chance to win funds if they pledged to mandate specific reforms, including test-based teacher evaluations in *all subjects* (for an account of Race to the Top's genesis, see "The Teachers' Unions' Last Stand," *New York Times Magazine*, May 17, 2010). Desperate for funds, states accepted this micromanagement. Duncan announced the winners in 2010, and they rushed to pass laws to fulfill their pledges. Other states followed suit in large part because the reform movement has so effectively popularized the notion of holding every teacher accountable with "objective, performance-based" measures.

Midway through 2011, the following states had passed laws or had legislation in the works: Alabama, Arizona, Colorado, Florida, Idaho, Illinois, Indiana, Louisiana, New Jersey, Michigan, Minnesota, Missouri, Nevada, New Hampshire, New York, Ohio, Oregon, Pennsylvania, Tennessee, Texas, Utah, and Washington. Many of the new laws require test scores to count for as much as 50 percent of a teacher's evaluation, but even 10 percent could distort the outcome, given the error-prone calculation methods. The rest of the evaluation includes a combination of "traditional measures" such as principals' observations, review of lesson plans, and portfolios of student work. All the new laws weaken protections for teachers.

Florida's new law, for example, requires the commissioner of education to come up with a value-added model that will determine 50 percent of every teacher's and principal's evaluation; the evaluations will decide salaries and dismissals. On April 4, 2011, Frederick Hess, director of Education Policy Studies at the conservative American Enterprise Institute (AEI) and a tireless reform advocate, wrote this about Florida's law in his *Education Week* blog:

> I'll bet right now that SB 736 is going to be a train wreck. Mandatory terminations will force some good teachers out of good schools because of predictable statistical fluctuations, and parents will be livid. Questions about cheating will rear their ugly head. A thrown-together growth model and rapidly generated tests, pursued with scarce resources and under a new Commissioner, are going to be predictably half-baked and prone to problems.

In the same post, Hess (whose work at AEI is supported by the Bill and Melinda Gates Foundation) explained that he backed the law when it was proposed in 2010:

> I thought it would knock down anachronistic policies governing tenure and pay—and problems with overreach and excessive prescriptiveness could be addressed later. . . . However, a year passed, proponents had a chance to reflect and reconsider, and there's no evidence that they improved their handiwork in any substantial way.

For most education reformers, better a train wreck than no reform. They want as much change as possible as fast as possible in order to take advantage of momentum and the favorable political climate. The rush to pass state laws has been their most successful strategy so far. They've skillfully built state campaigns, spending millions to support friendly candidates and lobby sitting lawmakers and their staffs. A nearly endless flow of money—from wealthy individuals, political action committees, and nonprofit organizations—funds the reformers' political operations just as it funds almost all the movement's activities.

Two groups in particular—Stand for Children (headquartered in Portland, Oregon) and Democrats for Education Reform (DFER, headquartered in New York City)—have played substantial roles by setting up branches in legislative battle states. Stand for Children's long list of contributors for general operations includes the Gates Foundation ($5.2 million between 2005 and 2010; see "Search Awarded Grants" at www.gatesfoundation.org) and the Walton Family Foundation (almost $1.4 million in 2010 alone; see the foundation's 990 IRS form, www.guidestar.org). DFER gets most of its money from financiers, especially hedge fund managers.

It's difficult to overstate the role of the mega-rich private funders: look into any education reform project—even those that appear to be individual or small local efforts—and you'll likely come across large foundations and financiers. This is typical: a small group of Indiana teachers lobbied successfully for the legislature to abolish seniority-based layoffs. They received media coverage but neglected to say that they had been recruited by Teach Plus, a Cambridge, Massachusetts-based group that operates on a $4 million grant given in 2009 by the Gates Foundation ("Behind Grass-Roots School Advocacy, Bill Gates," *New York Times*, May 21, 2011).

Evaluating Teachers: It's Not Rocket Science

While education reformers push a top-down pseudoscientific procedure, the programs for assessing teacher performance that actually work take a radically different approach. They're based on two assumptions: first, administrators and teachers should design and implement a program together, and, second, it should incorporate "professional development" (showing teachers how to improve). One such program, called Peer Assistance and Review (PAR), is being used successfully in seven school districts around the country: in Toledo, Ohio, since 1981; Cincinnati, Ohio, since 1985; Rochester, New York, since 1987; Minneapolis, Minnesota, since 1997; San Juan, Puerto Rico, since 2000; Montgomery County, Maryland, since 2001; and Syracuse, New York, since 2005.

A PAR program has two main components: one is a district PAR panel made up of seven to twelve members, half of them teachers and half administrators; the second component is a corps of Consulting Teachers (CTs). Typically, teachers who want to become CTs apply to the panel. Those who are chosen take a leave of absence from their classrooms for three to five years and assume responsibility for a caseload of ten to twenty teachers who are either new or low-performing. The CTs observe "their" teachers at work regularly during the school year, provide intensive mentoring, keep detailed records of progress and problems, and report to the panel on each teacher's development. They also recommend retaining, dismissing, or giving the teachers more assistance. The panel reviews reports and records, interviews each teacher, and makes a decision. The CTs receive extra pay for their service and then return to teaching (see "A User's Guide to Peer Assistance and Review" at the Harvard Graduate School of Education website).

Research on PAR programs shows that some teachers initially balk at being judged by their peers; some principals initially oppose giving up their authority over evaluations. Yet once the programs are in place, they get strong support. The advantages are many: more thorough assessments of teachers, more considered personnel decisions, speedier removal of ineffective teachers, opportunity for the best teachers to share their expertise, better trained first-year teachers, real improvement for some veteran teachers, and more time for principals to do their other work. Last but not least, the teachers' union is a partner from the start, so a culture of cooperation develops between union and administration on evaluations. Sometimes cooperation grows strong enough to improve relations on other issues. Consider the 2010 salary decisions in Maryland's Montgomery County school system ("Helping Teachers Help Themselves," *New York Times*, June 5, 2011):

> Last year when Larry Bowers, the district's finance director, said the schools could not afford a scheduled 5.3 percent raise, the teachers' union agreed. "Saved us $89 million," Mr. Bowers said. . . . Mr. Prouty, the union president, said he knew Mr. Bowers was telling the truth. "We formulate the budget; we know where the money is, which makes us much more trusting," said Mr. Prouty, whose members also agreed to forgo a raise next year.

PAR looks like a win for students, teachers, and administrators. Presidential candidate Barack Obama endorsed it in a November 20, 2007 education policy speech: "Teacher associations and school boards in a number of cities have led the way by developing peer assistance and review plans that do exactly this—setting professional standards that put children first." So why haven't education reformers made PAR or similar plans the center of their project? Why have their reforms brought us Arne Duncan and Race to the Top instead of Obama's 2007 thinking? Why should Maryland, a Race to the Top winner, be obliged to mandate a teacher-evaluation program that might ruin Montgomery County's excellent PAR plan (see "New Teacher Evaluation Plan Approved in Maryland," *Washington Post*, June 21, 2011)?

A Reform with No Appeal for "Reformers"

PAR-type plans don't appeal to education reformers for at least four reasons. First, although reformers claim they're not anti-teacher, but simply want to get rid of bad teachers, their rhetoric doesn't make distinctions: they end up portraying public school teachers in general as lazy, greedy, and just biding time until they can collect their pensions. The movement has eroded respect for teachers to the detriment of everyone with a stake in public education, especially children. PAR-type plans do the opposite: they empower teachers as professionals who are able to mentor and assess their peers and pass judgment. Second, PAR has no mathematical bells and whistles to impress non-experts; it makes no pretense of being "scientific." Paradoxically, the state laws backed by education reformers leave at least 50 percent of a teacher's evaluation—the part composed of traditional, non-test-based methods—unimproved. PAR instead turns these methods into a rigorous procedure carried out by a trained staff. Third, standardized testing and value-added modeling are growing industries with thousands of employees, many of them high-salaried. The new state laws greatly expand their markets; PAR doesn't. Ultimately, the testing industry is likely to be the only beneficiary of the education reformers' effort to transform teaching.

Finally, there are the unions. A virulent anti-teachers-union ethos pervades the education reform movement: the unions quash reforms out of self-interest—period. Success for reformers requires weakening or eliminating the unions. Once again, PAR-type plans do the opposite: they make teachers' unions a partner; the plans depend on union-management cooperation.

Many education reformers insist they don't oppose unions in general, only teachers' unions ("I'm a lifelong Democrat" is a common refrain). But many members of the broad reform coalition are fundamentally anti-union. For them—free-marketers, social conservatives, Christian fundamentalists, Republican politicians and their supporters—education reform makes great sense politically. The National Education Association (NEA), with approximately 3.2 million members, is by far the largest union in the United States; the American Federation of Teachers (AFT), with close to 1.5 million members, is the third or fourth largest. (These figures are approximate because it is difficult to compare union membership numbers meaningfully. Three main sources for data include LM-2 forms unions file with the federal Labor Department, figures provided to the AFL-CIO by affiliated unions, and union press packets. The figures vary depending on whether they include retiree members, seasonal workers, Canadian members, and agency fee-payers, workers in a bargaining unit who pay a fee to the union but are not members. Finally, some public employees, including some teachers, belong to a state or city union affiliated with two national unions.)

According to the Bureau of Labor Statistics, together the NEA and AFT account for about 30 percent of the nation's 14.8 million unionists. Crippling such a large portion of the labor movement debilitates the rest. It also undermines the Democratic Party in elections. The NEA and AFT, along with two other public sector unions (SEIU and AFSCME), constitute the strongest, most active component of the party's institutional base, especially at the state and local levels. Up to the present, they've provided the party with ground troops and funds. Although the Democrats now rely on corporate money almost as heavily as the Republicans, disabling the Democrats' union-based, grassroots operation serves Republicans well.

This is, of course, why Republican governors, galvanized by their 2010 election sweep, are going after all public-sector unions. Under the guise of dealing with budget shortfalls, they are rolling back not only salaries and pensions but also rights of unions to bargain for members, collect dues, and raise funds for political work. With relentless attacks on the teachers' unions, the education reformers have been immensely helpful—purposely or indifferently—to the Republicans.

Where Are We Headed?

I've focused my investigation on teacher evaluations, the use of tests, and protections against corruption and favoritism. Education reformers are making a mess in all three policy areas. Using too broad a brush, they also depict classroom experience and college and graduate degrees in education as irrelevant to good teaching. As an alternative, they promote high-speed licensing programs (typically subsidized by private funders) which place neophytes with a month or so of training into low-income schools. The aggregate effect of the reforms is to de-professionalize teaching: more rote test preparation and mindless data recording, exposure without remedy to arbitrary treatment, constant job insecurity, and the education equivalent of piece work (the higher the test scores, the more you earn). When teaching becomes tedious and nerve-wracking to the point that "employees" want out, the reformers' standard response is: in the twenty-first century, no one should expect to have a lifetime career.

Crusading with the zealots' mix of certainty and fervor, education reformers have made this a wretched time to be a public school teacher. Indeed, fewer and fewer people are interested in trying. The number of Californians seeking to become teachers dropped 45 percent from 2001-2 to 2008-9 (see "State's Teacher Supply Plummets," *California Watch*, December 14, 2010). In 2011, due to declining interest, Yale ended both its undergraduate teacher preparation and certification program and its Urban Teaching Initiative, a tuition-free master's degree program for students committed to teaching in New Haven's public schools. Teachers all over the country—in affluent districts as well as high-poverty schools—are dispirited. In New York City, 50 percent of new hires leave after five years in the classroom.

Meanwhile, parents worry that obsessive testing is hollowing out the substance of learning. They rightly expect good teaching to offer much more than the largely meaningless higher scores that consume education reform thinking. Yet the Obama administration is now promoting more testing—tests in all subjects, pretests in the fall, interim tests during the school year, and testing in pre-kindergarten and kindergarten.

And what about the schools that do need significant improvement? The good news comes from schools scattered around the country where teachers and principals have created successful models that shun the reform approach. Each school has its own story (see some other chapters in this volume for examples), but they share these features: a talented principal, a teaching staff that signs on and helps design a plan that fits their students' needs, experienced teachers who coach colleagues, regular meetings to assess and revise the plan, a concerted effort to engage parents, union cooperation, and understanding that improvement is an ongoing process.

Brockton High School in Massachusetts was once the kind of giant "dropout factory" (over 4,000 students) that education reformers insist on shutting down. Instead, the staff transformed the school dramatically with a program that emphasizes literacy skills, especially writing, in every subject, even physical education (see "School of Thought in Brockton, Mass.," a report on the PBS program *Need to Know*, February 3, 2011, and "4,100 Students Prove 'Small Is Better' Rule Wrong," *New York Times*, September 27, 2010). Eight K-8 schools in Chicago's lowest income neighborhoods transformed themselves using a program called Strategic Learning Initiatives, based on twenty years of research at the University of Chicago. Its award-winning parent engagement component includes workshops on what children will study, helping with homework, and parenting skills. Parents who've attended the workshops are then trained to lead the next series for other parents (see "Focus on Instruction Turns Around Chicago Schools," *Education Week*, January 5, 2010).

I've mentioned just two examples, but there are others. Education reporters should be tracking down these local stories: they comprise the mostly unknown, now threatened, but positive side of change. Here is how George H. Wood, principal of a rural school in Appalachian Ohio, contrasted his own experience with the reformers' agenda in a June 16, 2010 blog post for the Forum for Education and Democracy:

For the past eighteen years, I have worked as a high school/middle school principal alongside a dedicated staff and a committed community to improve a school. In that time, we have increased graduation and college-going rates, engaged our students in more internships and college courses, created an advisory system that keeps tabs on all our students, and developed the highest graduation standards in the state (including a Senior Project and Graduation Portfolio).

But reading the popular press and listening to the chatter from Washington, I have just found out that we are not part of the movement to "reform" schools. You see, we did not do all the stuff that the new "reformers" think is vital to improve our schools. We did not fire the staff, eliminate tenure, or go to pay based on test scores. We did not become a charter school. We did not take away control from a locally elected school board and give it to a mayor. We did not bring in a bunch of two-year short-term teachers.

Nope, we did not do any of these things. Because we knew they would not work.

Most Americans would agree that a strong democracy requires high quality, universally available public education. Without it, a society can't maintain an informed, civic-minded, adequately cohesive citizenry. Education also enriches life: it is a great good in itself. Only a public system can provide that benefit for tens of millions of children.

Notwithstanding the indispensability of public education, good schools staffed by excellent teachers cannot offset the problems of poverty. Education reformers occasionally pay lip service to this fact, but they continue to push policies that divert resources, energy, and attention from real solutions: health care that begins prenatally, decent housing, preschool, parenting education, and jobs that pay a living wage.

With ill-conceived policies and tremendous waste, the self-proclaimed reformers are dragging public education down the wrong road. Citizens who care about children must stop them.

Chapter 5

The Bipartisan, and Unfounded, Assault on Teachers' Unions

Richard D. Kahlenberg

Teachers' unions are under unprecedented bipartisan attack. The drumbeat is relentless, from the governors in Wisconsin and Ohio to the film directors of *Won't Back Down* (2012), *Waiting for Superman* (2010), and *The Lottery* (2010); from new lobbying groups like Michelle Rhee's StudentsFirst and Wall Street's Democrats for Education Reform to political columnists such as Jonathan Alter and George Will; from new books, like political scientist Terry Moe's *Special Interest* (2011) and entrepreneurial writer Steven Brill's *Class Warfare* (2011) to even, at times, members of the Obama administration. The consistent message is that teachers' unions are the central impediment to educational progress in the United States.

Part of the assault is unsurprising given its partisan origins. Republicans have long been critical, going back to at least 1996, when presidential candidate Bob Dole scolded teachers' unions: "If education were a war, you would be losing it. If it were a business, you would be driving it into bankruptcy. If it were a patient, it would be dying." If you're a Republican who wants to win elections, going after teachers' unions makes parochial sense. According to Moe, the National Education Association (NEA) and American Federation of Teachers (AFT) gave 95 percent of their contributions to Democrats in federal elections between 1989 and 2010 (283). The nakedly partisan nature of Wisconsin governor Scott Walker's attack on public sector collective bargaining was exposed when he exempted from his legislation two unions that supported him politically: those representing police and firefighters.

What is new and particularly disturbing is that partisan Republicans are now joined by many liberals and Democrats in attacking teachers' unions. Davis Guggenheim, an avowed liberal who directed Al Gore's anti-global warming documentary, *An Inconvenient Truth* (2006) and Barack Obama's convention biopic, was behind *Waiting for Superman*. Normally liberal *New York Times* columnist Nicholas Kristof regularly attacks teachers' unions, as does Brill, who contributed to the campaigns of Hillary Clinton and Barack Obama, yet compares teachers' union leaders to Saddam Hussein loyalists and South African apartheid officials. A string of Democratic schools superintendents (including New York City's Joel Klein and San Diego's Alan Bersin) have blamed unions for education's woes. Even President Obama strongly supports nonunionized charter schools and famously applauded the firing of every single teacher in Central Falls, Rhode Island.

The litany of complaints about teachers' unions is familiar. They make it "virtually impossible to get bad teachers out of the classroom," says Moe (5). Critics claim they oppose school choice, oppose merit pay, and oppose efforts to have excellent teachers "assigned" to high poverty schools where they are needed most.

Growing Democratic support of these criticisms has emboldened conservatives to go even farther and call for the complete abolition of collective bargaining for teachers a half century after it started. Writing in *Education Next* (Winter 2012), conservative education professor Jay Greene pines for a "return to the pre-collective bargaining era." Teachers' unions "are at the heart" of our education problems, Moe says. "As long as teachers unions remain powerful," he writes, the "basic requirements" of educational success "cannot be met." The idea that policymakers can work with "reform" union leaders is, in his view, "completely wrong-headed," "fanciful and misguided" (6, 242, 244, 342).

Critics suggest that collective bargaining for teachers is stacked, even undemocratic. Unlike the case of the private sector, where management and labor go head to head with clearly distinct interests, they say, in the case of teachers, powerful unions are actively involved in electing school board members, essentially helping pick the management team. Moreover, when collective bargaining covers education policy areas—such as class size or discipline codes—the public is shut out from the negotiations, they assert. Along the way, the interests of adults in the system are served, but not the interests of children, these critics suggest.

The critics' contentions, which I sum up as collective bargaining and teachers' unions being undemocratic and bad for schoolchildren, have no real empirical support. Democratic societies throughout the world recognize the basic right of employees to band together to pursue their interests and secure a decent standard of living, whether in the private or public sector. Article 23 of the 1948 Universal Declaration of Human Rights provides not only that workers should be shielded from discrimination but also that "Everyone has the right to form and join trade unions for the protection of his interests."

Collective bargaining is important in a democracy, not only to advance individual interests, but to give unions the power to serve as a countervailing force against big business and big government. Citing the struggle of Polish workers against the Communist regime, Ronald Reagan declared in a Labor Day speech in 1980: "where free unions and collective bargaining are forbidden, freedom is lost."

In the United States, thirty-five states and the District of Columbia have collective bargaining by statute or by state constitution for public school teachers; the rest explicitly prohibit it, are silent on the matter, or allow the decision to be made at the local level. It is not an accident that the states that either prohibit collective bargaining for teachers or by tradition never had it are mostly in the Deep South, the region of the country historically most hostile to extending democratic citizenship to all Americans.

The argument that collective bargaining is undemocratic fails to recognize that in a democracy, school boards are ultimately accountable to all voters—not just teachers, who often live and vote outside the district in which they teach, and in any event represent a small share of total voters. Union endorsements matter in school board elections, but so do the interests of general taxpayers, parents, and everyone else who makes up the community. If school board members toe a teachers' union line that is unpopular with voters, those officials can be thrown out in the next election.

The title of Moe's most recent book, *Special Interest: Teachers Unions and America's Public Schools* (2011), invokes a term historically applied to wealthy and powerful entities such as oil companies, tobacco interests, and gun manufacturers, whose narrow interests are recognized as often colliding with the more general public interest in such matters as clean water, good health, and public safety. Do rank and file teachers, who educate American school children and earn about $54,000 on average, really fall into the same category?

Albert Shanker long ago demonstrated that it was possible to be a strong union supporter and an education reformer, a tradition carried on today by AFT president Randi Weingarten. Local unions are sometimes resistant to necessary change, but the picture painted by critics of unions is sorely outdated. Unions today support school choice within the public school system, but oppose private school vouchers that might further Balkanize the nation's students. Unions in New York, Pittsburgh, and elsewhere favor teacher merit pay so long as it includes school-wide gains to reward effort while also encouraging cooperation between teachers. While unions disfavor plans to allow administrators to "allocate" teachers to high poverty schools against their will (a policy reminiscent of forced student assignment for racial balance during the days of busing), both the NEA and AFT favor paying bonuses to attract teachers to high poverty schools.

On the issue that arouses the most controversy, getting rid of bad educators, many teachers' unions today also favor weeding out those who are not up to the job not based strictly on test scores or the subjective judgment of principals, but through multiple measures of performance, including "peer review" plans. In peer review, expert teachers come into a school and work with struggling educators; many of those educators improve, but when the expert teachers do not see sufficient improvement, they recommend termination (the final decision rests with the superintendent and/or school board). The average fifth-grade teacher has a powerful self-interest in getting rid of an incompetent fourth-grade colleague, which is part of why peer review programs in places like Toledo, Ohio, and Montgomery County, Maryland, have resulted in increases in teacher terminations compared to previous systems in which administrators were in charge. In Montgomery County, for example, administrators dismissed just one teacher due to performance issues between 1994 and 1999, but during the first four years of the district's peer review program, 177 teachers were dismissed, not renewed, or resigned.

Moreover, there is no strong evidence that unions reduce overall educational outcomes and are, as Moe and other critics suggest, at "the heart" of our education problems. If collective bargaining were really a terrible practice for education, we should see stellar results in the grand experiments without it: the American South and the charter school arena. Why aren't the seven states that forbid collective bargaining for teachers—Arizona, Georgia, Mississippi, North Carolina, South Carolina, Texas, and Virginia—at the top of the educational heap? Why did the nation's most comprehensive study of charter schools (88 percent of which are nonunion), conducted by Stanford

University researchers and sponsored by pro-charter foundations, conclude that charters outperformed regular public schools only 17 percent of the time, and actually did significantly worse 37 percent of the time? Why, instead, do we see states like Massachusetts, and countries like Finland, both with strong teachers' unions, leading the pack?

Union critics like Moe reply, reasonably enough, that the South suffers from lots of other impediments to high achievement such as higher levels of poverty, a history of segregation, and lower levels of school spending. Well, yes, but this response begs a question: if factors like poverty and segregation matter a great deal more to student achievement than the existence of collective bargaining, why not focus on those issues instead of claiming that the ability of teachers to band together and pursue their interests is the central problem in American education? Moreover, a 2002 review of seventeen studies by researcher Robert Carini, "Teaching Unions and Student Achievement," finds that when demographic factors *are* carefully controlled for, "unionism leads to modestly higher standardized achievement scores" (10, 17).

Critics of unions point out that teacher interests "are *not the same* as the interests of children" (see, e.g., Terry M. Moe, "The Staggering Power of the Teachers' Unions," *Hoover Digest* [2011]). That's certainly true, but who are the selfless adults who think only about kids? For-profit charter school operators whose allegiance is to shareholders? Principals who send troublemakers back into the classroom because they don't want school suspension numbers to look bad? Superintendents who sometimes junk promising reforms instituted by predecessors because they cannot personally take credit? Mayors who must balance the need to invest in kids against the strong desire of many voters to hold down taxes?

Do the hedge fund billionaires who bankroll charter schools have only the interests of children at heart? Might it not be in the self-interest of very wealthy individuals to suggest that expensive efforts at reducing poverty aren't necessary, and that a nonunion teaching environment will do the trick? When hedge fund managers argue that their income should be taxed at a 15 percent marginal rate, they limit government revenue and squeeze funds for a number of public pursuits, including schools. Is that putting the interests of kids ahead of adults, as the reformers suggest we should always to do? Moreover, is the bias of Wall Street—that deregulation is good and unions distort markets—really beneficial for low-income children? Why aren't union critics more skeptical of deregulation in education, given that deregulation of banking, also supported by Wall Street, wreaked havoc on the economy? And is the antipathy of hedge fund managers toward organized labor generally in the interests of poor and working-class students, whose parents can't make ends meet in part because organized labor has been eviscerated in the United States over the past half century?

On many of the big educational issues—including levels of investment in education—the interests of educators who are in the classroom day in and day out do align nicely with the interests of the children they teach. Unlike the banks that want government money to cover for their reckless lending, teachers want money for school supplies and to reduce overcrowded classes. Yes, teachers have an interest in being well compensated, but presumably kids benefit too when higher salaries attract more talented educators than would otherwise apply.

Overall, as journalist Jonathan Chait noted in the *New Republic* (April 7, 2011), politicians, who have short-term horizons, are prone to under-investing in education, and teachers' unions "provide a natural bulwark" against that tendency. Because most voters don't have kids in the public school system, parents with children in public schools need political allies. The fact that teachers have, by joining together, achieved some power in the political process surely helps explain why the United States does a better job of investing in education than preventing poverty. The child poverty rate in the United States is 21.6 percent, fifth highest among forty Organisation for Economic Co-operation and Development (OECD) nations. Only Turkey, Romania, Mexico, and Israel have higher child poverty rates (OECD Family Database, chart CO2.2.A). Put differently, we're in the bottom eighth in preventing child poverty. By contrast, when the interests of children are directly connected with the interests of teachers—as on the question of public education spending—the United States ranks close to the top third. Among thirty-nine OECD nations, the United States ranks fourteen in spending on primary and secondary education as a percentage of gross domestic product (chart PF1.2.A).

Moreover, the United States would probably rank even worse on the poverty score were it not for the influence of teachers' unions and the American labor movement generally. Education reformers like Michelle Rhee have adopted the mantra that poverty is just an "excuse" for low performance, blithely dismissing decades of evidence finding that socioeconomic status is by far the biggest predictor of academic achievement. If we could just get the unions to agree to stop protecting bad teachers and allow great teachers to be paid more, Rhee says, we could make all the difference in education. The narrative is attractive because it indeed would be wonderful if student poverty and economic school segregation didn't matter, and if heroic teachers could consistently overcome the odds for students. But educators like Albert Shanker, head of the AFT in 1974–1997, knew better. He believed strongly that teachers' unions should be affiliated with the AFL-CIO, in part because teachers could do a much better job of educating students if educators were part of a coalition that fought to reduce income inequality and to improve housing and health care for children. Teachers know they will be more effective if children have full stomachs and proper eyeglasses, a central reason the AFT remains an active part of the broader labor movement trying to help rebuild the middle class.

While many divide the world between teachers' unions and reformers, the truth is that unions have long advocated a number of genuine reforms—inside and outside the classroom—that can have a sustained impact on reducing the achievement gap. They back early childhood education programs that blunt the impact of poverty and have been shown to have long-lasting effects on student outcomes. They back common standards of the type used by many of our successful international competitors. And in places like La Crosse, Wisconsin, Louisville, Kentucky, and Raleigh, North Carolina, teachers have backed public school choice policies that reduce concentrations of school poverty, thereby placing more low-income students in middle-class schools and increasing their chances of success.

Moreover, by democratizing education and giving teachers a voice, unions can strengthen schools by tapping into the promising ideas teachers have for reform. At the same time, giving teachers greater voice reduces frustration and turnover. It is well documented that while teacher turnover is high in regular public schools, it is even higher in the largely non-unionized charter sector. As researchers David Stuit and Thomas M. Smith have written in a research brief published by the National Center on School Choice (June 2010): "The odds of a charter school teacher leaving the profession versus staying in the same school were 130 percent greater than those of a traditional public school teacher. Similarly, the odds of a charter school teacher moving to another school were 76 percent greater." Some charter advocates have tried to spin the higher turnover rates as a virtue, but according to researcher Gary

Miron's testimony prepared for a hearing of the House Committee on Education and the Workforce (June 1, 2011), "attrition from the removal of ineffective teachers—a potential plus of charters—explains only a small portion of the annual exodus."

Critics of unions also fail to understand that the union leaders benefit immeasurably from the insights of their members. In a much-discussed twist in *Class Warfare*, Brill suggests that AFT president Randi Weingarten be appointed chancellor of New York City public schools: once liberated from her obligation to represent teachers, she could use her savvy and smarts to improve education. But this suggestion misses the crucial point that much of a union leader's strength comes from the fact that she or he constantly interacts with teachers and learns from them how education reform theories work in actual practice.

Other union critics also try to unfairly drive a wedge between teachers and their elected union leaders. In *Waiting for Superman*, for example, columnist Jonathan Alter claims: "It's very, very important to hold two contradictory ideas in your head at the same time. Teachers are great, a national treasure. Teachers' unions are, generally speaking, a menace and an impediment to reform." Interestingly, Moe, citing extensive polling data, concludes in *Special Interest* that his fellow critics like Alter are wrong on this matter. Moe finds that among teachers, "virtually all union members, whether Democrat or Republican, see their membership in the local as entirely voluntary and are highly satisfied with what they are getting" (109). In a 2008 poll conducted by Public Agenda, 75 percent of teachers agreed, "without collective bargaining, the working conditions and salaries of teachers would be much worse"; and 77 percent agreed that "without a union, teachers would be vulnerable to school politics or administrators who abuse their power."

Finally, teachers' unions, more than any other organizations, preserve the American system of public schools against privatization. Other groups also oppose private school vouchers—including those advocating on behalf of civil liberties and civil rights, school board associations, and the like. But only teachers' unions have the political muscle and sophistication to stop widespread privatization. Today, vouchers and similar schemes serve one-third of one percent of the American school population. This fact infuriates union critics, including those that see large profit potential in privatization, and delights a majority of the American public.

Most of the public also supports collective bargaining for teachers and other public employees. A *USA Today*/Gallup survey (February 28, 2011) found that 33 percent of Americans oppose ending collective bargaining for public-sector employees. A *Wall Street Journal*/NBC poll (February 24–28, 2001) found that while most Americans want public employees to pay more for retirement benefits and health care, 77 percent said unionized state and municipal employees should have the same rights as union members who work in the private sector.

The public is right on this question. Teachers should not have to go back to the pre-collective bargaining era, when they engaged in what Shanker called "collective begging." Educators were very poorly compensated; in New York they were paid less than those washing cars for a living. Teachers were subject to the whims of often autocratic principals and could be fired for joining a union.

Many states are facing dire budget crises, and unions need to be smart about advocating strategies that keep fiscal concerns in mind. That means moving beyond traditional efforts to pour more money into high-poverty schools. Magnet schools, which give low-income students a chance to be educated in a middle-class environment, are an especially promising investment. But this kind of engagement in education policy involves moving in a direction opposite of the one advocated by Rhee, Walker and other Democrat and Republican union critics.

As Shanker noted years ago, restricting bargaining to the issue of wages (as many states are now trying to do) is a clever trap in which critics can suggest that teachers care only about money. Collective bargaining should be broadened, not constrained, to give teachers a voice on a range of important educational questions, from merit pay to curriculum. This could help improve the battered image of teachers' unions. But, more important, it could help students.

Chapter 6

Free-Market Think Tanks and the Marketing of Education Policy

Kevin G. Welner

"For about two years now, President Obama and Secretary of Education Arne Duncan have been co-opting much of the GOP playbook on education. They support charter schools. They endorse merit pay. They decry teacher tenure and seniority. On alternating Thursdays, they bracingly challenge the teachers' unions." So begins a December 2010 article in *National Review Online*, authored by Frederick M. Hess of the American Enterprise Institute (AEI) and Michael Petrilli of the Fordham Institute. Later in the article, Duncan receives praise from these conservative pundits for embracing spending limitations on American schools and welcoming—in place of those resources— "productivity" increases.

The Duncan-Obama approach should sound familiar, even to those who do not follow education policy discussions. Defund, deregulate, de-unionize, and shift to the private sector. Reallocate policy-making authority from democratic institutions to a wealthy oligarchy. Corporate-endowed think tanks like AEI have been successfully promoting this road map for everything else, so why not education?

But education is different in one disquieting way: many self-identified progressives have climbed on board the bandwagon. Some, in fact, are driving. Although the economic analyses offered by groups like the Brookings Institution and the Center for American Progress generally explore how to soften the sharp edges of market capitalism, their respective education divisions are busily promoting free-market policies in our children's schools.

Arianna Huffington warns against deregulation of the financial sector, but she's all for it in the educational sector. Nicholas Kristof worries about a "hedge fund republic," but joins in the hedge fund managers' campaign to criticize teacher-union contracts. Jonathan Alter of *Newsweek* sees dangers in unregulated markets yet pushes for more markets in education. As anyone who has watched *Waiting for Superman* (2010) can attest, Alter is particularly hostile toward teachers' unions. Director Davis Guggenheim is another example: a hero of the left for *An Inconvenient Truth* (2006), but a hero of the right for *Superman*. Media stars such as John Legend and Oprah Winfrey have also joined in, as have (to some extent) venerable civil rights organizations such as the United Negro College Fund and National Council of La Raza.

The most engaged in this neoliberal education campaign are organizations focused on school choice: Democrats for Education Reform (and their 501(c)(4) Education Reform Now Advocacy), Education Sector, and the Progressive Policy Institute; as well as service-oriented groups like New Leaders for New Schools, the Knowledge Is Power Program (KIPP) and Green Dot charter networks, Teach for America, the New Teacher Project, Stand for Children, the New Schools Venture Fund, and even the leadership of the Harlem Children's Zone.

These groups, it should be stressed, are very careful to avoid being characterized as politically on the right or affiliated with Republican political efforts. Their collaborators, however, do not show any such reluctance. Rightwing, free-market think tanks have joined with neoliberal education groups in pushing for choice and privatization policies. These think tanks and similar organizations are active in every state, and many more are pursuing a national agenda. Together, these groups have launched a potent attack on the progressive foundations of American schooling, and they are framing this attack as a "civil rights struggle."

After years of hammering home the theme of "failing public schools," the campaign is now increasingly focused on teachers' unions and the existing system of teacher education, preparation, and certification. Deregulation is consistently put forward as the best way to address unmet needs. Additional attacks are leveled at legal and political efforts toward an equitable distribution of educational resources and at democratically elected school boards and neighborhood schooling. Offered in their place are school choice, mayoral control, and free-market entrepreneurialism. Under the new model, accountability and sound policy making are found not in traditional democratic structures but in a fundamentalist view of the power of the market as exerted through parental choice. Efficiency and quality are to be achieved through choice combined with publicized test scores.

By any measure, the free-market campaign in education has shown extraordinary results. Conservative education policy is now pervasive and deeply engrained among a growing faction of powerful and wealthy Democrats. As suggested by the opening quotation from Hess and Petrilli, education has emerged as a key potential area of accord between the White House and the Republican-led House. Only minimal compromise will be necessary because the two sets of positions are already so well aligned.

Of course, most people and organizations on the left are justifiably disgusted by the lack of progress the nation has made toward providing equitable educational opportunities for children of color and those living in poverty. And when confronted with repeated disappointments, it is not surprising that many people are willing to grab attractive-sounding alternatives. It is small wonder that some progressives find themselves drawn to organizations such as the Black Alliance for Educational Options. BAEO was started in 2000 with funding from the Walton Family Foundation and the Lynde and Harry Bradley Foundation—two philanthropies that have offered enormous support for school choice as well as support for a broad portfolio of anti-union, deregulation, and privatization endeavors. What BAEO and similar organizations do is help make the public face of school choice more attractive to progressives than the movement of decades ago, which was dominated by transparently anti-public school activists.

Such efforts point to what should be the fundamental progressive response—the critique that many progressives seem hesitant to seize: that educational opportunities should be among the most precious public goods. While public education does provide an important private benefit to children and their families, it also lies at the center of our societal well-being. Educational opportunities should therefore never be distributed by market forces, because markets exist to create inequalities—they thrive by creating "winners" and "losers." These forces are already at play in the housing market, and school reform should attenuate the resulting inequities, not exacerbate them, as we see happening with unconstrained school choice.

Reformers appeal to the urgency of confronting "failing schools," but the logic of their argument leads inevitably to students' dependence upon parents who know how to maneuver within the system to gain private advantage. This is an abandonment of the goal of a comprehensive public sector that provides equitable, universal opportunities. Such consequences are anathema to progressives when free-market ideas are applied to health care; there is no reason they should be welcome when applied to the education of the nation's children.

*   *   *

The shift to the current focus on deregulation and free-market solutions was not a mere happenstance. A great deal of time, money, and effort orchestrated the shift in a very purposeful, calculated way. As an example, consider the case of Linda Darling-Hammond.

During his 2008 presidential campaign, Barack Obama assembled what he called a "team of rivals" (evoking Abraham Lincoln) for his education advisers. The team was primarily composed of neoliberals, but among those leading the team was someone with a progressive perspective—Stanford professor Linda Darling-Hammond. She is widely recognized as one of the most accomplished and respected scholars in the field; teacher preparation and teacher quality are her particular areas of expertise.

Immediately after the election, Obama announced that Darling-Hammond would head his transition team for education, and speculation was strong that she was the front-runner to become secretary of education. What followed in November and December 2008 were repeated condemnations of Darling-Hammond—in the *Washington Post, New York Times, Newsweek,* and *New Republic,* among others—with the unremitting charge that she was a defender of the status quo and an enemy of reform. In his *New York Times* column (December 5, 2008), David Brooks wrote that his negative assessment was preceded by "a flurry of phone calls from reform leaders nervous that Obama was about to side against them" by choosing Darling-Hammond as education secretary. Her primary crime, in their view, was a 2005 research article in *Education Policy Analysis Archives* titled "Does Teacher Preparation Matter?" which was skeptical of dazzling claims by and about Teach for America. In the end, the media and political campaign against Darling-Hammond was both ferocious and successful.

*   *   *

In part, the success of the campaign reflects the rise of private advocacy think tanks, whose "research" has helped legitimate the conservative educational agenda. I have learned a lot since I helped to start the Think Tank Review Project (thinktankreview.org) five years ago. The project—now called Think Twice—applies academic peer review standards to reports from think tanks and publishes reviews on the project website. Think tank reports have become widely influential for policy makers and the media. Their influence is due not to the superiority of their research but rather to the think tanks' proficiency at packaging and marketing their publications—many of which are of very weak quality. We have found that these advocacy reports have often attained greater prominence than the most rigorously reviewed articles addressing the same issues published in the most respected research journals. This should be a matter of concern. If all documents labeled "research" are indiscriminately received and reported as of equal worth, without review or critique by independent experts, their value is obviously not dependent on quality or rigor. These attributes are beside the point. Value is instead tightly linked to the ability of the researchers to gain attention and influence policy. Private think tanks, which produce their own in-house, non-refereed research, accordingly become sensible investments for individuals and groups hoping to advance their agendas.

In January each year, the Think Twice project hands out its Bunkum Awards, highlighting nonsensical, confusing, and disingenuous education think tank reports from the past year. Only those reports judged to have most egregiously undermined informed discussion and sound policymaking are recognized. Past winners include the "Time Machine" Award given in 2010 to a report from the Reason Foundation. In a truly breathtaking innovation, the Foundation's 2009 *Weighted Student Formula Yearbook* attributed positive reform outcomes to policy changes that had not been made yet. Another winner was the Manhattan Institute, which received the "Who Reads Warning Labels?" Award in 2007 for its 2007 report, "How Much Are Public School Teachers Paid?" which argued that teachers are better paid than most white-collar professionals. The study used hourly earnings data to support its contentions. But, our reviewers noted, "This approach is fundamentally flawed because the [dataset's] calculation of weeks and hours worked is very different for teachers and other professionals. In fact, the Bureau of Labor

Statistics—which publishes the [dataset]—has explicitly warned its users not to use hourly rates of pay in this exact same context."

An attack on preschool policies by the Hoover Institution won the "Misdirection" Award in 2010 for its courageous effort to keep policy makers from noticing approaches that actually work to help children. Rather than acknowledging a mountain of empirical, peer-reviewed, and widely accepted evidence, the author of Hoover's *Reroute the Preschool Juggernaut* (2009) cherry-picks a few weak studies to criticize proposals for universal preschool. Our reviewer summed up this work as "errors, exaggerations, misrepresentation, and logical inconsistency." Among the reviewer's catalog of fourteen major errors, he notes that actual costs are exaggerated by a factor of two while immediate and long-term well-documented effects are underreported or not reported accurately.

This tactic—the selective use of earlier research to bolster what appear to be pre-determined findings—is one we have seen repeatedly. Other harmful patterns and practices that are pervasive in the publications of advocacy think tanks include methodological weaknesses, such as failure to account for selection bias or the confusion of correlation and causation, failure to provide the data on which the report's findings are based, overstated conclusions, and unsupported recommendations based on improbable inferential leaps.

In 2011, economist Jesse Rothstein of the University of California, Berkeley examined a December 2010 report from the Gates Foundation. The report, "Working with Teachers to Develop Fair and Reliable Measures of Effective Teaching," had been trumpeted in newspapers and other media outlets across the country as proof of the validity and usefulness of value-added models, which are used to estimate students' likely achievement in a given year. The report used student test scores to gauge teacher effectiveness—a confirmation of a policy supported by the foundation. But Rothstein found that the study's own data "undermine rather than validate value-added based approaches to teacher evaluation," earning it the "Mirror Image (What You Read Is Reversed)" Award in 2011. As presented in the Gates report, the study purportedly showed that teachers whose students show gains on the state test also produce gains on a separate test of deeper conceptual understanding, administered by the researchers. Rothstein's review, however, explained that these correlations are very weak—that over 40 percent of those teachers whose students' state exam scores place them in the bottom quarter of effectiveness are in the top half on the alternative assessment.

In report after report from market-oriented organizations, privatization reforms in particular have been offered as the pre-ordained solution for any number of educational problems, from school funding to high school drop-out rates to the weaknesses of the No Child Left Behind Act. Indeed, a person reading these reports could not fail to conclude that the public nature of public education is the root cause of all that ails schools—everything else is a symptom.

*   *   *

Just a few decades ago, the Think Twice project would have had much less work to do. Public policy think tanks began fairly modestly with the founding of such institutions as the Brookings Institution (1927), American Enterprise Institute (1943), and Hoover Institution (1959). In the 1970s, a number of influential think tanks such as the Heritage Foundation (1973) and Cato Institute (1977) were founded, and since the 1970s the number of think tanks has increased dramatically. The most active and powerful tend to be free-market think tanks like those above. To date, the Think Twice project has published a hundred reviews that highlight a well-financed, tightly interconnected group of policy actors working in a growing alliance of free-market organizations.

In addition to national organizations, a very visible and influential network of state-level free-market think tanks has been built, including the Pioneer Institute in Massachusetts, Mackinac Center in Michigan, Buckeye Institute in Ohio, and Commonwealth Foundation in Pennsylvania. They have induced major shifts in the nature of policy discussions. While university-based scholars produce the most research, publications of private think tanks are disproportionately represented in the reporting of major national newspapers. Market-oriented think tanks in particular have proliferated, buoyed by very large gifts from a relatively small number of benefactors. For instance, as my colleagues and I have noted in *Think Tank Research Quality* (2010), between 1985 and 2000, three staunchly right-wing funders—the Lynde and Harry Bradley Foundation, Sarah Scaife Foundation (controlled by billionaire newspaper publisher Richard Mellon Scaife), and John M. Olin Foundation—awarded grants of more than $100 million to just fifteen market-oriented think tanks. Further funding was provided by these foundations to other think tanks, and additional funders have also supported the network.

With funding from right-wing donors, market-oriented think tanks have been able to engage in aggressive outreach to media and policy makers to promote their favored ideas. Conservative donors have demonstrated a greater willingness than progressives to spend their money on developing and supporting institutions that adhere to their ideological premises—and to fund activities that directly engage with the political process. By contrast, most nonconservative grant makers tend to support community-based projects that address urgent needs and to shy away from politics. Furthermore, few progressive foundations are willing to fund the operating expenses of institutions with strong communication strategies and clear public policy goals. It is not surprising, then, that institutions funded by conservatives produce a much greater level of activity aimed directly at influencing policy, such as publication of research reports, briefing documents, legislative analyses, and commentaries, as well as networking and briefings for policy makers and reporters.

The pattern, seen cumulatively over the past several decades, is that the right has focused tremendous resources on marketing its ideas and building networks of powerful allies that will push those ideas; the left has not. As a result, the messages promoted by conservative think tanks have influenced even progressives who otherwise bring to bear a healthy skepticism regarding market-based proposals for solving problems of social inequality.

Changing this dynamic requires finding a way to limit the sway of power and money over school reform. Redressing the imbalance between the influence of vulnerable communities affected by school reform and that of billionnaires convinced they know what is best for those communities demands learning from the methods of the Scaifes, Olins, and others. Just as there are no quick fixes to the crises—educational and otherwise—facing America's low-income communities of color, there are no quick fixes to these participatory and political inequalities. To bring voices from vulnerable communities to the fore will require new networks of progressive educators, families, organizers, researchers, advocates, and policy makers as well as benefactors willing to invest heavily and for the long term in research, implementation, and communication—to engage with the politics as well as the substance of education.

Chapter 7

The Price of Human Capital: The Illusion of
Equal Educational Opportunity

Harvey Kantor and Robert Lowe

In his oft-quoted Fifth Report to the Massachusetts Board of Education, Horace Mann sought to popularize the idea that education had individual as well as collective economic benefits. This 1841 report became one of the most well known of Mann's twelve reports to the board, though Mann himself worried that such an appeal would exacerbate the materialism that he hoped the common schools would combat. At the time, however, the Massachusetts Board was under attack from opponents of a centralized school system, and Mann thought that by showing how schooling benefited the economy he might convince the board's opponents of the value of the state's investment in public education. Accordingly, he replaced his usual arguments about its moral and civic value with a demonstration of its monetary value to both workers and manufacturers in the Commonwealth. Arguing that the key to prosperity was an educated populace, he even sought to calculate the rate of return to the state's investment in education by asking a small sample of Massachusetts businessmen to assess the difference in productivity between literate and illiterate workers.

Though Mann's argument about economic efficacy helped save the Board of Education, until the end of the nineteenth century most common-school promoters continued to prioritize the civic and moral purposes of education. Since then, however, those ideas have been eclipsed by ones like those Mann articulated in his Fifth Report, particularly about the school's role in the production of what we now call human capital. Arguments about the school's civic and moral purposes have not disappeared, of course. They appear regularly on political leaders' lists of desirable educational goals. But over the last hundred years those ideas have been increasingly subordinated to the notion that the primary purpose of education is to equip students with the skills they presumably need to improve their own economic opportunities and to make the nation more prosperous and secure.

Nowhere has the influence of this way of thinking about education been more evident than in the history of federal education policy. It is especially evident today, for example, in programs like President Barack Obama's Race to the Top Fund, which explicitly links federal aid to his desire to restore the nation's competitive edge in the international marketplace. But the influence of ideas about human capital formation on federal education policy began nearly a century ago when they provided the chief justification for passage of the Smith-Hughes Vocational Education Act in 1917. And they have provided the main rationale for nearly all the federal government's most important educational initiatives ever since—including the National Defense Education Act (NDEA) in 1958, the Elementary and Secondary Education Act (ESEA) in 1965, and, most recently, the No Child Left Behind Act (NCLB) in 2001. Indeed, given the longstanding opposition to federal involvement in education, it's hard to imagine that these programs could have passed on any other terms.

Taken together, these initiatives helped justify the expansion of elementary and secondary education to working-class youth, immigrants, women, and people of color as well. As a result, the public high school today is more inclusive than it was at the end of the nineteenth century when it graduated only 3 percent of the eligible age group. Yet, if the programs spawned by the federal interest in developing human capital contributed to the democratization of secondary schools, they have also had less desirable consequences. They seldom provided the economic benefits their proponents promised, but operated instead to displace economic anxieties onto the schools, deflecting attention from the need for more assertive labor market polices. At the same time, they protected the educational advantages of the nation's most affluent and privileged citizens. This is true even though the conception of equal opportunity that has informed them has actually grown more robust over time as policy has shifted from a focus on teaching specific vocational skills to working-class and immigrant youth to a focus on equipping all students—rich and poor alike—with the cognitive skills that a more fluid, knowledge-based economy presumably requires.

Consider, for example, the movement for vocational education that culminated with the passage of the Smith-Hughes Act, the first major program of federal assistance to public education. In the first two decades of the twentieth century, no other reform attracted such a broad spectrum of supporters or generated such high expectations for success. Business executives, labor unions, social reformers, as well as many educators all argued that vocational training in schools, particularly trade and industrial education, would be an antidote to poverty, youth unemployment, and the threat of national economic decline. Yet even allowing for the rhetorical oversell that usually accompanies new programs, the payoff to investment in vocational education fell far short of what proponents assumed it would be. Not only did graduates seldom find jobs in the areas for which they had been trained, but most evaluations of vocational programs found that on average their graduates earned no more than graduates from the regular course of study. Indeed, most evaluations concluded that vocational education functioned mainly, in the words of one 1938 report, as a "dumping ground" for working-class and immigrant youth who had been pushed out of the labor market and pulled into school by tougher enforcement of child labor and compulsory education laws but whom educators did not think were capable of doing more advanced academic work.

It is important not to overstate these failures. Some young people did benefit from vocational education. Yet even in cases where it helped them get jobs, it ultimately did as much to harden as to reduce class and racial disparities in schools and in the labor market. Commercial education courses, for example, provided working- and middle-class young women a path out of domesticity into paid labor, and, in some cities, trade and technical schools provided a small number of immigrant and working-class boys with access to the more privileged sectors of the blue-collar work force, where technical skills were highly valued. That, however, is also why vocational educators typically excluded African American and Latino youth. They were channeled into courses in the "trowel trades" and domestic work or, as they began to attend high school in greater numbers, placed in the general education track that prepared them for neither work nor college.

Theoretically, of course, school officials and political leaders could have adopted policies that expanded access to the labor market by encouraging all students to enroll in courses that would prepare them for college, even if they were unlikely to go beyond high school. That was what the National Education

Association Committee of Ten had recommended in 1893 and what some policy makers recommend today. But at the turn of the century most educators rejected this idea. They believed it was inefficient and undemocratic because it didn't help students adjust to the demands of society and denied those headed for working-class jobs the same opportunity to prepare for their likely future occupations that the academic curriculum had long offered to middle-class youth bound for college and the professions. Once we recognize that the academic course of study was becoming more tightly linked to the most desirable jobs, however, the assumption that working-class students were more suited for vocational than academic study appears less as an expression of democracy than as a way for a relatively elite population to preserve access to college and subsequently to managerial and professional positions—at a time when students from poor and working-class families pressed for access of their own.

Partly for these reasons, vocational education fell out of favor. But the assumptions about human capital formation that informed it continued to shape educational policy long after enthusiasm for it had dimmed. Following the Second World War, for example, the Cold War inspired a shift in policy interest from preparing working-class young people for working-class jobs to providing equal opportunity for the development of high-level technical skills to counter the threat of Soviet technical superiority. A concern with national security, heightened by the launching of Sputnik, made it possible for many members of Congress to overcome their fear that federal involvement in education would erode the power of local school boards, thereby paving the way for the passage of the NDEA in 1958. "The present emergency," it declared, "demands that additional and more adequate educational opportunities be made available." Nonetheless, although its investment in support for mathematics, science, and foreign language instruction provided some financial heft to efforts already in place, the NDEA did little to create a serious intellectual experience for the vast majority of high school students. Its main concern was "to identify and educate more of the talent of our Nation." Consequently, it invested in both testing to determine who had the most talent and in guidance that would direct those students to challenging courses— and to college.

This agenda meshed perfectly with the proposals of James Bryant Conant's highly influential *The American High School Today* (1959). Published a year after Congress passed the NDEA, its affirmation of the comprehensive high school served as a blueprint for school districts across the country. Although Conant believed that all students needed a core of academic subjects, he maintained that there should be ability grouping and then a high-level academic track for the top 15 percent and a vocational track for those deemed to have limited academic talent. In harmony with the spirit of NDEA, he was committed to a broader view of equality of opportunity than earlier advocates of vocational education. He wanted to ensure that students who had high scores on aptitude tests did not choose the vocational track and that schools did not succumb to the pressure of affluent parents to place modestly talented students in a curriculum that was too advanced for them. This idea of equality as meritocracy made it possible, to use Thomas Jefferson's phrase, to rake some diamonds from the rubbish, enabling some outstanding students from disadvantaged backgrounds to get superior educations. Neither NDEA nor Conant, however, had anything to say about how socioeconomic differences produced test-score inequalities that were then reproduced by placement in the different tracks of the comprehensive high school.

The Cold War not only inspired the development of human capital to compete with the Soviet Union scientifically, but also inspired a concern to improve the image of American democracy in competition with the Soviet Union for the loyalties of people in Africa, Asia, and South America. The Supreme Court decision in *Brown v. Board of Education* (1954) satisfied this ideological concern by appearing to demonstrate that American democracy would no longer tolerate racial segregation. NDEA, however, paid no attention to matters of racial inequality. In fact, it passed only because proponents allayed the fears of Southern Congress members that greater federal involvement in education would lead to interference with their segregated institutions.

In contrast to the meritocratic emphasis of NDEA, which actually reinforced race and class inequalities in education, federal policy since 1960, beginning with Title I of the Elementary and Secondary Education Act of 1965, has tried to address these inequalities. Inspired by the civil rights movement, Title I signaled a shift from the international focus of the Cold War to a domestic focus on poverty—the realm Commissioner of Education Francis Keppel called our "nearest foreign country." In introducing the legislation that became the centerpiece of the Great Society and the war on poverty, President Lyndon Johnson stated, "Poverty has many roots, but the taproot is ignorance." The solution was to provide funding to schools with concentrations of the poor in order to "contribute particularly to meeting the special needs of educationally deprived children." In this way the poor would be able to accumulate the human capital necessary to find employment, which would enable them to escape from poverty.

In addition to distracting attention from the ways labor market inadequacies contributed to poverty, there were two major problems with Title I. First, despite an initial investment of slightly more than one billion dollars, the political viability of the program depended on the wide distribution of its funds. As a result, more than nine in every ten school districts ultimately shared the money, making it impossible to concentrate significant resources in the schools and districts with the largest number of poor students. Second, the practice of Title I was governed by the conviction that poor children, especially if they were African American or Latino, were hampered in school because they had cultural deficits that required compensatory education. Although Title I did not specify interventions, the typical practice emphasized pullout programs that focused on low-level skills to make up for what students presumably lacked—and this required them to miss regular classroom instruction.

These limitations became evident once evaluations were conducted. Early on, most of these evaluations found few positive effects. Some studies even found that the achievement of students in the program declined, though this was partly because of the wide dispersal of funding. Later evaluations, conducted once funds were better targeted to the students they were intended to help, were somewhat more encouraging, but they still paled in comparison to the program's original promise to help poor children escape from poverty. By the early 1980s, most concluded that the major benefit of the program was to keep the achievement gap between rich and poor students from getting worse.

Only modestly redistributive and built on the assumption that poor children were deficient rather than that schools were organized to hinder their capacity, Title I was a poor substitute for the more capacious view of equality of educational opportunity that integration promised. But because it distributed its funds so widely, it generated a broad constituency of support from new groups of service providers and recipients, both Republicans and Democrats in Congress, and education interest groups like the National Education Association, which rallied to defend the program whenever it was attacked. As a result, Title I turned out to be remarkably resilient, despite its relatively slight impact on student achievement. It survived Ronald Reagan's attempt to turn it into a block grant in 1981, and it continues to be the chief mechanism for distributing federal dollars to the schools, which it does according to the redistributive premises put in place in 1965.

Whereas Title I was motivated by a desire to use education to help children from low-income families escape what Lyndon Johnson referred to as the "cycle of poverty," the movement that culminated with the passage of the NCLB in 2001 had little to do with fighting poverty. It was motivated instead by a desire to upgrade the quality of the nation's labor force and thereby increase the capacity of its businesses to compete in the international marketplace. But as with the Great Society's poverty warriors, the businesspeople, politicians, educators, and other social reformers who fretted about the nation's lagging economic performance never questioned the idea that the solution to the problems they faced lay primarily with strategies of educational reform aimed at the development of human capital.

At the outset, NCLB did appear to embrace a more robust vision of equal opportunity than Title I of ESEA. Rather than trying to change the character of low-income children, as Title I seemed interested in doing, NCLB aimed to change the schools. By providing test score data to compare schools with students from different backgrounds and sanctioning those that did not bring all groups up to a minimum standard of academic achievement, NCLB countered the idea that low-income children and children of color were somehow incapable of achieving. Instead, it promised to offer proof that schools and educational practices, not children and their parents, were to blame for racially and economically disparate outcomes. It then promised to press inadequate schools to address those disparities.

But this vision of reform was even more pinched than the preceding one. It rightly rejected the array of stigmatizing practices that accompanied earlier compensatory programs and that had long depressed the educational achievement of low-income children. In doing so, however, it also minimized the idea that there was any connection between the conditions of educational provision and school achievement, let alone that equality required the redistribution of income. By setting uniform standards for all students and holding local schools accountable for meeting them, it sought instead to discipline teachers and administrators to raise achievement levels regardless of the often great disparities of resources available in different schools.

Over the last decade, the limits of this strategy have become all too apparent. Touted as a program to reduce the achievement gap so that all students would have an equal chance to acquire the academic skills needed in the twenty-first-century economy, NCLB was rarely effective. Most often, it functioned to protect the educational advantages of the most privileged, just as federal policy has done so often in the past. This time, however, the familiar result didn't come about because educators formally limited access to the most challenging academic classes or because they isolated poor students in pullout classrooms. It was because teachers and administrators in low-income city schools faced the impossible requirement of annual increases in the test scores of multiple subgroups—including special education students—so that all of them attained the same level of proficiency. In order to meet this goal and avoid the NCLB's penalties for failure, these educators focused narrowly on preparation for the tests in reading and mathematics at the expense of other subjects. In contrast, their counterparts in middle-class suburban schools, confident that their students could succeed on the tests without special preparation, continued to offer an enriched curriculum. In this way, the disaggregation of test scores by subgroup, which was the legislation's most progressive feature, actually worked to produce less than progressive results.

Though the rhetoric around NCLB was all about eliminating the achievement gap between rich and poor, any program that directly attacked the sources of the educational advantages of affluent over poor children was unlikely to have won political support. As a result, NCLB focused on saving the children in urban schools while leaving the district lines that protected the suburban schools and their mostly white, middle-class students intact.

None of this long history has done much to dampen enthusiasm among policy makers today for developing human capital in schools as a way to solve the economic challenges facing the nation and to equalize educational opportunity. Economic problems, such as stagnant wages and rising income inequality, for example, have more to do with the absence of strong labor market institutions, the adoption of regressive tax policies, and the social norms that enable vast accumulations of wealth for a few than they do with the quantity and quality of education students receive. Yet the commitment to addressing these problems through ostensibly better education policies not only remains unabated, but, if anything, has been enhanced by the now commonly held belief that the economy's shortcomings stem from too much government intervention rather than too little. In this environment, a "supply-side" strategy like human capital formation has particular appeal, even to many of those who were once skeptical about it.

Some of Obama's supporters hoped he might chart a different course. But his vision of education policy has done little to alter these preferences. His call for the nation to "out-educate" our international competitors continues to assign to the schools responsibility for solving problems that are beyond educational correction while the policies he has adopted—such as Race to the Top—pose no challenge to the jurisdictional arrangements that have long protected the educational advantages of the affluent. Instead, following the trajectory set in motion by NCLB, they are confined to the technical problems of how to manage schools better, measure achievement more precisely, encourage teachers to work harder, and manipulate incentives to stimulate the growth of charter schools.

No less than when Horace Mann wrote his Fifth Report, Obama's strategy might be the only way in the current political climate to win backing for more spending on education. But the history of past policy suggests that we have paid a steep price for it. We should be thinking instead about how we might establish conditions both inside and outside the schools that will engage students in the kind of serious intellectual work that the Committee of Ten called for more than a century ago, rather than pursuing policies that will only add another dimension of inequality to an already unequal system.

Chapter 8

Educational Movements, Not Market Moments

Janelle Scott

For at least two decades, conservatives have argued that school choice was the last unachieved civil right. In 2010, some powerful moderate voices echoed their view and invoked the name of Rosa Parks to support it. At a September 15 screening of the documentary *Waiting for Superman*, which claims charters are the solution for the persistent failure of urban public schools, secretary of education Arne Duncan announced that the film signaled a "Rosa Parks moment" that would initiate a new movement for school choice. On September 24, he repeated that message on the *Oprah Winfrey Show*, promoting the film: "When the country looked at Rosa Parks and looked in her eyes and saw her tremendous dignity and saw her humanity, the country was compelled to act."

In so doing, Duncan and his allies—philanthropists, policy advocates, and leading pundits—reduced the 1955 Montgomery bus boycott to a single act by one brave woman. In fact, that pivotal event was the work of thousands of African Americans and their supporters who struggled for nearly thirteen months to desegregate public transportation in the capital of Alabama after Parks's refusal to give up her seat to a white customer. Moreover, the concerns of civil rights activists extended far beyond transportation; they were fighting to end America's version of apartheid and achieve the full rights of citizenship. As the movement grew, it also advocated the end of poverty and the withdrawal of U.S. troops from Vietnam.

This misunderstanding of the history of the civil rights struggle reveals one of the key flaws in the push for market-based educational solutions. The top-down, managerial, singleminded approach pursued by Duncan and his allies ignores the vital, grassroots efforts underway in low-income communities, many of which directly challenge the market approach to schools that embraces competition, choice without equity provisions, and privatization. These local activists are deeply concerned with a range of problems that prevent public schools from giving poor and working-class children a good education: rampant unemployment, the lack of affordable housing, environmental degradation, and a flawed immigration policy. They want the state to distribute equitable and sufficient resources across communities, not simply to individual schools and parents. And they worry that choice stands to further stratify communities by race and poverty.

*   *   *

Advocates for market-based reforms are disconnected from such grassroots concerns. They take an elitist approach, claiming to know what is best for communities of color. In searching for spokespeople—exemplars of struggling parents and students to represent the need for market-based reform—they neglect the vibrant efforts of those working for educational equity for entire communities.

A good example of inequity concerns the huge gap between funding for urban and suburban school districts. In 2011, a broad swath of entrepreneurial school reformers, pundits, and even some from the civil rights community compared two African American women—Kelley Williams-Bolar from Akron, Ohio, and Tanya McDowell from Norwalk, Connecticut—to Rosa Parks after they were arrested for falsifying their addresses so their children might gain access to schools with more resources outside their urban neighborhoods. Comparisons to Parks were widespread—a Google search of "Williams-Bolar Rosa Parks" yields over twelve thousand results. For example, in a February 2011 post, Kyle Olson, a blogger for *Big Government*, appealed to education reformers to take advantage of the "human face" Williams-Bolar had provided to advocate for an expansion of school choice. His post juxtaposed the classic photograph of Parks being fingerprinted by Montgomery police officers with Williams-Bolar being handcuffed in Akron.

Olson and his fellow market advocates might have thought to ask Williams-Bolar how she saw herself, and why, if charter schools were the salvation, she had bypassed the six community schools (as charters are known in

Ohio) operating in Akron. While she acknowledged that the Copely-Fairlawn school district—the suburban district she had sought out—had higher
performing schools, she wanted to send her daughters there so that they
could go to their grandfather's home nearby after school while she had to
be at work. The girls were too young to be home alone. In fact, on February
3, 2011, she told the *Akron Beacon Journal* in an article entitled, "Center to
File Mother's Appeal," "I'm not perfect and I'm not a Rosa Parks. I'm just a
mom looking out for her kids." Although better schooling was one issue for
Williams-Bolar, safety and security for her daughters, given her need to work
to support them, was a key motivation for her breaking the law. For her and
many who seek safer, better schools, there is no real choice.

*   *   *

The problem lies in the rigid boundaries decreed by courts, beginning in the
1970s, which effectively exempted suburban schools from the requirement
to take part in metropolitan desegregation plans. Many suburban districts
such as Orland Park, Illinois, and Clifton, New Jersey, actually employ private
detectives to investigate the validity of enrolled students' addresses; in some
cases they follow parents who have dropped their children off at school to
verify that they live within the attendance boundaries. Clifton offers a reward
for tips leading to the discovery of address fraud. The Copely-Fairlawn district's private detective followed Williams-Bolar as she drove her daughters to
school, leading to her arrest for fraud.

   With suburban schools off-limits, school choice largely operates inside
urban school districts, and market advocates who decried Williams-Bolar's treatment did not call for a movement to eradicate district attendance
boundaries. Some choice plans, such as magnet schools, mean to facilitate
desegregation on a voluntary basis and do, on the whole, promote integration. Others, such as charter schools and vouchers, offer few ways to promote
equality of opportunity beyond individual parental empowerment. Many
urban parents do avail themselves of these latter options. But this amounts
to choosing between problematic traditional public schools and alternatives
they have had little role in shaping; they may be participating in an individual
moment of empowerment, but their choice making is not a part of a broader
movement for equality of opportunity for all students.

   Contemporary school reformers have not helped matters by undercutting democratic processes. Most favor abolishing elected school boards and local school councils. Yet, the latter were hard won by community control activists frustrated by earlier eras of school reform featuring centralized, managerial leadership dominated by white men inattentive to the needs of poor students and students of color. Both Chicago and New York City recently did away with their elected boards of education and put mayors in charge of their schools. In many cities, private organizations have been given the power to set up and expand charter schools.

And the making of urban educational policy is shaped by unprecedented amounts of private money. For example, under Michelle Rhee, former chancellor of Washington, D.C., schools, several foundations, including the Walton Family Foundation and the Robertson Foundation, pledged millions of dollars to underwrite school reform, money contingent on implementation of the reforms. This practice, increasingly common in cash-starved school districts, stands to distort the policy process and limit the influence of local community movements that have long fought for voice and control under more traditional school governance forms.

Because most elite reformers are disconnected from local struggles, they do not engage the issue of socioeconomic inequality, even as the United States is experiencing the most profound wealth gap since the 1920s. African American and Latino parents cannot be solely focused on securing better schools for their children as long as so many are unemployed or underemployed and have neither safe nor affordable housing.

Civil rights organizations such as the NAACP have long opposed market-based educational polices that do nothing to address racial segregation and class stratification in minority communities. This stance brings them into coalition with teachers' unions, which are portrayed as the prime villains in the accounts of school reformers. But, in fact, teachers' unions—often with African American members in the lead—have consistently supported lawsuits to desegregate schools and bring about fiscal equity between urban and suburban districts.

*   *   *

And, though one wouldn't know it from the mass media, the cause of integrated schools continues to generate broad-based multiracial support in many localities, as the recent struggle in Wake County, North Carolina,

illustrates. Since 2000, a student assignment plan has been in place that resulted in no school having more than 40 percent of its students classified
as living in poverty. This plan also achieved a great deal of racial diversity.
In 2010, newly elected school board members affiliated with the Tea Party
movement tried to block this successful socioeconomic integration plan in
favor of a school choice plan that would almost certainly have resegregated
schools by race and class. Students, civil rights groups, parents, and teachers
took to the streets and testified in packed school board meetings in their efforts to uphold the socioeconomic integration plan. At a July rally in support
of the plan, George Ramsey, a former Enlow High School student, argued,
"Putting back up the walls that this school system worked so hard to tear
down only sends us back." The market reformers were noticeably silent about
these protests, though in 2011, organizing in support of the integration plan
resulted in the ousting of school board members who were determined to
dismantle it.

Grassroots activists have also opposed the larger attempt to put private
agencies in charge of setting up and managing schools. For at least a decade, organizers across the country have fought against school privatization in San Francisco, New York City, Philadelphia, and other cities. For
example, New York's first foray into private management of charter schools
over a decade ago resulted in a racially charged mobilizing effort, with the
community organizing group Association of Community Organizations
for Reform Now (ACORN) leading the opposition. The for-profit school
management company Edison Schools (now Edison Learning) and the New
York City Department of Education joined in efforts to convince parents in
Harlem and Brooklyn to vote to have their schools taken over and managed
by the firm. Though turnout was low, ultimately parents voted against the
proposal.

Under the supervision of Mayor Bloomberg, in the years following the
controversial Edison takeover proposal, charter schools managed by charter management organizations have expanded in New York City, bypassing
the need for parents in existing schools to vote for conversion by starting
new schools altogether. These schools have expended significant resources to
market themselves to parents, and, indeed, many of them have been in high
demand from parents. Yet opposition also exists. More recently, organizers
have pushed back against the growth of charter schools in Harlem and the

privatization and state takeover of schools in New Orleans after Hurricane Katrina.

Not surprisingly, market reformers have been highly critical of these opposition efforts. For example, Dennis Walcott, the black chancellor of New York City schools, accused the NAACP and teachers' union of playing the "race card" when, in June 2011, they filed suit to stop charter schools from taking up space in existing schools. Walcott and his supporters dismissed the overcrowding and inequitable distribution of scarce resources by accusing his critics of racial manipulation.

Yet such detractors, who would otherwise lend their support solely to the expansion of market-based schooling options, miss a vital opportunity to collaborate with organizations that are seeking to increase educational opportunity for all students. Groups like Rethinking Schools and its affiliate, NOT Waiting for Superman, as well as other organizations such as Parents Across America, Class Size Matters, New York Collective of Radical Educators, Forum for Education and Democracy, Coalition for Essential Schools, and A Broader, Bolder Approach to Education are examples of organizations advocating for an alternative vision of good public education. These organizations promote public schools that are open, nested in communities, have excellent teachers and school leaders, and are well resourced, diverse, and democratic. Despite a lack of funding and political support, they have the potential to reorient current efforts toward more democratic, high-quality, and representative public education. Their task is to build networks that bridge communities, as the civil rights movement did decades ago.

*   *   *

The current generation of school reformers is, of course, motivated by good intentions. And they are undoubtedly sincere in their stated desire to emulate the goals and heroes of the Civil Rights movement. Arne Duncan consistently spoke in support of Wake County's integration plan. But tensions persist over the advocacy of school choice as the prevailing civil rights issue when its focus is frequently on individual parental empowerment. We see this focus in the attempt to make "National School Choice Week," first launched in January 2011, an event in which parent and student stories of struggle and triumph in relation to market policies are featured in national and local news media. The message is that individual rights equate a mass movement. It is clear that leading school reformers seem to largely view the great civil rights struggle as the work of atomized individuals and consistently denigrate contemporary activists whose ideas of how fix urban schools clash with their own.

Certainly, the liberty and dignity of each individual were key tenets of the civil rights movement. But freedom activists kept their eyes on the prize of benefits for entire communities and worked to democratize schools and other institutions so they would not continue to be ruled by those who already enjoyed the privileges of wealth and a place at or near the top of the racial hierarchy. Today, when the economic crisis has eroded the gains of the black and Latino middle classes and deepened the poverty of other Americans of color, school reformers continue to insist that poverty and unemployment are "no excuse" for not performing well on standardized tests and deride critics of the privatizing and segregating effects of some choice policies as being defenders of an unequal status quo. In fact, these market critics seek a much more equitable schooling system that would disrupt what Jonathon Kozol famously termed, in the title of his popular 1991 book, *Savage Inequalities*.

Can we imagine Martin Luther King, Jr., A. Philip Randolph, Ella Baker, or Rosa Parks marching on Washington to secure the right for parents to compete in lotteries for spaces in free-market schools? Rather than these figures, the managers of such reforms in fact seem to be emulating another iconic cultural figure: Milton Friedman, the Nobel Prize-winning libertarian economist whose 1962 best-selling book was entitled *Free to Choose*.

PART II

Education, Race, and Poverty

Chapter 9

Public Education as Welfare

Michael B. Katz

Welfare is the most despised public institution in America. Public education is the most iconic. To associate them with each other will strike most Americans as bizarre, even offensive. The link would be less surprising to nineteenth-century reformers for whom crime, poverty, and ignorance formed an unholy trinity against which they struggled. Nor would it raise British eyebrows. Ignorance was one of the "five giants" to be slain by the new welfare state proposed in the famous Beveridge Report. National Health Insurance, the cornerstone of the British welfare state, and the 1944 Education Act, which introduced the first national system of secondary education to Britain, were passed by Parliament only two years apart. Yet, only a few scholars have even suggested that education might form part of the American welfare state.

This mutual neglect by students of welfare and education is a mistake. In the rest of this chapter, I explain why. I also describe where public education fits in the architecture of the welfare state and why this attempt to join the negative and positive poles of social policy matters. To the first question—why—my answer stresses economic redistribution. To the second question—how—the answer is that education is a special track in the public welfare state. To the last question—why it matters—the answer is twofold: both the welfare state and education are enormous and in one way or another touch every single American. It behooves us to know how they work. Even more, insight into links between public education and the welfare state illuminate the mechanisms through which American governments try to accomplish their goals and show how institutions whose public purpose is egalitarian in fact reproduce inequality.

The definition and boundaries of the welfare state are not transparent; they remain contentious topics. Elsewhere, in *The Price of Citizenship: Redefining the American Welfare State* (2001, updated edition 2008), I have explained that the "term 'welfare state' refers to a collection of programs designed to assure economic security to all citizens by guaranteeing the fundamental necessities of life: food, shelter, medical care, protection in childhood and support in old age. In America, the usual restriction of the definition of welfare state to government programs excludes the vast array of private activities that address economic security and the needs associated with poverty and dependence." The way to understand a nation's welfare state is not to apply a theoretically driven definition but, rather, to examine the mechanisms through which legislators, service providers, and employers, whether public, private, or a mix of the two, try to prevent or respond to poverty, illness, dependency, economic insecurity, and old age.

Where does public education fit within this definition? To begin, on a concrete level, for more than a century schools have been used as agents of the welfare state to deliver social services, such as nutrition and health. Today, in poor neighborhoods, they often provide hot breakfasts among other services. More to the point, public school systems administer one of the nation's largest programs of economic redistribution. Most accounts of public education finance stress the opposite point by highlighting inequities, "savage inequalities," to borrow Jonathan Kozol's phrase, that shortchange city youngsters and racial minorities. To a large part, these result from the much higher per pupil spending in affluent suburbs than in poor inner cities, where yields from property taxes are much lower. All this is undeniable as well as unacceptable.

But tilt the angle and look at the question from another perspective. Consider how much the average family with children pays in property taxes, the principal support for schools. Then focus on per pupil expenditure, even in poor districts. You will find that families, including poor city families, receive benefits worth much more than they have contributed. Wealthier families, childless and empty-nest couples, and businesses subsidize families with children in school.

There is nothing new about this. The mid-nineteenth-century founders of public school systems, like Horace Mann, and their opponents under-

stood the redistributive character of public education. To build school systems, early school promoters needed to persuade the wealthy and childless
that universal, free education would serve their interests by reducing the in-
cidence of crime, lowering the cost of poor relief, improving the skills and
attitudes of workers, assimilating immigrants, and even saving them money
in the long run. So successful were early school promoters that taxation for
public education lost its controversial quality. With just a few exceptions, debates focused on the amount of taxes, not on their legitimacy. The exceptions
occurred primarily around the founding of high schools, which working-
class and other voters correctly observed would serve only a small fraction of
families at a time when most young people in their early teens were sent out
to work or kept at home to help their families. For the most part, however,
the redistributive quality of public education sank farther from public con-
sciousness. This is what early school promoters wanted and had worked to
make happen. When they began their work in the early nineteenth century,
"public," as used in education, usually referred to schools widely available
and either free or cheap, in short, schools for the poor. School promoters
worked tirelessly to break this link between public and pauper that inhibited
the development of universal public education systems. So successful were
they that today the linkage seems outrageous, even though in cities where
most remaining affluent families send their children to private schools, the
association of public with pauper has reemerged with renewed ferocity.

As a concrete example, here is a back-of-the-envelope illustration. In
2003–2004, public elementary and secondary education in the United States
cost $403 billion or, on average, $8,310 per student (or, taking the median,
$7,860). Most families paid nothing like the full cost of this education in
taxes. Property taxes, which account for a huge share of spending on public
schools, amount to an average of $935 per person, or, for a family of four,
something under $4,000, less than half the average per pupil cost. As rough as
these figures are, they do suggest that most families with school-age children
receive much more from spending on public education than they contribute
in taxes. (A similar point could be made about public higher education.)

Taxpayers provide this subsidy because they view public education as
a crucial public good. It prevents poverty, lowers the crime rate, prepares
young people for the workforce, and fosters social mobility—or so the story
goes. The reality, as historians of education have shown, is a good deal more
complex. Public education is the mechanism through which the United

States solves problems and attempts to reach goals achieved more directly or through different mechanisms in other countries. International comparisons usually brand the United States a welfare laggard because it spends less of its national income on welfare-related benefits than do other advanced industrial democracies. But the comparisons leave out spending on public education, private social services, employer-provided health care and pensions, and benefits delivered through the tax code, a definitional weakness whose importance will become clearer with the description of the architecture of the welfare state which follows.

In *Social Control of the Welfare State* (1976), sociologist Morris Janowitz pointed out that "the most significant difference between the institutional bases of the welfare state in Great Britain and the United States was the emphasis placed on public education—especially for lower income groups—in the United States. Massive support for the expansion of public education . . . in the United States, must be seen as a central component of the American notion of welfare." In the late nineteenth and early twentieth centuries, while other nations were introducing unemployment, old age, and health insurance, the United States was building high schools, which experienced a huge surge in enrollment. "One would have to return to the 1910s to find levels of secondary school enrollment in the United States that match those in 1950s Western Europe," point out economists Claudia Golden and Lawrence F. Katz in *The Race Between Education and Technology* (2008:26). European nations were about a generation behind the United States in expanding secondary education; the United States was about a generation behind Europe in instituting its welfare state. In "Education and Social Security Entitlements in Europe and America" (1981), political scientist Arnold J. Heidenheimer observes that, "Public social insurance and some other kinds of income maintenance programs were introduced in the United States with about a one generation lag behind Europe. . . . the broadening of U.S. post-primary school opportunities occurred a generation earlier than in Europe, and European systems have only in the past few decades allowed their secondary and tertiary systems to enter the take off stage" (269).

With education considered a component, it becomes clear that the American welfare state focuses on enhancing equality of opportunity in contrast to European welfare states, which historically have been more sympathetic to equality of condition. In the United States, equality always has been primarily about a level playing field where individuals can compete unhindered by obstacles that crimp the full expression of their native talents; education has served as the main mechanism for leveling the field. European concepts of equality more often focus on group inequality and the collective mitigation of handicaps and risks that, in the United States, have been left for individuals to deal with on their own.

Public education is part of the American welfare state. But which part? How does it fit into the welfare state's complicated architecture? In *The Price of Citizenship*, I have described the architecture of the American welfare state in detail. Here I summarize it briefly. The American welfare state consists of several components, each of which is rooted in a different place in American history. Think of the welfare state as a largely unplanned structure erected by many different people over centuries with its parts loosely coupled. This rickety, ungainly structure—which no sane, rational person would have designed—consists of two main divisions: the public and private welfare states, with subdivisions in each. The divisions of the public welfare state are public assistance, social insurance, and taxation. Public assistance, throughout most of its history called outdoor relief, originated with the Elizabethan poor laws brought over by the colonists. It consists of means tested benefits. Examples are, before 1996, Aid to Families with Dependent Children (AFDC), and after 1996, Temporary Assistance to Needy Families (TANF), the programs current-day Americans usually have in mind when they speak of "welfare." Social insurance originated in Europe in the late nineteenth century and made its way slowly to the United States. The first form of American social insurance was workers' compensation, instituted by several state governments in the early twentieth century. Social insurance benefits accrue to individuals on account of fixed criteria such as age. They are called insurance because they are allegedly based on prior contributions. The major social insurances—Social Security for the elderly and unemployment insurance—emerged with a bang in 1935 when Congress passed the Social Security Act. Social insurance benefits are much higher than benefits provided through public assistance, and they carry no stigma. The third track in the public welfare state is taxation. Both federal and state governments administer important benefits through the tax code rather than through direct grants. This is the most modern feature of the welfare state. The major example of a benefit aimed at poor people is the Earned Income Tax Credit, which expanded greatly during the presidency of Bill Clinton.

Within the private welfare state are two divisions: charities and social services, and employee benefits. Charities and social services, of course, have a long and diverse history. In the 1960s, governments started to fund an increasing number of services provided through private agencies. (In the United States, governments primarily write checks; they do not usually operate programs.) More and more dependent on public funding, private agencies increasingly became, in effect, government providers, a transformation with profound implications for their work. Employee benefits constitute the other division in the private welfare state, dating primarily from after the Second World War. They expanded as a result of the growth of trade unions, legitimated by the 1935 Wagner Act, and 1949 decisions of the Labor Relations Board, which held that employers were required to bargain over, not provide, employee benefits.

Some economists object to including employee benefits in the welfare state, but they are mistaken. Employee benefits are the mechanism through which the United States has chosen to meet the health care needs of a majority of its population. About 60 percent of Americans receive their health insurance through their employer, and many receive pensions as well. Without employer-provided health care and pensions—if trade unions had bargained hard for a public rather than a private welfare state—the larger American welfare state would look very different. Moreover, the federal government encourages delivery of health care and pensions through private employers by allowing them to deduct the cost from taxes, and it supervises them with massive regulations, notably the Employee Retirement Income Security Act (ERISA), passed in 1974.

The first thing to stress about this welfare state as a whole is that its divisions are not distinct. They overlap and blend in complicated ways, giving the American welfare state a mixed economy not usefully described as either public or private. At the same time, federalism constrains its options, with some benefits at the center, provided by the federal government, and others offered through state and local governments. Throughout the twentieth century, a great problem facing would-be welfare state builders was designing benefits to pass constitutional muster.

How does public education fit into the odd, bifurcated structure of America's welfare state? Public education shares characteristics with social insurance, public assistance, and social services. At first, it appears closest to social insurance. Its benefits are universal and not means tested, which makes them similar to Social Security (although Social Security benefits received by high-income individuals are taxed). But education benefits are largely in-kind as are many other welfare state benefits such as food stamps, housing, and medical care. (In-kind benefits are "government provision of goods and services to those in need of them" rather than "with income sufficient to meet their needs via the market.") Nor are benefits earned by recipients through prior payroll contributions or employment. This separates them from Social Security, unemployment insurance, and workers' compensation. Public education is also an enormous source of employment, second only to health care in the public welfare state.

Even more, public education is primarily local. Great variation exists among states and, within states, among municipalities. In this regard, it differs completely from Social Security and Medicare, whose nationally set benefits are uniform across the nation, and is more like unemployment insurance, workers' compensation, and TANF (and earlier AFDC), which vary by state, but not by municipality within states. The adequacy of educational benefits, by contrast, varies with municipal wealth. Education, in fact, is the only public benefit financed largely by property taxes. This confusing mix of administrative and financial patterns provides another example of how history shapes institutions and policy.

Because of its differences from both social insurance and public assistance, public education composes a separate division within the public welfare state. But it moves in the same directions as the rest. The forces redefining the American welfare state have buffeted public schools as well as public assistance, social insurance, and the private welfare state.

In *The Price of Citizenship*, I argue that, since the 1980s, pursuit of three objectives has driven change in the whole giant welfare state edifice. These objectives are, first, a war on dependence in all its forms—not only the dependence of young unmarried mothers on welfare but all forms of dependence on public and private support such as the dependence of workers on paternalistic employers for secure long-term jobs and benefits. Second is the devolution of authority, meaning the transfer of power from the federal government to the states, from states to localities, and from the public to the private sector. Last is the application of free-market models to social policy. Everywhere, the free market triumphed as a template for a reengineered welfare state. This is not a partisan story. Broad consensus on these objectives crossed party lines. Within the reconfigured welfare state, work in the regular labor market emerged as the gold standard, the mark of first class citizenship which carried with it entitlement to the most generous benefits. The corollary, of course, was that failure or inability to join the regular labor force meant relegation to second-class citizenship where benefits were mean, punitive, or just unavailable.

The war on dependence, the devolution of authority, and the application of market models also run through the history of public education in these decades. The attack on "social promotion"; emphasis on high-stakes tests; implementation of tougher high school graduation requirements; and transmutation of "accountability" into the engine of school reform: all these developments are of a piece with the war on dependence. They reject any paternalistic coddling and call for individual students to stand on their own with rewards distributed strictly according to personal merit. Other developments point to the practice of devolution in public education. A prime example is the turn toward site-based management, that is, the decentralization of significant administrative authority from central offices to individual schools. The most extreme example is Chicago's 1989 school reform, which put Local School Councils in charge of each school, even giving them authority to hire and fire principals. At the same time, however, a countervailing trend, represented by the federal No Child Left Behind Act (NCLB) and the imposition of standards, limited the autonomy of individual teachers and schools and imposed new forms of centralization. In this slightly schizoid blend of local autonomy and central control, trends in public education paralleled developments in the administration of public assistance: the 1996 federal "welfare reform" legislation mandated a set of outcomes but left states autonomy in reaching them. In both education and public assistance, the mechanism of reform became the centralization of acceptable outcomes and the decentralization of the means for achieving them.

As for the free market as a template for reform, it was everywhere in education as well as the rest of the welfare state. Markets invaded schools with compulsory viewing of advertising on Chris Whittle's Channel One, "free" TV news for schools, and kickbacks to schools from Coke, Pepsi, and other products sold in vending machines—money schools desperately needed as their budgets for sports, arts, and culture were cut. Some school districts turned over individual schools to for-profit corporations, such as Edison Schools, while advocacy of vouchers and private charter schools reflected the belief that blending competition among providers with parental choice would expose poorly performing schools and teachers and motivate others to improve.

Unlike the situation in the rest of the welfare state, educational benefits cannot be tied to employment. But they are stratified nonetheless by location, wealth, and race. The forces eroding the fiscal capacities of cities and old suburbs—withdrawal of federal aid and a shrinking tax base—have had a devastating impact on public education and on children and adolescents, relegating a great many youngsters living in poor or near-poor families to second-class citizenship. In the educational division of the public welfare state, test results play the role taken on elsewhere by employment. They are gatekeepers to the benefits of first-class citizenship. The danger is that high-stakes tests and stiffer graduation requirements will further stratify citizenship among the young with kids failing tests joining nonworking mothers and out-of-work black men as the undeserving poor. In this way, public education complements the rest of the welfare state as a mechanism for reproducing—as well as mitigating—inequality in America.

Chapter 10

In Search of Equality in School Finance Reform

Pamela Barnhouse Walters, Jean C. Robinson, and Julia C. Lamber

If any reform promised to bring about equality of educational opportunity, it was arguably school finance reform. By eliminating the large differences in per-pupil spending among school districts in the same state, it would have leveled the playing field between high-spending versus low-spending districts. Yet, after four decades of effort, fewer than half the states have made serious attempts to equalize school financing (almost always in response to decisions from state supreme courts ordering them to do so). Furthermore, even in the states that have attempted to do so, the reforms have met considerable political and popular resistance. In most states in which the courts have ordered an overhaul of public school financing, the legislatures have at best tinkered around the edges of an equalizing reform. Some have ignored the rulings outright. As a result, there continue to be large differences in funding between high-spending and low-spending districts in just about every state.

School finance reform challenges the very foundation on which American inequality of educational opportunity rests. That is our historical reliance on local property taxes as the primary means of financing K-12 public education, coupled with the segregation of poor from affluent communities by school district boundaries. The result is the familiar patchwork pattern of "good" and "bad" public schools: with rare exceptions, to find the best public schools we need to look to affluent suburbs, and to find the worst we have only to turn to our central cities. School finance reform would have dismantled this system that typically relegates children from poor communities to low-quality public schools (and, as is less often publicly recognized, reserves the best public schools for children in affluent communities).

Popular and scholarly writing on school finance reform generally depicts it as a failed effort. We concur, but we believe that before addressing the question of the overall failure, we must explore a prior and equally important question: given its radically redistributive potential, how did school finance reform ever get any political traction? After all, the United States is hardly known for its commitment to redistributive social policies.

How did policy makers come to make a commitment to school finance reform in the first place, and how did reform efforts, once undertaken, get blunted, derailed, and sometimes outright defeated? An interesting complication to the story is that school finance reform efforts have been turned back even as the abstract principle on which they are based, the promise of equality of educational opportunity, retains its longstanding pride of place in American political culture. As it turns out, equality means different things to different people. This range of meanings is the key to understanding why school finance reform originally got its political legs and why it has been hobbled.

Political resonance notwithstanding, equality remains only vaguely defined and understood. When Americans embrace equality as an abstract principle, they generally fail to understand that *by definition* some groups reap huge benefits from the inequality endemic to American public schooling. Similarly, little attention is paid to the fact that the "good" education privileged children generally get needs to be a *better* education than what is available to most others. That's because a "good" education is what economists call a *positional* good: its value rises in inverse proportion to its scarcity. Instead of focusing on the benefits that unequal schooling provides to the winners (here, students in resource-rich school districts), public attention focuses on the need to alleviate the sufferings of the losers (students in resource-poor districts). The undeniable reality that doing so will reduce the *relative* educational advantages enjoyed by the privileged is rarely acknowledged. Prior to and during policy adoption, school finance reform was framed as an effort that would remove barriers to access to education on the part of previously disadvantaged groups (students in poorly funded public school districts). In this version of what equality means, it is framed as nothing more and nothing less than a benefit to the disadvantaged, which obscures the fundamentally redistributive nature of the reform.

But as equalizing reforms unfold, the threat they pose to the most privileged students becomes impossible to gloss over or ignore. And at that point popular support for "equality" weakens. As policy makers began to take steps to implement court-mandated school finance orders, people began to understand that students in resource-rich districts (especially wealthy suburbs) might have their *relative* advantage diminished. Their schools might no longer be the best by such a wide margin. At that point, opponents of school finance reform took advantage of the vagueness and flexibility of the meaning of equality as they found ways to resist the reform without repudiating the principle of equality. One way they resisted was to reframe what equality means by offering definitions of "equal" or "equality" that sound like equivalents but in fact have quite different implications for forms of redress. The terms "equity," "fairness," and "adequacy" were offered as apparent synonyms at different times. Opponents made particularly good use of the concept of fairness by arguing that an equalization of educational resources would actually be "unfair" to the formerly advantaged. Another way opponents resisted was by in effect "trumping" equality claims by invoking other core political values as more important (without directly denying the importance of equality). The main trump cards were calls for local control and state fiscal responsibility.

*   *   *

The first suits challenging unequal school funding were filed in 1968, in Texas and then California. Between 1968 and 1973, school finance reform came to be regarded in highly positive terms within federal policy circles. Indeed, in 1972 a federal legislative proposal to equalize funding across school districts came close to passing. The key reason why such a radically redistributive reform gained strong national political traction in the early 1970s is that school finance reform was closely linked to the politics of school desegregation and the practice of busing to achieve racial balance in American public schools.

The Texas and California suits capitalized on the cultural legitimacy of the principle of *racial* equality established by the black civil rights movement during the 1960s. In both cases, the plaintiffs, Mexican American families in poorly funded districts, undertook the suits as remedies for racial discrimination in public education. In the national policy discussion that began after the suits were filed, school finance reform was similarly understood to be at least in part a remedy for racial discrimination and segregation. The racial equality argument, one that was very difficult to repudiate in the context of the late 1960s and early 1970s, was in effect flexibly extended to be about disparities in educational resources between school districts.

The political resonance of arguments about equality notwithstanding, the success of early efforts at school finance reform hinged to a large extent on the *protections* from racial equality it promised whites. Leaving minority students in predominantly minority schools while improving the resources available to minority schools was a way to avoid jeopardizing the "good" schools enjoyed by whites. This motivation for school finance reform gained additional momentum once school busing became a national political controversy. The 1971 United States Supreme Court decision in *Swann v. Charlotte-Mecklenburg Board of Education* brought busing from the South to the rest of the country and triggered widespread opposition to the practice. In 1972, President Richard Nixon packaged proposed legislation to increase federal funding for poor school districts with an initiative to dismantle busing. The racial implications of the former were explicitly acknowledged, while the latter was cloaked in a language of equality. In a televised address, the president said his proposed Equal Educational Opportunities Act would "improve the education of minority children in the central cities without busing them to the suburbs." In exchange for halting busing, he pledged to "guarantee that the children currently attending the poorest schools in our cities and in rural districts be provided with education equal to that of the good schools or their communities." Among the means by which this would be accomplished was a provision that each school district must spend as much on schools in poor areas as it did on schools in wealthy areas or become ineligible for federal funds. Even though the proposed legislation ultimately died in the Senate later in 1972, the national debate about school finance reform during this period assumed it would happen. Indeed, it was the morally correct course of action.

The public debate over Nixon's proposed legislation focused little attention on the redistributive consequences of the initiative. The fact that privileged children would lose some of their substantial educational advantage over others was obscured by popular opposition to the perceived greater evil of busing, which would allow racial minorities to "infiltrate" white schools. In this context, those who opposed racial integration could support school finance reform by framing it as an effort to alleviate the worst of the educational deprivations suffered by children in resource-poor school districts that would (coincidentally) have no adverse effects on white, suburban schools. It might even leave them untouched. Political support for Nixon's proposal for federal school finance reform must be understood, then, not as an embrace of the principle of true equality, which requires redistribution, but rather as a rejection of racial integration in public schools.

The window of opportunity for school finance reform to become a federal policy initiative closed in 1973, when the U.S. Supreme Court in *San Antonio Independent School District v. Rodriguez* ruled that education was not a fundamental right guaranteed by the Constitution. After *Rodriguez*, legal redress for funding inequality could be found only by appeal to state constitutional guarantees. School finance reform moved to state supreme courts and state legislatures.

*   *   *

Part of the changing political discourse about what school funding equalization would really mean involved a change over time in the language state courts used in deciding school finance cases. All state constitutions have education provisions requiring systems of free public education. Some state constitutions, like Ohio's, also require that these educational systems be "thorough and efficient." These education clauses, along with state equal-protection provisions, provide the basis of modern school finance lawsuits. But the court decisions do not turn on or at least cannot be explained in terms of the constitutional language or provisions.

Early rulings by state supreme courts were based on a logic and language of equality, although "equity" often appeared side-by-side with "equality" in early decisions. The murkiness of the concept of equality was as apparent in court rulings as it was in general political debate. Throughout the era (1973–1989) in which school finance scholars generally agree that the courts used a standard of "equality" to render their decisions, the courts never offered a clear standard for what would constitute "equal." Eschewing the most straightforward definition of equality—parity or a fifty-fifty division—the courts in practice defined equal opportunity to mean equality with some allowance for disparities without any clear guidance on how big those disparities might be. That lack of guidance left ample room for political opponents to reframe what equality or equal opportunity meant.

Equity has none of the connotations of sameness or parity that equality does; instead, it foregrounds fairness and justice, which might not demand equal shares. Nonetheless, in the early decisions a language of "equity" was sometimes used as if it were a synonym for "equality." In 1976 in *Serrano v. Priest (Serrano II)*, the California Supreme Court ordered a new state finance system to fix "inequities," not "inequalities." In 1986, in *Serrano v. Priest (Serrano III)*, the California court found "the progress toward equitable financial treatment of students since 1974 a remarkable accomplishment," and that although differences in spending remained, those differences were justifiable. In practice, "equity" allowed for more discrepancies between groups than did "equality," even if the exact degree of discrepancy permitted remained similarly unspecified. The principle of equity appears regularly in state school finance decisions throughout the 1970s and 1980s.

The language of school finance reform changed in 1989 when, in *Rose v. Council for Better Education*, the Kentucky Supreme Court ruled that each child should be given "an equal opportunity to have an adequate education," a standard that required all schools to have "sufficient" and "substantially uniform" (but not necessarily equal) funding. The *Rose* decision marked a turn in school finance litigation: from that point forward, most cases were decided in terms of adequacy rather than equity. Although the changes to the state finance system allowed by the court privileged adequate over equal, they provided no more guidance about exactly how big the disparities might be than had the courts that decided equality cases.

This discursive turn from equality to adequacy serves, in effect, to limit the resource claims that can be legitimately made by the least advantaged group. They may have the right to an improvement in resources, but not necessarily to any closing of the gap between school districts with the worst versus best resources. A metric of adequacy also diverts public attention from what consequences, if any, the reform has for the educational resources enjoyed by the most advantaged groups. It both delegitimizes redistribution as a goal and obscures any potential redistributional consequences of the reforms.

*　*　*

Although the vagueness of the court's definition of equality gave political opponents of school finance reform considerable room to offer their own definitions, the substitution of equity for equality provided even greater opportunities for deflecting the equalizing potential of the reform. Equity is closely associated with a standard of fairness. The claim that school finance reform should be fair provided a big opportunity for opponents to argue that the reform was in fact *unfair*, unfair to those whose privileged public educations would be jeopardized, that is. The (un)fairness arguments are among the few times when the redistributive consequences of these reforms were explicitly acknowledged.

The most striking unfairness arguments used by school finance opponents are those that call such efforts "Robin Hood" plans. That is, reforms that would (unfairly) steal from the rich to give to the poor. The Robin Hood label was used to great effect in many states, including Texas, Vermont, and Ohio. The basic argument is that wealthy school districts deserved to keep the resources they generated through their own taxes; it was unfair to require them to share those resources with districts that generated less tax revenue per pupil for the schools. Shortly after the *DeRolph* decision in Ohio, for example, the *Columbus Dispatch* adopted an editorial position against it, lamenting that "healthier districts which demonstrate a willingness to fund educational excellence would be penalized via a court-ordered leveling" (July 17, 1994). A state representative from a property-rich Ohio school district complained in the *Cleveland Plain Dealer* that *DeRolph* would require the people of his district to give their money away to other people who wouldn't help themselves ("Funding Decision Forces Legislators to Examine Plans," July 3, 1994). In a March 28, 1996, editorial discussing New Jersey's school finance reform efforts, the *New York Times* objected that cutting funds to high-performing districts would be "in effect punishing them for achieving excellence."

Depicting school finance reform as unfair allowed opponents to fight against it without embracing inequality. Another form taken by attempts to counter equality claims was an argument that some other legitimate political value or state interest took priority over equality or, in our words, trumped it. The most common competing claim that opponents made was an appeal to local control. Arguments concerning the need for fiscal responsibility, that equality was just too expensive (and thus fiscally irresponsible), constituted another form of competing claim.

The principle of local control as a means of fighting school finance reform appeared early. Commenting on California's school finance reform efforts, for example, a 1972 *New York Times* article observed that "taxpayers and officials" were most worried about "the possible loss of local control, the fear that once

money is no longer raised locally, decisions will no longer be made locally either" ("Property Tax Reform Enthusiasm Lags," December 19). A California
official similarly worried in the *Los Angeles Times* that, by limiting localities'
ability to raise property taxes, school finance reform would "cripple" local government ("Passage of Tax Reform-School Financing Bill Urged by Riles," July
19, 1972). Given the near-sacred status of local control in American political
culture, such arguments come as no surprise. What was not openly acknowledged, however, is that local control is what allows resource-rich school districts with the best schools to provide those superior resources to their own
schools rather than dilute them by sharing with others.

The local control argument continued to be regularly deployed by opponents. Throughout the 1990s, for example, local control was part of the rhetoric used to oppose the Ohio Supreme Court's decision in *DeRolph v. State*.
Governor George Voinovich responded to the decision with the complaint
that "the court decided they were going to meddle in and decide how we were
going to run our school systems" ("Governor Rips Schools Ruling," *Columbus Dispatch*, March 26, 1997); the state budget director was quoted as saying
that "this decision will likely result in a significant state tax increase and an
erosion of local control of schools" ("Budget Process to Go On," *Columbus
Dispatch*, March 26, 1997). An editorial the previous day in the same paper
argued that the ruling would result in the "loss of local control of schools."

A state's duty to be fiscally responsible was similarly a call used to blunt
school finance reform without directly repudiating the principle of equality.
It first appeared in political resistance to the California Supreme Court 1976
decision in *Serrano II*. Faced with state legislation that would have increased
funds for poor districts without reducing funds for wealthy oness—an initiative that would have required a massive tax increase—the voters of California
in 1978 passed the infamous Proposition 13, which limited local property tax
rates and thus crippled the state's ability to fund its public schools at former
levels. Again in California, when the state supreme court decided in 1986
in *Serrano III* that sufficient progress had been made toward making school
finance equitable, it went on to rule that the remaining disparities in funding,
even if significant, were "justified" by other compelling state interests, such as
a need for state financial stability at a time of fiscal crisis.

Similar arguments for fiscal responsibility were used to good effect by
opponents of school finance reform elsewhere. In Ohio, for example, State
Senator Eugene Watts, an opponent of the *DeRolph* decision, was quoted as

saying, "we will not be bullied or browbeaten into surrendering our constitutional duty, and into bayoneting the people of Ohio with a massive—and
unnecessary—tax increase" ("Two Senators Propose to Amend State Constitution," *Columbus Dispatch*, March 4, 1999). As part of his opposition to the
first *DeRolph* decision, Voinovich similarly voiced the (negative) view that
it would require a "massive tax increase on the people of Ohio" ("Decision
Spurs Tax-Hike Fear," *Columbus Dispatch*, July 9, 1994). In New Jersey, home
to one of the longest-running school finance reform battles, in the mid-1990s
Governor Christine Todd Whitman complained that following the court
ruling would drain state resources, to little good effect, because "pouring"
money into failing schools was not the answer ("Showdown over a Financing Gap," *New York Times*, November 26, 1996). Critics' charges that school
finance reform would erode local control or was fiscally irresponsible had the
same effect as labels of unfairness: they allowed opponents to fight the reform
without taking a stand against equality.

*   *   *

The irony in the story of school finance reform, then, is that Americans appear to be willing to follow through on a political commitment to equality
only when its redistributive consequences are downplayed or glossed over.
Once it becomes apparent that an initiative to create greater equality in school
resources will threaten the easy access children in resource-rich districts have
to public schools that are hands-down superior to most other schools, school
finance reform meets strong political opposition. The fact that existing inequalities in public schools can be defended with words that on the surface
look like close cousins of equality is, however, the ultimate irony.

Resolving this impasse requires changing the conversation. We need to
move away from a focus on redistributing resources across the extant system
of school districts and revisit the basic structure of inequality of education in
this country. The new conversation about promoting equality of educational
opportunity would have to include a rethinking of the sacrosanct status of
school district boundaries. The relatively small step of consolidating small
school districts into larger ones would increase socioeconomic diversity
within districts and couple the fates of affluent and less affluent students to
each other, almost certainly to the benefit of those who had previously resided
in poorly funded districts. A more politically ambitious effort would abolish

school district boundaries altogether, or make them moot with respect to access to resources, by funding all schools from a central state budget.

The new conversation would usefully revisit the sacredness of local control in American political culture. Most other advanced, industrial democracies fund and control education at the national level and, as a result, offer far greater equality of educational opportunities and resources to their citizens. An updated version of President Nixon's Equal Educational Opportunities Act would be a step in the right direction.

This new conversation would also need to acknowledge that educational reform cannot be a stand-alone effort. The problems of poor-quality urban public schools, in particular, are not the result of education policy and practice alone. Any successful effort to bring the educational opportunities available in public urban schools closer to what is enjoyed in our better schools must be combined with efforts to address other problems, such as housing, transportation, and employment.

We understand that it would be politically difficult to turn the conversation in the directions we suggest. But if our goal is to make significant progress in closing the gap in resources and opportunities between our best and worst schools, we need to do more than tinker around the edges of the current system. We need to muster the political will and build the political coalitions necessary to make such a reexamination of the fundamentals possible.

Chapter 11

"I Want the White People Here!": The Dark Side of an Urban School Renaissance

Maia Cucchiara

Grant Elementary, part of Philadelphia's beleaguered public school system, stands among rows of historic townhouses in Philadelphia's revitalized downtown (all school, neighborhood, and individual names in this chapter are pseudonyms). Beginning in 2004, Grant was the focus of an aggressive campaign by parents, school district administrators, and local civic leaders to market this and other downtown schools to the middle- and upper-middle-class professionals living in the area. Many Philadelphians, concerned about both the quality of the schools and ongoing middle-class flight, supported the campaign. This is understandable. After all, an influx of middle-class parents in Philadelphia's schools could generate additional resources and higher standards in these schools—no small thing in a city littered with failed reform efforts. And the middle- and upper-middle-class parents who came to Grant as a result of this campaign did improve the school in many ways. Yet the story this chapter tells—the story of an urban school "renaissance"—is more complicated than those involved at Grant might have expected. The effort to attract a particular constituency to the school had a number of inequitable consequences, most notably the marginalization and exclusion of low-income and minority families. Thus, while the marketing of Grant did result in enhanced programming and facilities at the school, it also made the public schools complicit in the larger project of reshaping urban public institutions so that they disproportionately serve the interests of the middle- and upper-middle classes.

This pattern is being repeated in cities across the country, as, rather than fleeing for the suburbs, urban middle-class families join together to make dramatic improvements to their local schools. Their efforts are generally celebrated in the local and national media, with middle- and upper-middle-class parents called "pioneers" or "reformers" and lauded for their donations of time, money, and other resources. In Chicago, for example, the effort to transform one neighborhood school (Nettelhorst Elementary) generated national publicity, including a book tour, media appearances, and commendation from public officials. Such a "solution" to the enduring problems of urban education uses the resources of the middle class to try to address what are largely structural challenges: inequitable school funding and the myriad consequences of poverty. Like other reform strategies that are currently popular—such as linking teacher salary to student test scores and alternative teacher certification—middle-class transformations of urban public schools negate the need for difficult conversations about resource distribution and the disenfranchisement of low-income urban communities. Yet, as I learned in my ethnography of Grant, the benefits of recruiting more middle-class families to urban public schools also come at a cost, namely, limited access and diminished status for some low-income and minority families.

*   *   *

The area surrounding Grant Elementary School is known as Cobble Square, a prosperous neighborhood in Philadelphia's downtown. Streets are lined with grand old homes, horse-drawn carriages carry tourists from one site to another, and some of the streets are paved with cobblestones. Though it has been there for decades, the school still does not quite fit into its historic surroundings: it towers over a nearby row of colonial houses, and its playground is bare and utilitarian compared to the lush window boxes and shaded sidewalks in the vicinity.

In 2000 Cobble Square was 91 percent white. It was also very expensive: the median residential sale price in 2005 was $679,000, compared to a citywide median of $86,000. The Grant catchment area included Cobble Square and a more diverse set of neighborhoods, including a heavily Asian community. Yet the marketing of Grant focused heavily on Cobble Square and other white and middle- to upper-middle-class neighborhoods in the larger

downtown area, which itself had become increasingly affluent over the previous decade.

In order to understand how the effort to market a public school to professional families was experienced by parents, I conducted a two-year ethnography (2004–2006) of Grant Elementary's Parent Teacher Organization
(PTO). The year I began my study, Grant served 471 students from kindergarten through eighth grade: 43 percent Asian American, 43 percent African
American, and 11 percent white.

While Cobble Square residents generally eschewed Grant in favor of one
of the local private schools, in 2003 a small group of parents from the community began to actively recruit other "neighborhood" parents to Grant. A local
business organization, the Center City District, which received money from
the state of Pennsylvania and a local foundation to market downtown public
schools to professionals living in the area, later complemented and expanded
on their efforts. The Center City District framed this campaign, known as
the Center City Schools Initiative (CCSI), as an effort to prevent middle- and
upper-middle-class families from moving to the suburbs, thereby promoting the revitalization of the downtown and Philadelphia's overall economic
growth. In a 2004 report titled, "Growing Smarter," the organization argued,
"Public schools in Center City can play a key role in enhancing the competitiveness and prosperity of Philadelphia by retaining the young *knowledge workers* who have been moving downtown in unprecedented numbers."
While the Grant parents' attempts to attract more Cobble Square families to
their school predated the CCSI (for example, the Grant PTO had established
a marketing and public relations subcommittee a year before this larger campaign was announced), many of their assumptions about the role schools
could play in making the downtown appealing to families, the ways an increase in middle-class families would benefit the schools, and the need to
create a more exclusive image for their school resonated with the Center City
District's approach.

Because so few Cobble Square families sent their children to Grant, the
school historically filled with children from across the city who applied to
transfer into Grant as a way of escaping the low-performing schools in their
own neighborhoods. A number of children (approximately fifty each year)
also transferred into Grant under the provisions of the No Child Left Behind
Act (NCLB), which allowed them to leave their failing schools for one of a
small number of Philadelphia schools with higher levels of student achieve-

ment. While the students from Cobble Square (whose families were targeted by the marketing campaign) were largely white and middle to upper-middle class, the students who transferred into Grant were generally African American and working class or low income. These differences in race and class became extremely significant to the marketing campaign, as Cobble Square parents strove to increase the number of families "like them" at the school.

*   *   *

A core group of mostly white middle- to upper-middle-class Cobble Square parents devoted untold hours to marketing Grant Elementary School to "neighborhood" (e.g., Cobble Square) families. They believed that if more neighborhood families sent their children to Grant, the school would improve in a variety of ways, from the resources available, to the expectations for behavior, to the academic achievement of all students. Their determination to increase the number of neighborhood families was such that one mother, an African American woman who transferred her children to Grant and was critical of the fixation on neighborhood families, derided it in an interview as a faith that "the more Cobble Square parents we have, the more our life will be saved."

Parents held open houses planned especially for Center City families, organized public meetings, produced fliers, and talked with neighbors on the sidewalk and in local playgrounds. Whenever possible, they sought to promote a positive image of Grant as a school where, in the words of a local newsletter, "great things are happening!" Their focus on neighborhood parents was explicit, and how a particular event or addition to the school's resources or programming would look to other Cobble Square families featured prominently in many parent conversations. Thus Sharon, a Cobble Square mother who spearheaded the marketing campaign, explained in an interview, "the biggest agenda for us is making the school a place that other Cobble Square parents would come to." Their assumption was that Cobble Square parents would be drawn to Grant only if they could be convinced that it was significantly different from the rest of Philadelphia's inner-city schools. For this reason, in hosting fundraisers, opera concerts, and other school-related events, they strove not only to showcase Grant's academics and programming but also to show that many of the families it attracted were far more affluent and sophisticated than the bulk of Philadelphia parents.

The CCSI, a partnership between the Center City District and the School District of Philadelphia, gave greater momentum and legitimacy to the efforts of Sharon and other parents to market Grant. When the CEO of Philadelphia's schools, Paul Vallas, came to visit Grant in spring 2004, he described the CCSI and the district's interest in making Grant and other downtown schools more appealing to families who might otherwise leave for the suburbs. Standing at the front of the school auditorium, a spacious but dimly lit room where rows of old-fashioned varnished wooden chairs faced a small stage, Vallas told an audience of about fifty parents about his plans for Grant, which included building a new play structure in the school's otherwise empty asphalt play yard. Noting that many people in the Cobble Square area (and in downtown more broadly) did not send their children to public school, he elaborated, "We are trying to make the schools more attractive, to physically upgrade them. This is part of the campaign to get more in the community to send their kids here . . . . You design it and present the plan. It will make the school much more attractive!" Like the Cobble Square parents, Vallas explicitly referenced the importance not just of improving Grant's overall appearance but of specifically selling the school to Cobble Square families (people "in the community"), who might otherwise make a different choice.

Nearly a year later, a district official attended a PTO meeting at Grant. As she joined a group of about twelve parents in the school library, she described the CCSI goal of improving customer service for Center City families, noting that "parents are the real customers and need to be treated that way." Though her phrase suggested that *all* parents had equal status as customers, the CCSI and the marketing of Grant actually distinguished between groups. The Cobble Square families became the most valued customers, the transfer students and their families the least. Transfer students did not live in Cobble Square or, for the most part, in the revitalized downtown. In contrast, they came from South, North, and West Philadelphia neighborhoods where poverty and school failure were endemic. And, as explained earlier, transfer students were generally (but not exclusively) African American and low-income.

When some parents, administrators, and teachers spoke of their goal of increasing the number of neighborhood families at the school, they contrasted these desirable families with those of the children who transferred to Grant. Amy is an Asian mother from South Philadelphia, an area plagued by tensions between the African American and Asian communities. In an interview in a local coffee shop, she explained the difference between the two groups in this way: "They're more willing to listen, the children who are from Cobble Square. They're more willing to listen, more willing to learn. Whereas the students from the not-so-advantaged homes, they don't tend to care about education as much. They just want to play." This parent's comment recalls the decades-old assumption that, while middle-class children make "good" students, low-income children, especially African Americans, are inherently uninterested in learning and difficult for teachers to manage.

A teacher was particularly forceful in her assessment of the difference between the two groups. She argued in an interview that Grant would be better if it served more children from the neighborhood and fewer who had to journey in from other parts of the city.

> I want to see parents that care about what's going on with the education, not ones that just throw their kid onto a bus and the kid comes here or throws the kid onto a train and the child comes here. . . . And the problem is, when you get the children from the families where the parents do not care and—what you're talking about this school, Grant School, it's in a very affluent area. And most times—oh, gosh, I don't even want to say it. When you're dealing with an affluent neighborhood, you're dealing with parents of interest. They care! As opposed to other areas. It sounds horrible, I know it does. But that's it. Realistic. I mean, that's the way it is. So if the common sense here is that if the neighborhood children came to this school and it's an affluent neighborhood and it's caring parents, then all the parents that send the children here, would care about their children, the education and maintaining Grant to where it's a very good learning environment.

Though the fact that transfer parents had gone to the trouble of securing a spot at Grant (not an easy task in a district with few high-performing schools) suggested that they were quite committed to their children's education, this teacher still assumed that, because many were low-income, they were uniformly less cooperative and caring than more affluent families. She also did not commend the efforts to which both students and parents went to make lengthy commutes to and from school possible. Instead, to her the act of "throwing" a child on the bus or train signaled disregard. In this way, the focus on attracting more neighborhood families both built on and legitimized widely held views about the superiority of the middle class and deficit assumptions about the poor.

*   *   *

The efforts of middle- and upper-middle-class families (and the district's interest in attracting and retaining such families to the school) did bring resources to Grant, including the new playground, a high-tech library, and an additional kindergarten teacher. However, low-income parents reported feeling excluded and marginalized by the campaign to remake Grant, particularly by what they saw as its messages about race, class, and who mattered. Sabrina, a low-income African American mother who transferred her two children into Grant from a school in their West Philadelphia neighborhood, was particularly vocal about how the campaign—particularly the repeated references at PTO meetings—to recruit more downtown families, affected her own sense of membership within the school community. In an interview conducted in her small living room, she explained:

> So, I can't talk about people's motives, but I can talk about how that made me feel. And that makes me feel like there is some sort of inner prejudice that you don't belong here. I know I told you this too before, but I think that [downtown] is looked upon differently, because of the status of people's jobs, like people own their own businesses, they are looked upon differently. Like they are giving them a higher status or something, you know.

Sabrina saw the focus on attracting "neighborhood" families as an effort to recruit a more affluent constituency to the school. She contrasted her own status—as someone not from downtown and not having a prestigious job or her own business—with that of the more desirable parents. In the end, she felt, her worth was diminished. While Sabrina was reluctant to call the focus on Cobble Square families racist, she definitely saw it as exclusionary. She continued, "I mean, you know, they go out to the communities and they try to recruit all these kids to keep it secluded, to keep it on that level of—I don't want to say race, but, you know, to keep it like Cobble Square."

Patricia, who transferred her son to Grant from a poor neighborhood in North Philadelphia, similarly characterized the marketing campaign as an effort to keep children from less affluent parts of the city out of Grant: "Personally, I think they're doing it because they don't want the other neighborhood children to come in their school. And they think that the other neighborhood children are disrupting their school; they think their school is going down." Thus, to Patricia, Sabrina, and many other low-income African American parents at Grant, the Cobble Square parents' attempts to transform the school by attracting middle- and upper-middle-class families was, essentially, an act of reclaiming Grant for a more privileged population.

*   *   *

In fall 2005, a School District of Philadelphia administrator who had been closely involved with the development of the CCSI spoke frankly about her concerns about its long-term impact. She listed the neighborhoods targeted by the initiative and explained,

> And, so, to me those areas are predominantly white. . . . So from a district perspective I was able to see a schematic of how many kids from outside of those catchment areas attend the three [downtown] elementary schools that they were focusing on. And I was disturbed to see that some of those kids, who had an opportunity to go to a school in a neighborhood where they had no real viable neighborhood option, may lose that option.

In other words, this administrator, like the parents quoted above and many other critics of the CCSI, worried that any increase in the number of neighborhood children at high-performing downtown schools would inevitably lead to a decrease in the number of spots available to children from other parts of the city, children whose neighborhood schools were not "viable" because they were so low-achieving.

And, in fact, these fears were justified. In fall 2005, when the marketing of Grant was still in its early stages, 237 students (49 percent of the school's population) transferred into the school from neighborhoods across the city. By 2009, after the campaign had been in effect for several years, this number had shrunk to 124 (21 percent). Meanwhile, the number of students coming from Grant's catchment area (Cobble Square and the adjacent neighborhoods) increased from 248 (51 percent) to 454 (79 percent). Grant's African

American population decreased by nearly 50 percent during this period. Similar patterns occurred at other high-achieving downtown schools targeted by the CCSI and have also been documented in other cities where large numbers of middle-class parents have enrolled their children in—and worked to transform—particular public schools. Thus, while renewed interest in public schools among middle- and upper-middle-class downtown families may have brought about some positive changes, it also resulted in a constriction of opportunity, as spots at those schools became less available to other Philadelphia students.

*　*　*

On the one hand, there is much to celebrate about a trend, evident in Philadelphia and other cities, of middle-class families remaining in the city and working to improve their local schools. In doing so, they contribute to the local tax base, bring their often-significant forms of social, cultural, and financial capital to the schools, and generate political support for urban public education (a resource that has long been in short supply). Indeed, in spring 2011, when the School District of Philadelphia faced its largest budget crisis ever and threatened to cut basic services, middle-class families (including many from the downtown area) were instrumental in securing additional funding. On the other hand, the positioning of middle-class families as the schools' last, best hope is troubling because of the corresponding positioning of low-income families—especially low-income families of color—as the problem. This so-called solution also draws attention away from the entrenched poverty and political disenfranchisement of many urban communities, the true causes of urban school failure.

In addition, the reclaiming of urban public schools by middle-class families can lead, as we have seen, to the displacement of other children, particularly those children who, arguably, most need high-quality schools. Thus, a private effort (such as the parents' campaign to market Grant) or a public-private partnership (the CCSI) can assume the mantle of pursuing a general good while actually disproportionately benefiting an already advantaged population. In Philadelphia, the use of public funds, including school district resources and a grant from the state, to attain this private advantage raises questions about new forms of inequality at play in twenty-first century American cities and the role of public institutions in creating them. It also suggests that a reliance on the seemingly neutral free market can serve the interests of a relatively privileged part of the population while diminishing the status of other groups. Policy makers, educators, and scholars would do well to ensure that whatever benefits middle-class parents bring to urban schools do not come at the expense of other parts of the population. This possibility is generally overlooked in the celebratory rhetoric about urban school transformations driven by the middle class.

Chapter 12

The Rhetoric of Choice: Segregation, Desegregation, and Charter Schools

Ansley T. Erickson

Over the last decade, talk of choice in education has reached an unprecedented pitch, and the talk has brought forth extensive dollars and human energy. Advocates for school choice, which has become a pseudonym for charter school reform, claim that changing how individual students end up at one school rather than another will contribute to significantly expanded access to quality education.

Forty years ago, many American communities began to reorganize student assignment on a massive scale. Court-ordered busing for desegregation radically altered how students were assigned to schools and on what criteria. It is worth looking at that historical moment to understand the nature and limitations of the present debate. Although desegregation may seem a remnant of a distant era, reinterpreting the history of desegregation raises important cautions for the current interest in charter schools.

A common thread runs through opposition to desegregation and advocacy for charter schools: the rhetoric of choice. This rhetoric emphasizes the power of individual action and decision-making and veils the deep influences of policy and politics. Examining the gap between the rhetoric and the reality clarifies the history of desegregation and contributes to a respectfully critical look at school "choice" in practice today.

* * *

It may seem odd to speak of desegregation and choice together, as the images desegregation calls to mind are often ones of compulsion—courts ordered districts to desegregate, students experienced "forced" busing, federal troops pried open the doors of Little Rock's Central High School. But the rhetoric of choice had an impact on desegregation, both as it happened and as its history has been written.

The accomplishments of desegregation were limited. Even at the peak of court-ordered desegregation, in the 1980s, 57 percent of black southerners attended schools that were majority black—and resegregation developed quickly and forcefully, so that by 2005 that figure had risen to 72 percent, similar to patterns in the North as well. The conventional wisdom holds that "choices" made by white parents derailed desegregation. That is, the courts may have compelled desegregation, but white parents made choices that undermined these mandates. Those with the means to do so moved to less diverse or less actively desegregating districts or sent their children to private schools. Exercising this choice, they helped remake the demographics of urban schools from the 1950s through the 1980s. Cities with diverse populations by race and class became predominantly black and predominantly poor. Desegregation plans that rearranged students across schools could not keep up with these shifting demographics. Myriad individual choices—some of them frankly racist—seemed the key factor in explaining the difficulties of desegregation and the resilience of segregation.

Contemporary observers and historians attached to these patterns the label "de facto segregation," a variant of the rhetoric of choice. The de facto model holds that current (and some past) school segregation comes from the actions of individuals as they enter the housing market, create or reinforce segregation, and then produce segregated schools. De facto segregation provides a description, but lacks the rigor of a real causal explanation. De jure segregation, usually juxtaposed with de facto segregation, comes from state action in explicitly discriminatory law or policy. By contrast, de facto segregation grows from vague "other factors," as Chief Justice John Roberts put it in the 2007 case *Parents Involved in Community Schools v. Seattle School Dist. No. 1.*

Such weak attention to causality should tip us off: "de facto" segregation does not exist. Although acts of individual racism helped shape desegregation,

individual "choice" was never as autonomous as the de facto logic suggested. A deep field of historical work on housing has shown that federal
policy frankly encouraged segregated white suburbs and segregated black
city neighborhoods. The seemingly autonomous, free-market, white house
purchaser was in fact responding to clear policy-based incentives and disincentives. Federal tax and lending policies made purchasing a suburban home
both a more possible and a more seemingly desirable choice than remaining
in city neighborhoods. Transportation policy helped, too, as low gas taxes
facilitated longer commutes on newly opened interstates linking suburbs and
the city—some of which opened just months before school desegregation via
busing began. These highways facilitated white families' departures to surrounding non-desegregating school systems. Simultaneously, without federally backed mortgages for existing urban homes or access to many suburbs
still barricaded by segregationist practices in the real estate industry, most
black families, and nearly all poor black families, remained anchored in urban centers. Individuals, both black and white, did make choices, but they
did so within boundaries formed by policy.

Despite its vagueness, the notion of de facto segregation has shaped much
jurisprudence on segregation and desegregation, including the 2007 *Parents
Involved* decision striking down voluntary desegregation plans in Seattle and
Louisville. A five-judge majority drew on a variety of arguments, including
the distinction between de jure and de facto segregation. Chief Justice Roberts's plurality opinion in the case argued that school districts with de facto
segregated attendance patterns rooted in historic segregationist policy had
neither the contemporary responsibility nor the right to consider race in student assignment. Roberts thus extended the basic logic of the 1992 *Freeman
v. Pitts* ruling: "Where resegregation is a product not of state action but of
private choices, it does not have constitutional implications." Justice Clarence
Thomas continued the rhetoric of choice when he described patterns of segregation in Seattle and Louisville as "racial imbalance" that "might" have resulted from past de jure desegregation, or from "innocent private decisions,
including voluntary housing choices." Justice Anthony Kennedy, who argued
that de facto segregation *could* be addressed constitutionally, left de facto segregation again without a clear definition, writing that while de jure segregation was "imposed by law," de facto segregation stemmed from "bias masked
deep within the social order."

Dissenting justice Stephen Breyer, in an opinion joined by Ruth Bader

Ginsburg, John Paul Stevens, and David Souter, argued that the de jure/de facto language was "meaningless." Breyer pointed out that school policies "have often affected not only schools, but also housing patterns, employment practices, economic conditions, and social attitudes." Nonetheless, the plurality in *Parents Involved* upheld the myth of de facto segregation and further buried the policy foundations of segregation in American education.

Recent historical work supports Breyer's view. Schools have done much more than receive the products of segregated residential patterns; aspects of school policy have helped construct segregation. When early twentieth-century planners imagined new modes of city design, they thought of schools and neighborhoods as mutually constitutive; many embraced segregation as an appropriate characteristic of both. Historian Karen Benjamin has shown in an article in the *Journal of Urban History* (2012) that in Raleigh, North Carolina, early twentieth-century decisions to build new segregated schools in particular areas supported a conscious strategy to invest in segregated white suburbs while concentrating black residents in one city quadrant. In Nashville, Tennessee, urban renewal projects of the 1950s and 1960s used schools as markers of neighborhoods and intentionally located new public housing nearby, building segregated housing and schooling in tandem. And the North was far from exempt: historian Andrew Highsmith's doctoral dissertation, "Demolition Means Progress" (2009) documents how in Flint, Michigan, a philanthropically supported "community schools" program explicitly made schools the hubs of segregated communities. Policies such as these laid the brick-and-mortar foundation for the segregated patterns of American cities today.

The rhetoric of choice and de facto segregation renders invisible the policies that fostered residential segregation and those that linked segregated schools to segregated neighborhoods. Such invisibility contributes to colorblind suburban innocence, as University of Michigan historian Matthew Lassiter phrases it in *Silent Majority* (2006), through which white suburbanites exempt themselves from culpability for segregation and inequality. Embracing the rhetoric of choice, these suburbanites imagine their own success as the product of autonomous hard work, skillfully overlooking their reliance on extensive and effective government subsidy in housing and beyond.

The powerful language of "choice" overwhelmed another reality in desegregation as well. *How* courts and school districts implemented desegregation continued many forms of inequality. Careful to document the many manifestations of white, middle-class resistance to desegregation, historians long neglected to consider what desegregation meant to black families and communities, and how it was experienced by black children. In the 1950s and 1960s, desegregation often brought the closure of black schools, on the racist premise that white students could not be well educated in these venues. Desegregation thus severed black neighborhoods from educational institutions. With busing in the 1970s and 1980s came new waves of school closings, along other with unequal practices: black students left their neighborhood schools at younger ages, spent more years riding buses, and rode for longer periods of time than their white peers.

These inequalities may have been described in the neutral language of logistical necessity, but in fact, they were attempts to accommodate white parental choice, to make it less likely that white, middle-class families would leave desegregating public school districts. The policy-smoothed route to the suburbs gave middle-class white families a stranglehold on city and metropolitan education policy. By threatening to withdraw, these families could turn desegregation plans to their benefit and away from equitable implementation.

Desegregation entailed many choices, but the rhetoric of choice as it makes its way into our histories acknowledges only some of these. That rhetoric fosters a very partial view of how desegregation unfolded, what impeded it, and what encouraged resegregation. The rhetoric of choice focuses on individual decisions and has failed to acknowledge how policy choices were equally if not more important in shaping desegregation. The policies that facilitated white suburbanization rested on other choices—to marshal political power on behalf of some Americans and not others, to let the resulting inequalities go unaddressed. To understand segregation and desegregation, past and present, this full range of choices has to become visible.

Montgomery County, Maryland, launched a desegregation program that demonstrates what is possible when policy tools previously arrayed against desegregation are instead aligned to support it. Through inclusionary zoning and the use of public housing funds to scatter subsidized-rent units across the area, Montgomery County distributed poor students throughout the county, as school assignment followed residence. In a careful evaluation of the effects of this program published by the Century Foundation (2010), researcher Heather Schwartz has shown that the kind of socioeconomic integration Montgomery County adopted had more impact on raising student performance than did compensatory programs targeted at the county's remaining schools with high concentrations of poverty.

Desegregation produced powerful myths about inequality that rendered invisible a vast web of explicit and intentional policies. These myths falsely portrayed desegregation's failures as the product of autonomous individual choice. Meanwhile, these myths obscured inequalities in desegregation. A new, but parallel, kind of mythmaking about choice is underway in today's charter school efforts.

*   *   *

Charter schools offer parents "choice" in schooling for their children. But the constraints on that choice are massive, based in historic and current policy, and yet rarely acknowledged. The first and most significant constraint is that, despite claims implying broad mobility for students, most charter schools remain creatures of the school district in which they reside. Charter admissions practices respect the jurisdictional boundaries that separate city districts from suburban ones or wealthier from poorer suburbs. Few state charter laws prohibit charter schools from enrolling out-of-district students, but most give priority to applications from students living in the district. Where there are more applicants than spaces, out-of-district students don't gain admission.

And school districts demonstrate striking segregation by race and income. School district lines cordon off the students and the resources of wealthy communities from poorer ones. In his early arguments for school choice, even Milton Friedman observed, in *Capitalism and Freedom*, that poor families had the least choice and the least effective mobility when it came to schooling, and that schools thus "produc[ed] further stratification" (92). Friedman saw this point as one of the many reasons for genuine school choice across district and private/public lines. Yet in most charter schools today, "choice" respects district lines and thus leaves the stratification they reflect unchallenged.

Combine charters' respect for jurisdictional lines with the fact that most suburban districts have been notably uninterested in charter schools, and you have what legal scholar James Ryan, in *Five Miles Away, a World Apart* (2010), labels the "suburban veto" of charter schooling. Parents in some suburban districts and even some well-resourced sections of urban ones, as in New York City, rally against charter proposals, for fear that charters will draw resources away from their valued public school systems. The suburban veto of charters is just the most recent incarnation of a core theme of education policy of the last fifty years, as Ryan rightly argues: the protection of suburban privilege, rationalized as a necessary concession to parental choice, as in desegregation, or expressed as an exemption from choice, as in charter schools.

The "suburban veto" has contributed to an increasing identification between charter schools and poor, urban students, one embedded in many state charter laws as well. For nearly a decade, Tennessee's charter-authorizing law restricted charter enrollment only to some students: those whose home school had failed to make adequate yearly progress under the No Child Left Behind Act or who had failed to reach proficiency in their grade 3–8 annual tests or were free-lunch eligible (a common indicator for poverty status). As these measures skew toward students of color, the charter law increased the likelihood that charters were segregated places on multiple measures. Tennessee's law was one of the more restrictive, and the state legislature revised the law in 2011 to open some charters more broadly. Yet there and in other states the identification between charters and urban, poor, and struggling students continues.

Charters demonstrate higher rates of segregation by race than do nearby public schools. Some charter advocates contest this finding, but accept that, at minimum, charters are as segregated as the very segregated public schools in our nation's metropolitan areas. Respect for district lines, charter laws that target poor students or those in failing schools, and the suburban veto together produce notably segregated student enrollments.

Some high-poverty, racially segregated schools can achieve remarkable successes, and some credit their segregation for part of their success—as they enjoy a strong community ethos or can target particular kinds of student need. But it is crucial to note that segregation does not imply that charters serve all the most needy students—as the disproportionately low levels of enrollment of English-language learners and students with special needs indicates—or that racial segregation means charters have reached the poorest students.

One reason segregation matters is that it creates political vulnerability for charter schools as individual institutions and as a reform strategy. The political challenges echo other past social policies that falter because political support wanes once they are identified as programs "for" poor people or people of color. Measuring charter funding is complex. Although some charter schools have received extensive funds from private philanthropy and some districts have provided valuable public subsidies, in many cases fewer public dollars flow to charters, on a per-pupil basis, than to district schools. The causes for this disparity vary: some state laws allocate fewer dollars per charter pupil or exclude charters from some forms of state aid. Some charters must use their per-pupil allocation to pay for services usually covered by district, rather than school, budgets. The question of whether charters serve the students needing the most expensive services further complicates the measure. Charter schools remain vulnerable to shifts in funding and political support, a vulnerability only heightened if they become identified as places for poor children residing in racially and economically segregated city neighborhoods. Efforts to intentionally diversify charter schools by facilitating enrollment across district lines, like that underway now in Rhode Island, not only bring the benefits known to accompany desegregated student experiences, but are more likely to encourage a more enduring base of political support for charters.

Some charter advocates use choice-talk to attempt to dismiss the fact of segregation in many charters, describing concentrations by skin color and class as "freely chosen," in Paul Peterson's words that contain echoes of the "de facto" language (*Education Next*, February 8, 2010). Segregation by race and/or class that emerged out of actual free choice—of schools across a range of geographic locations, with differing demographics and pedagogical approaches—would be one thing. Many of the early advocates for charter schools found the image of such broad choice inspiring and motivating. Charter schools differ as widely as parents' reasons for choosing them, but many promise more orderly school climates, more committed teachers, and higher levels of academic achievement. But even when they realize these promises, most charter schools offer much less than "free choice." For most families, and particularly for poor families, charter schools in their best form have brought the meaningful, but more restricted possibility of attending better or similarly performing schools in their neighborhood or nearby, with similarly or more segregated student populations. But considering the growing power of urban-focused, consciously branded charter networks, charters are rarely vehicles of desegregation or jurisdictional boundary-crossing, and common measurement on narrow test-score matrices limits pedagogical variation.

*   *   *

If the rhetoric of choice is in fact so distant from the reality, why does it remain so powerful? Because, like the powerful myth of de facto segregation, it offers an appealingly simple, yet fundamentally false line of thinking about what makes segregation and inequality, and what could create greater equality. For some students and some families, charter school choice is transformative. But building policy on those instances of transformation reflects reticence to confront, or in some cases willful ignorance of, where broader patterns of inequality and segregation come from, of how much American policy choices over decades have constrained some individual choices and enabled others.

During the post-Second World War boom in suburbanization and sharp segregation in the metropolitan United States, white middle-class families had extensive policy encouragement to "choose" the suburbs. Today, in another era of sharp segregation by race and class, the rhetoric of choice promises poor families of color a tool to overcome the reality of unequal education rooted in layers of policy. Yet "choice" today comes without the policy supports—in housing, transportation, movement across jurisdictional lines— that middle-class white families enjoyed earlier.

When we trace the rhetoric of choice across the decades, we see that it has migrated from describing an obstructionist power held by white, middle-class families to a supposedly curative one increasingly offered to poor families of color. Rarely in American history have public goods moved from doing service for the elite and powerful to being tools for disadvantaged communities. When the rhetoric suggests that choice has become such a tool, we should pay close and skeptical attention.

Both our historical understanding of desegregation and our present-day discussion of charter schools suffer from the distorting rhetoric of choice. Choice alone did not sink desegregation; nor will it alone galvanize educational equality. We need a better way to think and talk about how both current and historic policy choices interact with individual choices, understanding that just as neither alone determines outcomes, any approach to educational improvement needs to take account of both. And we need just as much careful attention to the fine details of implementation as to the grand rhetoric.

Chapter 13

Criminalizing Kids: The Overlooked Reason for Failing Schools

Heather Ann Thompson

The nation's school dropout rate reached crisis levels in 2009, and test scores posted by its poorest public schools were also grim. According to a report in *The Hill* on March 10, 2010, only 70 percent of first-year students entering America's high schools were graduating, with a full 1.2 million students dropping out each school year. Four months earlier, *Time*'s Detroit blog noted that in 2009 the Detroit public school system reported math scores that were the worst in forty years of participation in the National Assessment of Educational Progress test (December 8, 2009). So great was the problem of "low performing" schools by 2010 that the U.S. Department of Education set up ten regional advisory committees "to collect information on the educational needs across the country" and President Barack Obama committed $3.5 billion to fund schools that were doing particularly poorly.

Politicians and policy makers offer various explanations for the dire state of public education in America. Some blame self-interested teachers' unions for abysmal graduation rates and test scores (see Kahlenberg's chapter in this book). Others argue that deepening poverty rates coupled with increasing racial segregation have undermined school success (see the other chapters in this section). All have missed the proverbial elephant in the classroom, which is the extent to which the nation's public school system has been criminalized over the last forty years. More specifically, they have failed to reckon with the devastating effect this unprecedented criminalization of educational spaces has had on the ability of teachers to teach and students to learn. If we are truly serious about fixing our nation's schools, and if we ever hope to roll back the resegregation and ever-deepening poverty of these same institutions, we must first recognize the enormous price public school children have paid for America's recent embrace of the world's most massive and punitive penal state—a vast carceral apparatus that has wed our economy, society, and political structures to the practice of punishment in unprecedented ways. We must challenge the view that society's interests can best be met by criminalizing the neediest citizens and the spaces in which they live, work, and learn.

*   *   *

Although most Americans are at least vaguely aware that this nation has beefed up its law-and-order apparatus considerably over the last five decades, few grasp what a dramatic and destructive political and policy shift has actually occurred. Before the early 1970s, the incarceration rate was fairly unremarkable. Indeed, according to the U.S. Department of Justice, Bureau of Justice Statistics, in the thirty-five years prior to 1970 the prison population in this country only increased by 52,249. In the subsequent thirty-five years, however, from 1970 to 2005, it increased by a staggering 1.26 million, a far larger percentage of the total U.S. population. While the incarceration rate of the nation as a whole rose to historic and even shocking levels after the 1960s, as Michelle Alexander notes in her path breaking study *The New Jim Crow* (2010), the rate for African Americans in particular became catastrophic. Eventually one out of every nine black men aged twenty to thirty-four would be in prison in America.

The origins of this deeply racialized crisis are complex, but the political backlash to the civil rights momentum of the 1960s was a central cause. As the 1960s unfolded, white fears of black agitation both implicitly and explicitly contributed to a complete overhaul of this country's criminal laws as well as its state and federal policies governing punishment. In short, the more contested urban spaces became in the 1960s, and the more they erupted in protest and outrage, the more certain were white voters that crime had become the nation's most pressing problem, that blacks were responsible for this breakdown of law and order, and that the way to deal with both blacks and crime was to beef up the carceral state.

Notably, however, at the very time the foundation of the carceral state was first being laid, namely when the Johnson administration passed the Law

Enforcement Assistance Act of 1965, which earmarked historically new levels of funding for the nation's criminal justice apparatus, the nation was not experiencing a crime wave. Indeed, the same states that were clamoring most loudly to bolster the criminal justice system in the mid-1960s were, according to data gathered by the federal as well as state governments, experiencing the lowest crime rate since 1910.

As the 1960s wore on, though, and not coincidentally because the federal reporting standards changed and more money was available to areas that reported high crime rates, the nation's crime problem seemed even graver than it was. With whites increasingly unnerved by the civil rights unrest continuing to engulf the country, all plans to give greater resources to police departments, pass more stringent laws, and make punishment for breaking those laws more punitive were enthusiastically embraced. Speaking to a reporter from the *New York Times* in 1964, one taxi driver bluntly articulated the white view that blacks' civil rights desires directly undermined public safety: "we have a terrific crime problem here and if you segregate [blacks], it's easier to police them" ("Johnson Prestige on the Line in Indiana," April 19).

As the twentieth century came to a close, policies born of white fear of urban unrest had led to the wholesale criminalization of urban spaces of color. Thanks to a revolution in drug legislation, to the enforcement of particularly aggressive new law-and-order policies such as Stop and Frisk, and to a simultaneous overhaul of sentencing guidelines, by 2010 the Justice Department reported that more than seven million Americans were trapped in the criminal justice system—on parole, on probation, or in prison—and the overwhelming majority of them came from poor inner-city neighborhoods. Indeed, it mattered little whether one came from an urban enclave of a southern state like Texas, a western state like California, or a northeastern state like Pennsylvania; law-and-order rhetoric dominated the political landscape and scarred the social landscape of America's inner cities. Indeed, by 2010, states across the country were spending as much as a billion dollars a year on myriad new anti-crime measures, leaving few resources to repair the damage caused to America's inner cities by this same turn to criminalization.

*   *   *

Arguably, nowhere was the cost of criminalizing urban spaces higher, and its consequences more painfully felt, than in our nation's public school system.

Even though America's school-age children had since time immemorial engaged in fights, been disrespectful to teachers, skipped classes, bullied one
another, and engaged in vandalism as well as other inappropriate behaviors,
in the late 1960s school systems began employing security staffs in order to
deal with such student conduct far more aggressively and punitively.

Not coincidentally, the districts most eager to bring a police presence
into city schools were those that had also experienced an upsurge of civil
rights activism on the part of their students. Detroit city schools, for example, got their greatest influx of police officers on the heels of some particularly dramatic Black Power protests in its institutions, such as those that
gripped Northern High School in 1969. Atlanta city schools also did not
bring a law enforcement presence to their buildings until similarly volatile
racial experiences in 1969, and, that same year, the state of Kansas decided
it was time to pass specific legislation so its educational facilities could hire
school security officers and "designate any one or more of such school security officers as a campus police officer" in order to "aid and supplement
law enforcement agencies of the state and of the city and county" (Kansas
State Statute 72-8222).

Forty years later, many urban schools, including those in which the civil
rights movement had placed so much hope, have come to resemble penal
institutions. This hyper-criminalization of inner-city public schools and students has been fueled by a growing conviction on the part of the nation's
politicians and the public alike that inner-city school kids had become particularly violent. Whereas school children of the 1940s disrupted the classroom by running in the halls, chewing gum, and littering, by the 1980s, it
would seem, young people were more likely to rape and rob.

As a fascinating piece by Barry O'Neil in the March 6, 1994, *New York
Times Magazine* has pointed out, however, evidence that schools were in fact
witnessing new levels of youth violence was always scant at best. Indeed, most
alarmist claims to that effect, it turns out, actually originated in a "fundamentalist attack on public schools" penned by born-again Christian T. Cullen
Davis of Ft. Worth, Texas. Remarkably, Davis's admittedly unscientific list of
numerous heinous acts committed by today's youth was, by the 1980s, being
cited as gospel by everyone from secretary of education William Bennett to
Harvard president Derek Bok to surgeon general nominee Joycelyn Elders
to right-wing television talk-show pundit Rush Limbaugh. By the 1990s, it
had become a given that the nation's inner-city youth were more violent than

ever, and that these animalistic kids needed new forms of surveillance, a new degree of punishment, and new levels of containment.

Thanks to the soon widespread belief that America's inner-city public schools now required military-like tactics to keep them safe, by 2011 the school district of Philadelphia, for instance, boasted "a huge security force consisting of 657 personnel, including 408 School Police Officers and 249 School Security Officers." The same January 2011 report, "Zero Tolerance in Philadelphia," that called attention to this huge school security force in Philly also reported that its school district had formed a newly intimate alliance with the city juvenile justice system in order to facilitate the monitoring and censuring of student conduct. Far away in Texas, legislation also came to mandate that "the juvenile justice community and the education community come together to help make safe schools a reality," and such laws operated in myriad other urban districts across the country as well.

Eventually America's public school students in poor neighborhoods found themselves in legal trouble not only for more serious offenses such as bringing a weapon to school, but far more often for much lesser "offenses" such as truancy. In a number of urban school districts, for instance, this age-old student behavior can now land a student's file on the desk of the district attorney or even lead that student to be shackled with an electronic tether otherwise intended for use on parolees.

Ironically, simultaneous to administrators' criminalizing truancy in new ways as the twentieth century wound down—ostensibly so that kids would spend more time in the classroom—the criminalization of other student behaviors was leading to record rates of expulsion. Of students expelled or arrested for acts such as smoking, talking back, having a cell phone in class, or having any sharp object in a backpack, an overwhelming number hadn't yet even entered high school. As the "Zero Tolerance in Philadelphia" report revealed, "nearly all of the students expelled in 2008–09 were between the ages of 8 and 14, and the most common ages of the expelled students were 11 and 12."

Once kicked out of school, young students find themselves sent to various special institutions that cities and counties have been forced to set up specifically to teach kids deemed too disruptive for the traditional classroom. According to an NBC affiliate in Miami, Florida, for example, instead of re-admitting eight-year-old Samuel Burgos to his elementary school a full year after expelling him for coming to school with a toy gun, Broward County

School District chose to assign him to "a correctional school for problem children" in a different city altogether (NBC Miami, September 16, 2010).

Older students in America's urban districts routinely risked not only expulsion but arrest as their schools increasingly embraced so-called zero tolerance policies. By the close of the 1990s, according to sociologists John Hagen, Carla Shedd, and Monique Payne in an article in *Sociological Review* (2005), not only did every single school in the nation's third largest urban center, Chicago, have police officers patrolling the hallways, but it had also passed a loitering law "which permitted police to arrest anyone whom they suspected of being a gang member for congregating with no apparent legal purpose." That particular "zero tolerance" policy "resulted in more than 42,000 arrests." It also led to a formal agreement between the Chicago public schools and the Chicago Police Department in which "the city police department [would] release to each school's administrators on a daily basis the names of youth arrested off campus," which, in turn, could be "used to justify school suspension and expulsion decisions."

By the new millennium, organizations such as the Education Law Project were reporting that urban school districts such as Philadelphia's had a student arrest rate "between 3 and 25 times higher than most of the other districts" in that state ("Zero Tolerance in Philadelphia," 6). A 2010 report by the American Civil Liberties Union has made clear that in this and other states, such as Florida, the overwhelming number of public school kids arrested had engaged in acts that even tough-on-crime prosecutors had to classify as a misdemeanor.

Clearly, not every child in America's inner-city public schools got expelled or arrested. All of them, however, no matter how well-behaved they were or how successfully they managed to dodge notice by school administrators or police, suffered the daily humiliations and hostile learning environments that post-1960s criminalization ensured. No student could escape the surveillance cameras and digital security systems, and all lived in fear of being patted down, wanded, and even strip searched at the whim of school police personnel. Without question such capricious and degrading treatment sapped student self-esteem. As one Philadelphia kid put it to a team studying zero tolerance policies in his school, "It makes it seem as though they expect us to be negative. I feel violated." Another explained further, "I have to go through the [metal] detector every day, making me feel like they don't trust me." Still another remarked on the treatment he endured coming into his school for the first time, "I had to take off my shoes and they searched me like I was a real criminal. . . [after that] I was making up every excuse not to go to school" ("Zero Tolerance in Philadelphia," 96, 97, 14).

Not going to school, either because students hoped to avoid the embarrassment of being searched, or because they had been expelled for having a pack of cigarettes or arrested for doodling on a desk or texting in a math class, clearly affected their ability to do well academically. Policy makers and politicians alike, however, have completely ignored this reality when they propose remedies for America's "dropout crisis" or its ever-widening "achievement gap." They not only have missed the fact that literally tens of thousands of children across the nation have landed in jail cells instead of classrooms, but also have failed to see the high price that even kids who managed to don a graduation gown rather than a prison jumpsuit have paid for the hyper-criminalization of city schools. As one student put it to criminologist Paul Hirschfield in an article in *Theoretical Criminology* (2008), "You're not expected to leave this school and go to college. You're not expected to do anything."

*   *   *

To be sure, a real barrier to any politicians, policy makers, and even many parents being willing to reckon with the steep costs of criminalizing our nation's public schools remains the belief that school districts must work hard to "keep schools safe." Even the nation's poorest inner-city parents, those who have made it crystal clear that they don't want armed police officers in city schools and that they object strongly to district-level measures that criminalize their children, fret mightily about the issue of school safety. Although the existence of metal detectors provides such parents some level of relief that guns won't be in their child's classroom, the price paid for this peace of mind—that their kids feel under siege and themselves risk arrest for the most benign of acts—is indeed dear. School administrators must begin to find ways to keep schools safe without turning them into prisons.

Just as we all need to reassess the roots of poor school performance, so must we rethink our views on school violence in America. Not only do our assumptions about a newly violent youth rest on a most dubious and nonscientific evidentiary foundation, but so does our belief that public schools are now more violent than ever before. To be sure, the phenomenon of bullying has always been, and remains, a problem in our nation's schools—both public and private. Notably, however, the sort of "violence" and types of "crimes" the post-1970 criminalization of public school students allegedly sought to address was already on the decline when the most draconian policies, such as zero tolerance, were implemented around the country, as were violence rates in society as a whole. According to national statistics provided by the Curry School of Education at the University of Virginia, school violence is today at a record low, despite the fact that juvenile expulsions and arrest rates have continued to skyrocket. Even though school districts have become more, not less, punitive each subsequent year since 2000, the data are clear: our nation's inner-city kids are not "super predators," nor are they wild animals who should be tamed with tasers and long terms behind bars.

Not only are urban schoolchildren less prone to violence today than they were in the early twentieth century, but they also do not engage in more lawless behaviors than their counterparts in other seemingly safer districts. Indeed, when one compares data from the nation's poorest inner-city schools with other schools in the state, one finds that, although inner-city kids are far more criminalized, their levels of violence are in fact no higher. For example, when researchers compared "School Safety Incident" data from the Philadelphia public schools in the 2008–2009 school year with like data from the rest of Pennsylvania, they found, "The rest of the state had more than five times as many incidents as Philadelphia ... [and yet] in Philadelphia, students were arrested for these incidents nearly *twice* as often as they were in the rest of Pennsylvania." Studies such as this one reveal that official ideas about violence and safety are highly subjective and that inner-city kids are "being criminalized more than their peers across the state for the same behaviors" ("Zero Tolerance in Philadelphia," 7).

Notwithstanding the paucity of evidence to indicate that today's youth in general, and urban youth of color in particular, should be policed to a historically and internationally unprecedented extent, the fact that juvenile arrest rates have soared in recent years has only fueled the political call for even greater criminalization of our nation's public schools. We as a nation must work hard to resist equating rising youth arrest rates with out-of-control youth violence and, instead, focus our attention on the very clear connections between the criminalization of public school kids and their poor academic performance. As a research report by the American Psychological Association concluded clearly in 2007, there is "a negative relationship between the use of school suspension and expulsion and school-wide academic achievement." Other research shows similar findings. Ultimately, these kids' notable academic underachievement does not stem from the fact that their teachers want decent pay and job security; it results from being treated day in and day out as the worst of the worst in society and being forced to learn not what analogies they might need to know for the SAT, but what rules of conduct might land them in jail. And while policy measures to fund and de-segregate our nation's schools would certainly help these kids perform better than they do, unless this nation is willing also to decriminalize the spaces where inner-city kids go to learn—five days a week, nine months a year, every single year of their lives from age five to eighteen—these spaces will remain deeply impoverished and intensely segregated bastions of despair.

PART III

Alternatives to Technocratic Reform

Chapter 14

Abandoning the Higher Purposes
of Public Schools

Deborah Meier

In September 1966 I wrote my first piece on education for *Dissent*, "A Report from Philadelphia: Head Start or Dead End?" I was teaching morning Head Start after a few years of subbing and kindergarten in Chicago, and on the way to teaching kindergarten in Central Harlem. I had just begun to contemplate that teaching might not be a time killer until my kids got older and I could work full-time at something politically or intellectually Important.

Now, forty-five years later, I think about these amazingly interesting years. But, had I written this fifteen years ago I would have been more optimistic and triumphant. The ease with which my colleagues and I found ways to rethink "ghetto" education for children in the early 1990s, despite a largely conservative political and cultural era, fooled me. Until the last decade, I thought that inch by inch we could create a new world. I wasn't really that naïve, but I acted as if I were.

In that first *Dissent* article I recounted both the whirlwind fun of opening a center in a Germantown, Philadelphia, church and the silly Fridays listening to our leader sing songs and teach us finger plays. My youngest son, frightened out of his local kindergarten by a teacher who threatened to keep him in school overnight if he didn't learn to tie his shoes, joined me in Germantown, and I fantasized about opening a kindergarten at the local school. Instead, we moved to New York City. By the time I was ready for full-time work, I was what was thought of then as a "school reformer." I was out to prove that the least-advantaged children would thrive best in precisely the kind of educational setting we established for the most advantaged, ideally in an economically and racially mixed school, and with more focus on building trust with the families being served.

We had unqualified success. Many of us in New York branched out to take leadership of one public school after another—often small schools of choice, all firmly entrenched in the public sector and with strong ties to the local unions. But we tended to forget the larger picture, as we focused more narrowly on schooling in general and our own ventures—schools and classrooms—in particular. Our work spread from a focus on early childhood to the possibilities of secondary schools. I became a secondary school principal, with an amazing amount of freedom—free even to ignore credit hours and local tests—as part of a national experiment with Ted Sizer, head of Brown University's education department.

Even as we enjoyed our triumphs, another train was leaving the station. At first, these new reformers didn't sound unfriendly and even picked up a lot of our language—about school autonomy, empowerment, family-teacher engagement, engaged learning, and a tinge of radical disregard for mere credit hours. Having been converted myself to choice and small schools as vehicles for change, I was friendly even to their more extreme views on these matters. I reminded impatient foundation reformers that they should worry less about scaling-up in a hurry, about building replica chain schools, and instead invest in people with similar ideas. They told us, bluntly, that our work was impressive and deserving of all the awards and degrees we received, but that we needed systemwide change, something faster and more far-reaching that could be carried out by ordinary people following a good recipe.

The orders were blunt. We must save the children right now, said the new reformers. We must hurry through the leisurely years that middle-class children are allowed for informal play and get poor children into the "real" stuff faster, even before they reached kindergarten. I, a long-time revolutionary, found myself counseling corporate foundations for more patience!

In my 1966 *Dissent* article, I "demolished" their arguments about "those children," myths I thought the War on Poverty was too easily buying. I claimed that teachers fell into three categories: public school traditionalists, reformers, and radicals. The first were those who felt that "the fault lies with the poor themselves." They placed the emphasis on discipline, rules, morality, authority, and the three Rs (reading, wRiting, and aRithmetic). The traditionalists failed to see that most public education for the poor was already just what they were aiming for. Progressive education—this is where Diane Ravitch and I sharply clashed—couldn't be the cause of urban school failure because it never existed on a large scale in public schools for the poor. The reformers, on the other hand, accepted the idea that schools should provide what many families lacked: good manners, patience, and the ABCs. They saw this, I thought, as a way to mold the poor into "something more akin to the successful middle-class five year olds." (In retrospect, the reformers as I described them presented a more benign version of current corporate reform agenda.) The "radicals," like me, aimed our attention at "remaking the school" rather than the child. We focused on the strengths of "lower-class children," which the "necessity to survive" in an unfriendly world had produced. The "culture of poverty," I argued, can't be overcome by pretending it doesn't exist. Instead, change begins with self-acceptance. They must find ways to utilize the "culture of poverty" itself, to begin with the child's own experiences, good and bad, to involve his parents and his community, and to let each child's growth develop from his already functioning personality rather than cut off from it and rootless.

It was, as my mentor Lillian Weber declared over and over, our task to promote continuities rather than use school as an "alternative." She founded the City College Workshop Center to share ideas about how such an approach might work. The usual "reform" packages might work with the exceptions, but not for most. Most children come to school with understandings and loyalties developed in the course of their own lives. If forced to, I noted in the *Dissent* essay on Head Start, he or she will "leave . . . what he learns . . . at the door when he goes out." In short, we had as our goal an adult who "will be able to decide for himself . . . what kind of person he wants to become."

I ended that piece with a reminder—to myself, I think—that "education alone will not resolve the issues at stake in the War on Poverty." But given that schools exist, they should for poor and rich alike rest on democratic purposes and "respect for the child's integrity." We can, I concluded, "accept society's need to reform itself or simply pretend to reform the child." Until we do the former, we are heading into a dead end.

And so we have. From the early 1990s on we've built a head of steam for precisely the "dead end" we predicted, and called it revolution and reform simultaneously. We've placed our focus on the need for so-called "mind workers" for the twenty-first century, a prognosis that's at best controversial. We've maladapted new forms of technology as the answer: plug them in earlier.

Even the coin of the realm of these new reformers—test scores—have failed for a very long time. In the 1970s and 1980s scores actually rose; since the early 1990s, we've experienced stagnation, even as test scores have become the new purpose for schools. The old elitism at least had some relationship to genuine achievement. The new one is fruitless. It's like focusing all driver education on longer and more frequent multiple-choice and short-answer tests. The road test is viewed, at best, as a luxury.

All the schools I've attended—as well as those we founded in East Harlem (and eventually throughout all the boroughs but Staten Island) and in Boston—rested on quite a different view of purpose and achievement. Our graduates truly had to present the evidence of their capacities and competencies to a committee of experts from different backgrounds (academic and nonacademic) in a lengthy (often an hour-long) interview based on a body of work that demonstrated these competencies. We built the competencies around "five habits of mind" we thought essential to a strong, involved, and informed citizenry (for example, being a good juror) in each of the usual academic domains as well as a few the school deemed equally important (like the arts and service to the community). No two schools used exactly the same formula but most used the same criteria—external and internal reviewers examining real accomplishments and making collective judgments of them and of the students' capacity to present and defend their work. It was preparation for this kind of "old-fashioned" examination process for which the school was responsible year after year. And it was from such experiences that faculty, families, and kids got their inspiration.

This "radical" idea has been around for centuries, waiting to be used by schools for ordinary children. It's how a good apprenticeship works—whether for a tool-and-die maker or a lawyer. It's how we review doctoral candidates in every university in the land. And the time it takes for such an approach or its many similar alternatives to work is part of, not separate from, the purpose of the school. It prepares kids to study and present and defend their ideas. Opinions come in many forms, but good ideas (in science, math, or social studies) all come with these same ingredients that our graduation requirements drew upon.

Never, in my worst nightmares of 1966, did I dream that we'd give up on public education as a vehicle for making a better future for all children. Never would I have dreamed that mayors of big cities would be given the power to transform public schools into private schools operated by trustees with no roots in the community, with low-paid teachers rotating in and out. Never once did I imagine that we'd literally turn schools over to chain store operators, to do with the poor whatever they chose—as long as they could produce test scores not much worse than their public rivals. But we have. And overcoming this fast-moving train will be harder than I thought.

Yes, schools can make a difference, but the kind of difference depends on the purposes of the school, and it's these higher intellectual, moral, and social purposes of the school that we are abandoning for the least advantaged. But, in the terms John Dewey set the challenge a century ago, we have given up too quickly. We forget that democracy is an unfinished project, dependent on building a citizenry in which all see themselves as members of the ruling class—with an education that befits such a dream.

Chapter 15

Equity-Minded Instructional Leadership: Turning Up the Volume for English Learners

Tina Trujillo and Sarah Woulfin

After taking a deep breath, Principal Forte pulled back her shoulders, glanced around her crowded office, and pondered the question. What was her most important responsibility as the principal of Jefferson Elementary School? (All names of schools and individuals in this chapter are pseudonyms.) It was to serve as an instructional leader by championing quality teaching for all children. She was keenly aware of the multiple constituencies in her school's students. And she worked tirelessly to make sure that English learners, that is, students whose first language was not English, received the attention they were due: "My job is to be the broker between the populations and to ensure that the volume gets turned up on the families whose voices aren't as loud . . . because it's really easy at an immersion school to listen to the voices that are privileged."

This position is what drew us to Jefferson's principal. In the eyes of the state, Jefferson's reforms appeared to be working. Its standardized test scores consistently rose over the past three years, both for the overall school and when broken down for Latinos, English learners, and poor students. Such steady gains were uncommon for a school with its demographic profile, but the real story of Jefferson was not about its test performance. It was about the broader notions of success that Jefferson's principal promoted, and the paths she took to get there.

We came across this uncommon leader during our research study of a half dozen public elementary schools engaged in reform. Over the course of six months, we collected interview, survey, and classroom observation data to compare Principal Forte and her teachers' instruction to that of other schools, all located in some of California's largest urban districts. Jefferson's leadership—and its classrooms—stood out from the rest.

In education, we hear a great deal about what good principals do. They are strong administrators, well versed in management principles. They set ambitious goals for raising test scores. They organize every part of their school efficiently around the test—from textbooks to teacher training. They are relentless in their drive for teachers to use instructional strategies that will raise scores.

Less often, we hear about another style of principal. They are social justice leaders. They carve out space for teachers to discuss their beliefs about students of different races, languages, or income levels. They call our attention to the social and political inequities that persist in their school and community.

Forte fit neither mold. As Jefferson's principal for four years, she knew that successfully leading a diverse, urban elementary school required more than just raising test scores. It also required more than simply endorsing principles of social justice. It demanded a complex blend of both. She concentrated on fostering pedagogy that was keyed to students' academic and cultural needs, while also working to amplify the voices of students that public schools have historically neglected. In her view, good teaching and equity went hand in glove: "My job is to help the teachers be the best . . . teachers they can be, and to especially help Latino families, and Chinese families to some degree, learn how to advocate for their children."

Her beliefs about leadership stemmed, in part, from her history. Forte had almost fifteen years of experience in public schools. Fluent in both English and Spanish, she had taught bilingual elementary classes and high school Spanish. After California voters passed Proposition 227, an anti-immigration law that largely displaced bilingual education with English-only programs, she found herself teaching newly arrived immigrants in English classrooms. At the time, she had minimal professional knowledge of how students become bilingual and literate in English, as well as their home language. She deepened her expertise in language acquisition through graduate studies and her own work improving struggling schools before district supervisors tapped her to lead Jefferson.

When Forte talked about the kinds of questions that motivated her work, she spoke not about the pressing issues for her district or state, but about the issues that most intrigued her as a bilingual educator with genuine curiosities about the cultural and cognitive dimensions of language. How do students transfer skills from Spanish to English? What are the most supportive instructional settings for students from different cultural and linguistic backgrounds? At Jefferson Elementary School, the answers to these questions became clear.

*   *   *

From the outside, Jefferson looked like an ordinary urban elementary school. An aged but clean 1950s exterior consisted mainly of faded orange concrete pods. One pod looked out onto a modest, grassy playground and a worn play structure. Another bordered splintered blacktop, cloaked in two painted blue world hemispheres, each with bright yellow continents. Tile mosaics and a student mural of violet butterflies perched on red daisies lit up another corner of the campus.

Walking inside the school revealed much more about Jefferson's character. Relics of faculty meetings in the teachers' lounge hinted at the principal's approach to reform—lists of strategies for teaching English learners posted alongside posters about the state test. Community outreach flyers and announcements of parent-led workshops, printed in English, Spanish, and Cantonese, were common around the building. The uneven pitch of students singing drifted out of open doors lining the hallways. Children and adults were warm and polite.

Because Jefferson was a neighborhood school, its student body represented the racial and linguistic diversity of its surrounding community. Latinos made up half the enrollment, Chinese almost a third. The rest were mostly white or African American. Over half were classified as English learners, and two-thirds qualified for free or reduced-price lunch.

Forte designed an elaborate instructional system based on these demographics: three separate language tracks tailored to its biggest groups of students. Each track—English language development, Spanish immersion, and Chinese bilingual—employed a distinct set of teaching strategies, many designed to support students to speak, read, and write in two languages. This instructional program embodied several key dimensions of Jefferson's leadership.

* * *

When researchers and policy makers talk about effective instructional leadership, especially against the backdrop of today's high-stakes accountability policies that trigger punitive consequences for schools with low scores, they often prop up a familiar model for leading schools. Settle on goals for standardized testing, standardize what teachers teach by aligning instructional materials with the content that is tested, make data-based decisions, and monitor students' and teachers' progress toward the test goals. The successful cases in the research on instructional leadership and school reform typically highlight principals whose schools have increased test scores or closed achievement gaps, presumably as a consequence of this model. Success is largely defined in terms of test performance.

These test-based definitions of success risk reducing teachers', families', and policy makers' conceptions of learning to discrete, easily measurable, quantifiable tasks. Such definitions are largely taken up in economic arguments as indicators of schools' effectiveness in preparing students for the workplace. Relying on this singular proxy for success emphasizes primarily economic purposes of schools. Yet, as other chapters in this book show, this emphasis distracts attention from other purposes because it takes time and other resources away from more complex instructional activities that target social, moral, or civic goals.

Forte's leadership differed from the conventional model in important ways. She eschewed the singular goal of raising test scores that has become ubiquitous for English learners and other groups who have historically performed poorly on standardized tests. She resisted pressures to standardize instruction across her classrooms. And she steered clear of traditional classroom inspections to monitor teachers' preparation for the state test. The result was an unconventional model for instructional leadership that promoted non-test-based goals for teaching and learning; resources that were distributed equitably, not equally; and diverse, equity-minded teaching techniques.

* * *

Today, most principals held up as exemplars recount how they heeded district, state, or federal calls for higher test scores. They tell stories about how they used the policies to set in motion dramatic reforms. Others recall their experiences in an unusually autonomous public school or one nurtured by an exceptionally enlightened district. Jefferson's story was different. Forte viewed herself as a buffer whose job it was to shield teachers from the on-slaught of policies about state curriculum standards and testing intended to change what teachers do.

Jefferson's principal, like many urban school leaders, lamented the re-quirements her central office placed on teachers that did not directly foster conversations about the details of their practice. District mandates for record keeping, faculty meeting agendas, and instructional materials were common. Yet Forte managed to meet district obligations without overwhelming her staff. She gathered information from teachers to complete their paperwork on her own. She set aside regular time for teachers to talk about instruc-tion within the district's parameters for teacher in-services, curriculum, and the like. She sought instructional support from central office administrators and school reform specialists who shared her instructional philosophy, while quietly dismissing the advice of supervisors that she found unconstructive. Her institutional savvy paid off; it minimized excessive district intervention in her classrooms and protected teachers' time to tackle the complexities of teaching English learners.

In faculty meetings, Jefferson's principal also played down California's heavy emphasis on standards-based test goals. In her view, state testing goals that measured students' mastery of curriculum standards were too vague. They weren't designed to encourage teachers to identify the specific instruc-tional steps necessary for children to develop particular skills. She put it this way: "If standard 3.5 says that students will be able to use literary elements like metaphor, simile, et cetera . . . then what do you want students to be able to say and do, write and produce? Do you want them just to be able to fill in a bubble test or do you want them to create their own similes and metaphors? Do you want them to be able to use them in narratives?" Teachers' real goal, in her view, was to identify chains of instructional decisions like this one, so these were the types of questions Jefferson's teachers routinely grappled with in meetings.

Forte also mediated between her district and her teachers when the dis-trict called for teachers to spend significant time "aligning" lessons from their language arts textbooks with the state curriculum—the current trend in which teachers match the content of their instruction to the content of their state test. Forte's main concern was for her teachers to talk about how to tailor their teaching to different students. In her words, alignment exercises "don't help teachers really talk about the *how* of instruction," so she discontinued the practice. In its place she set aside bi-weekly meetings for teachers to exchange ideas about daily instructional strategies and adapt them for English-learner students.

*   *   *

There is another growing trend in today's urban districts and schools that seek rapid gains on state tests. They homogenize. By standardizing teachers' curricula, instructional strategies, materials, and other parts of classrooms, leaders try to maximize students' exposure to the content that will appear on the test. This behavior is particularly common in schools serving high numbers of English learners and poor children of color.

Jefferson's leader bucked this trend, too. In fact, she did the opposite. Forte differentiated instructional staff and services based on the varying degrees of need among her three main groups of students.

In one case, rather than equally assigning the same number of reading specialists across all three instructional tracks in the school, she concentrated them chiefly among English learners and Latinos, since these were the students with the greatest literacy needs. When faced with parent resistance, she explained that these were the children that required the most services; Chinese-speaking and English-only speaking children received less because they required less. Most of the time, she found that parents accepted this logic.

In another case, she creatively funded a collection of intervention services specifically aimed at poor Latino students, for this was the population her school was least successful in reaching. Part of the obstacle had nothing to do with classroom teaching. Long work shifts, minimally educated parents, and impoverished households all set poor Latino kids behind their middle-class, English- and Chinese-speaking peers. Forte accepted that the achievement gap existed before kids ever walked through her door. This fact was beyond her control, yet she worked doggedly on what her school could control: its response. One by one, she adapted every staff member's role to focus on the students who struggled most: "my parent liaisons tutor, my secretaries tutor, everybody in this building does something to change the achievement levels of the kids in this building." At Jefferson, extended school days for Spanish-speaking Latino students; after-school enrichment programs; tutoring; and differentiated access to reading specialists all supplemented poor Latino children's experiences beyond the classroom walls.

* * *

Another oft-heard refrain about school improvement is a managerial one; effective principals talk about their close supervision of what happens inside classrooms. They monitor. They track teachers' progress by regularly analyzing test data or inspecting classrooms to ensure teachers are doing what is expected. Here, too, Jefferson's leader deviated from the norm.

Forte spent time in classrooms, but not to check teachers' compliance with rules or regulations. She studied the way her teachers taught. She routinely wrote down teachers' questions for students of different races, languages, and gender. Then, she used the information as a basis for one-on-one conversations with teachers about what she observed. The purpose was to stretch teachers' thinking about their questioning to identify when they asked more or less challenging questions of students from different backgrounds. She recalled how conversations unfolded: "They call on Juan and say, 'What color is the horse in the story?' Then, they call on Mary and say, 'How did the horse decide to leave the stable?' . . . I say, 'Here are the questions you asked the . . . English speakers. Here are the questions you asked the English learners.'"

In this way, Jefferson's leader used not numbers from standardized tests or perfunctory classroom inspections, but rich information that came out of the daily work in classes. Her discussions with teachers got inside their classrooms' core and revolved around the moment-to-moment decisions that were the essence of teaching. And she did it in a way that brought to the fore issues of race and language in teachers' instruction. The effects of this coaching were evident inside of classrooms.

* * *

Visits to English language development (ELD) and bilingual classrooms revealed areas in which Forte realized her goals. They also showed how instruction for Jefferson's English learners sometimes marched to two different beats.

Teachers repeatedly said that they heeded the principal's call to provide exciting, engaging instruction. One fifth-grade teacher echoed many when he shared what went through his mind when planning a lesson: "All the standards aside, if they're not interested, then it's just a lot of standards." Pedagogy at Jefferson also frequently differed according to students' needs, and classrooms tended to center more on students than teachers. That is, on most days it was easy to find students eagerly solving problems together, debating with one another, or experimenting—not just sitting, watching their teacher. And, across every ELD room, students could be found reading a variety of texts were keyed to their specific reading levels—from *Nelson the Baby Elephant* to *The Adventures of Thomas Edison*. In many classes, students participated in projects that blended academic standards with visual and performing arts.

In one fourth-grade ELD room, students performed theatrical renditions of "Little Red Riding Hood" and other fairy tales, using specially designed books with scripts for developing reading fluency, oral speaking, and presentation skills. Absorbed in small groups, students of varying ability levels weighed the pros and cons of each book, and ultimately agreed on one to read and perform. In a back corner, an energized foursome decided who would star as the wolf, the grandma, the hunter, and Red Riding Hood herself. Smiling and giggling, they diligently rehearsed the script before acting out an eerie stroll through a forest, an ominous encounter with a duplicitous wolf, and a cheerful resolution of the wolf's betrayal. In this room, students drove the particulars of the tasks and collaborative activities allowed stronger readers to support weaker ones. The result was a lively atmosphere in which ELD students actively engaged in learning that was fun and challenging, and that targeted several literacy skills at once.

Down the hall, an animated teacher presented many opportunities for bilingual second graders to read, speak, and actively listen. After gathering students on a checkered rug, she hooked the students with a colorful, oversized book about butterflies. Students shared what they already knew about butterflies and what they saw in the book before the teacher introduced the book's vocabulary. As the teacher pointed to the word "metamorphosis" on a white board, she asked students to clap out its syllables before she defined the term. The youngsters sat motionless, engrossed in the text. The teacher walked through the illustrations and read their captions. Students wondered aloud about why caterpillars do the things they do, and they eventually assembled in small groups to make a sentence with their new word—metamorphosis. The series of tasks supported English learners' literacy development with visual representations of the text and careful introductions to complex vocabulary—larva, chrysalis, and pupa. It melded literacy and science. It cultivated academic language by introducing students to the notion of captions in expository text. And it provided several chances for English learners to simultaneously build oral language and social skills.

Today's zeal for testing demands that virtually every urban public school serving disadvantaged communities make hefty gains on standardized assessments. Measurable results are the bottom line for the district, state, and federal authorities that watch over these schools. Despite this reality, Forte managed to infuse a broader set of aims for teaching and learning into her classrooms, even when teachers prepared students to take the state test.

In addition to teaching the conventional, standards-based content that was measured by the state assessment, several of Jefferson's teachers explicitly taught their students test-taking strategies—from carefully reading directions to filling in computer-scanned circles. Interviews with teachers brought to light the ways teachers sensed pressures to boost students' test scores, regardless of the principal's intentions to buffer teachers from unnecessary district intervention or unconstructive testing messages.

Throughout testing season, Jefferson's ELD teachers could be found leading a range of lessons to prepare for the test. Yet the pedagogical features of their instruction varied widely. Large and small group activities took place, and many lessons contained a blend of lecture, practice, and music. In one fourth-grade room, students diligently filled out test booklets for twenty-five minutes until an enthusiastic teacher interrupted the monotony with a spirited song about trying their best on the test. He strummed his guitar. Students sang and laughed. Some even danced. Afterward, the teacher reviewed answers to test questions with the whole class before coaching small groups in strategies for demonstrating their knowledge and skills on the test.

Thus, a delicate tension existed between test-centered and child-centered instruction in Jefferson's classrooms. While teachers prioritized students' needs and preserved diverse, engaging forms of instruction, testing and accountability mandates never fell far from their radar.

*   *   *

Texts on educational leadership tend to portray a fairly simple, managerial project. This portrayal trivializes the multiple, frequently conflicting realities in which school leaders live. Layered underneath the testing demands on urban schools are pedagogical considerations, social and political concerns, organizational anomalies, and many other forces.

This is why Forte's leadership is instructive. It offers a case of an urban leader who muddled through these realities and pushed an agenda for more than just test scores. Crafting multiple instructional programs, each tailored to her students' unique needs, was of paramount importance. Creating access for less privileged families was another goal. Distributing resources based on linguistic, cultural, and other needs represented another. Steady test gains were less central, but still present in her thinking, as classrooms showed. Jefferson's principal maintained social, civic, and political goals for students, not just test-based ones.

And so, Jefferson's leadership was complicated because our social world is complicated. Purely managerial models for improving schools fall short, as do models that narrowly conceive of educational equity or social justice. In this case, a principal tried to advance an equity-oriented model of leadership that emphasized high quality teaching and that increased resources for historically under-resourced groups, but that never completely dispensed with testing mandates.

In the end, Jefferson's leader cultivated a set of classrooms that sometimes inspired and often showcased complex pedagogy for English learners, yet still revealed a strong sense of pragmatism about the broader policy environment in which the school was nested. But at Jefferson the connections between testing policies and classroom practice were not tightly scripted. Improvisation occurred, and two distinct harmonies could be seen and heard throughout its classrooms. Teachers strove to prepare kids for the realities of high-stakes testing while also engaging them in ways that fostered deep literacy skills and strategies. The result was a school that embraced multiple notions of success for English learners and a principal who contributed a complicated model of equity-minded instructional leadership to the public school system and to the ways we can imagine urban school reform.

Chapter 16

Professional Unionism: Redefining the Role of Teachers and Their Unions in Reform Efforts

Claire Robertson-Kraft

Education policy makers have long searched for a system that will recognize and reward outstanding practice, support instructional improvement, and ultimately hold educators accountable for performance. But we are now at a moment when these ideas are more at the forefront of the public conversation than ever before. For states and districts to secure grants from President Obama's Race to the Top Fund, they were required to develop new ways to measure effective teaching and propose plans to use this information in decisions related to compensation, career advancement, and tenure. The availability of federal funds resulted in a flurry of activity and, in the past year, several states have rewritten their education laws so that student performance data can be included in teacher evaluation systems. Although the broader public still does not agree on how best to measure performance, it is clear that they will continue to demand measurable evidence of success.

As Richard Kahlenberg discusses in his chapter on unions in this book, it has become popular in the rhetoric of reformers to cast teachers' unions as the chief obstacle to making these changes. Critics contend that unions have more power than any other interest group and only a limited vested interest in improving student achievement. Chief among their concerns are that unions protect ineffective teachers from being dismissed, allow for evaluation systems that fail to differentiate teacher performance, and promote a salary schedule that rewards seniority rather than teaching excellence. To exacerbate matters, they argue that, with a base of over three million members, teachers' unions have used their political power to thwart flexibility and stifle innovation. In the current climate, this perspective has become the prevailing wisdom among an increasingly influential group of education reformers, resulting in legislation in several states that would either eliminate or significantly limit the collective bargaining rights of teachers.

It's no secret that existing systems rate virtually all teachers good or great and fail to recognize excellence or address poor performance, and that these practices make it challenging for districts to develop a high-quality teaching force. However, there's little evidence that vilifying teachers unions will help solve the problem. To the contrary, whether districts can successfully sustain reform initiatives of this type has historically been shown to depend in large measure on teacher buy-in, particularly from the unions.

If current reforms are to be effective over the long term, they must be done with teachers and not to them. This will mean changing the way unions represent teachers and teachers' unions and school districts conduct their business. Above all else, meaningful reform will require teachers and administrators to work as partners. Rather than eliminate unions, a philosophy of "professional unionism" should lay the foundation for any comprehensive reform effort. In a professional model, unions collaborate with school districts to ensure that teachers play an active role in the implementation of new initiatives. If unions do not adapt to meet the demands of the changing context, they may face irreversible decline.

*   *   *

Collective bargaining agreements, as the product of negotiations between local school boards and teachers' unions, are ultimately instruments of policy. Not only do they directly influence the operation of the school district, they also shape the context for teachers' work. In *United Mind Workers* (1997), Charles Kerchner, Julia Koppich, and Joseph Weeres discuss two very different approaches to collective bargaining—traditional contracts, which reflect industrial-style unionism, and reform contracts, which represent a shift to professional unionism. The industrial model of union-management relations currently in place in most school districts across the country emerged nearly fifty years ago under the leadership of United Federation of Teachers (UFT) president Al Shanker. In 1962, the UFT led a successful teacher strike in New York City resulting in the first collectively bargained contract. This watershed moment in union history transformed the role of unions and changed the balance of power between teachers and administrators. In the following years, union membership in New York City increased dramatically, and, in just over a decade, school teachers became among the most unionized workers in the nation.

The collective bargaining laws that became widespread in the 1960s and 1970s emphasized the distinct and competing interests of labor and management, their adversarial relationships, and the union's obligation to protect its members. Industrial contracts came to be characterized by three hallmarks:

- Separation of Labor and Management. Traditional contracts clearly delineated labor and management roles. The assumption was that union and management had conflicting interests and different spheres of work.
- Adversarial Labor-Management Relations. The industrial model assumed that labor and management were fundamental adversaries and that collective bargaining was the primary means to resolve conflict.
- Limited Scope of Bargaining. The scope of bargaining was limited, typically restricted to wages, hours, and working conditions. In this model, teaching was considered a largely standardized type of work, and collective bargaining agreements sought to establish uniform conditions for the teaching workforce.

*   *   *

Over the past several decades, this model of industrial unionism has been under attack by a growing number of educational reformers. States and districts have set out to change teacher policy by setting new educational standards and developing accountability mechanisms for measuring performance. Concurrently, public sector unions have been enfeebled by the decline in the private sector union movement. In the 1960s and 1970s, union loyalty was an expectation among many Americans and, during this period, teachers put their livelihood on the line to defend their rights. Today, in a more conservative era, unions are often seen as directly in conflict with the power of individuals and the market. In 2011, a Pew Research Center survey revealed that public perception of labor unions had reached its lowest level in a quarter of a century, with only 45 percent of those surveyed having a favorable view ("Labor Unions Seen as Good for Workers, not U.S. Competitiveness").

In addition to external forces, the demand for change has resulted from shifts in the demographics of the teaching force. It was projected that between 2000 and 2010, approximately two million of the nation's three million teachers would retire. Among those were the teachers who established unions in the 1960s and 1970s and deeply understood the origin and importance of collective bargaining. These teachers were replaced with a younger workforce less likely to participate in the life of teacher organizations, dismissing union activities as irrelevant to their practice. Given this, it's not surprising that research by the Public Agenda Foundation has demonstrated that newer teachers do not understand much about unions' traditional function in protecting workers' rights, have different expectations for their role from their veteran colleagues, and as such, are more likely to favor differentiated roles and alternate forms of compensation. A related study presented by Susan Moore Johnson to the American Educational Research Association in 2008 revealed that these newer teachers did not intend to make teaching a lifelong career and were focused on teaching for a few years before pursuing other opportunities. Unions now face the challenge of simultaneously responding to the professional concerns and aspirations of this bifurcated membership.

* * *

During the 1960s and 1970s, unions came together to fight for what they saw as the priorities of their time—fair treatment, better pay, and adequate working conditions. Today, education reform battles are focused on improving the conditions of teaching and learning, which has created a new source of tension between management and union leadership in many districts. The 2012 teacher strike in Chicago, the first in the city in twenty-five years, epitomizes this more adversarial approach to labor-management relations. Traditional collective bargaining arrangements, such as the one in Chicago, tend to promote uniformity, making it challenging to collaboratively implement new types of reform-oriented practices. Despite the prevalence of the industrial model of unionism, several districts are experimenting with progressive practices through alternate forms of bargaining.

In contrast to the industrial model of union-management relations, which assumes that labor and management are fundamental adversaries, trust and shared power lie at the heart of this new model of professional or reform unionism. This approach, discussed by Kerchner, Koppich, and Weeres in *United Mind Workers*, is outlined in Table 16.1.

Table 16.1. Professional (Reform) Bargaining

Blurs distinction between labor and management	Reform contracts bridge labor-management divide by identifying collective aspects of education work. Under these contracts, unions and management assume joint responsibility for improving quality of the teaching force.
Expands bargaining scope to include education policy issues	Proponents of professional unionism urge that unions must organize around issues of educational quality and school innovation. They should collaborate with districts to create a more attractive working environment by ensuring teachers have the support to improve instruction and by offering new opportunities for career and professional growth.
Promotes collaborative or interest-based bargaining	A more collaborative approach to negotiation focuses not on dividing fixed resources but on expanding the proverbial pie. Collaborative or interest-based bargaining urges parties to overcome competitive tendencies and focus on finding common ground. In contrast to industrial bargaining, interest-based bargaining is not viewed as a zero-sum game.

The concept of professional unionism first emerged in the late 1980s and early 1990s, when local unions in Cincinnati, Toledo, Minneapolis, Rochester, Columbus, and Montgomery County, Maryland, began to adopt innovative approaches to labor-management relations and to broaden their contracts to embrace reform-oriented issues. These contracts focused on the teaching

Table 16.2. Principles of Individual Versus Professional Unionism in Practice

Contract issue	Traditional contract (industrial model)	Reform contract (professional model)
Relationship between union and management	Separation of labor and management	Blurred labor-management distinctions
Style of negotiations	Adversarial	Collaborative
Bargaining type	Positional bargaining	Interest-based bargaining
Scope of negotiations	Limited	Expanded
Teacher differentiation	All teachers are treated the same: • Standardized salary schedule and single role of "teacher" • Seniority-based transfer rights	Teachers are treated differently based on skills and interests: • Differentiated pay and career roles • Site selection of teachers over seniority rights
Professional development and evaluation	Contract limits professional development and evaluation: • Purposefully limited offerings • No career development • Pro forma evaluation	Contract emphasizes professional development and evaluation: • Expanded offerings • Differentiated teacher roles • Standards-based evaluation
Focus of protection	Individual teachers	Teaching profession

Information in this table is based on Julia Koppich's 2007 working paper prepared for the School Finance Redesign Project. Resource Allocation in Traditional and Reform-Oriented Collective Bargaining Agreements, Working Paper 18, Center on Reinventing Public Education, School Finance Redesign Project, University of Washington, Seattle.

profession, rather than individual teachers, by addressing issues such as career development, differentiated pay, new teacher induction, and standards-based evaluation processes. Most importantly, over time, relationships came to be characterized by collaboration and mutual trust. Table 16.2 provides an example of the differences between industrial and professional unionism in practice.

*   *   *

Unfortunately, professional unionism has only taken hold in a handful of districts across the county. Led by what former Denver Classroom Teacher Association (DCTA) union leader Brad Jupp refers to as "exorbitant actors," these leaders challenged existing trends and chartered new ground in labor-management relations. One such union—the Toledo Federation of Teachers in Ohio—provides a powerful profile of what professional unionism looks like in practice.

Following a teacher strike in the late 1970s, tensions in Toledo over an escalating number of teacher terminations had begun to affect the relationship between labor and management. Spearheaded by Toledo Federation of Teachers (TFT) president Dal Lawrence, the district brought representatives from union and management together in a collaborative setting to discuss how best to support new teachers and create professional standards of excellence. The product was the Toledo Plan, as it came to be known, which provided new and struggling veteran teachers with professional development to bring their work to acceptable standards and included an evaluation system that detected and screened out those who showed little aptitude for the classroom. In 1981, the Toledo Public School System became the first district to institute this type of intern-intervention program, which has come to be commonly known as peer assistance and review (PAR).

Most notably, the oversight for the program illustrates the principles of joint union-management collaboration in action. As the governing body for the program, the Intern Board of Review is made up of five union representatives, appointed by the TFT, and four management representatives selected by the assistant superintendent. The chair rotates annually between the president of the TFT and the assistant superintendent. The board is responsible for all aspects of the program, including accepting or rejecting the evaluation recommendations of the consulting teachers, assigning and monitoring consulting teachers, planning and implementing applicable in-service activities, and managing the budget. Through extensive observations and assistance, consulting teachers provide the Board of Review with their recommendation, and six votes from the board are required to reverse the consulting teacher's recommendation. The board recommendation is then sent to the superintendent, who recommends to the Toledo Board of Education employment, non-renewal, or termination.

Although PAR can be quite expensive, Harvard Graduate School of Education researchers discovered that administrators and union leaders in PAR districts believed the program's benefits—higher retention rates among new teachers, a professional culture focused on standards of practice, targeted assistance for struggling teachers, and a path to dismissal that protects due process but does not result in costly arbitration—far outweighed the costs. While the primary goal of PAR is to develop teachers' effectiveness, the program also ensures that teachers who do not meet expectations are removed from the classroom. In fact, PAR programs in districts such as Toledo now dismiss ineffective teachers at much higher rates than when evaluations were conducted solely by administration. Most important, however, the program emphasizes the value of creating a professional conversation around improved instruction. In so doing, it builds a solid partnership between unions, teachers, and administrators that encourages them to work collaboratively to enhance quality teaching.

*   *   *

To be sure, moving to a model of professional unionism will be challenging, and it would be naïve to assume that districts and teachers unions can easily bring about these changes in practice. Union leaders will need to unlearn existing habits and develop new practices focused on meeting the needs of a shifting membership. But other cities can learn from the efforts of districts such as Toledo that have sustained a model of professional unionism over time. The following recommendations are drawn from their experience.

Embrace change. To embrace a professional model, school district and teacher union leadership need to acknowledge that they have entered into a new era in public education where student performance is more central to decision-making than ever before. Now that the goals for student learning have increased substantially, what we expect of teachers and teaching must change as well. Union leaders will have to persuade long-time members that accepting change does not mean abandoning the more traditional focus on industrial issues; it merely requires taking on an expanded role. They must also respond to the needs of the next generation of teachers, who have been shown to be more likely to support differentiated pay and embrace opportunities for collaboration and career advancement.

Cultivate strong leadership. The quality of leadership at the district and union level is a necessary prerequisite for facilitating a reform-oriented approach. After thirty years of research, Susan Moore Johnson has concluded, as she put it in an article in *Teacher Unions and Education Policy: Retrenchment or Reform?* (2004), that "individuals—not impersonal, autonomous, inevitable processes—determine the character and shape that collective bargaining will take and the outcomes it will yield" (47–48). Indeed, the experience of Dal Lawrence in Toledo provides evidence for this assertion. Strong leadership cannot exist just at the union level, however. Rather, labor and management must both recognize that they have a common interest in improving student achievement and that each has specialized knowledge to contribute to the quality of decisions. Districts must identify the characteristics of effective leaders and institute mechanisms for cultivating this type of leadership over time. Finding leaders of a certain caliber will inevitably require a bit of chance, but districts can also work to build organizational infrastructure and provide external support to institutionalize these practices.

Build organizational infrastructure. In districts where reform-oriented practices take hold, collaboration becomes embedded in the way the district conducts business. Unfortunately, most districts do not have the organizational capacity to rapidly transform practice. Successfully altering labor-management relations will require instituting systems and procedures to sustain reforms over time. Toledo created various structures to foster investment in the reform process: for example, building-level teams, school improvement committees, school steering committees, leadership teams, advisory councils. These structures can become vehicles for creating a dense internal organization within the union that facilitates the development of new leadership.

Promote an expanded role for teachers. If reforms are to be sustained, districts and unions alike need to operate with the philosophy that teachers should be empowered to have a voice in policy development. Change should not be imposed through top-down command and control or additional bureaucratic regulations; rather, policy makers should find ways to expand teachers' roles through initiatives such as PAR.

With the increased focus on reforming the school system, policy makers are becoming even more demanding and public perceptions are shifting, making change seem inevitable. The tradition of adversarial relations and mistrust marking most relationships between teachers' unions and management has hindered movement toward professional unionism. Together, labor and management need to commit to moving beyond this partisan anger to foster a workplace culture where improving student performance is at the heart of school improvement efforts.

It is essential that as policy begins to hold teachers accountable for their students' performance, it also ensures they are given a say in key decisions that affect instructional practice. In turn, unions must play a key role in improving the quality of education by collaborating with school districts to ensure that their members meet the standards necessary to foster student learning. Ultimately, the best chances for successful implementation of new reforms lie not in eliminating unions, but with progressive educators and union leaders who willingly work together to improve public schools. Now is the time for teachers and their unions to redefine their role with management and assume a seat at the policy decision making table.

Chapter 17

Pushing Back: How an Environmental Charter School Resisted Test-Driven Pressures

Paul Skilton-Sylvester

Who would believe that Albert Shanker, the late, controversial president of the American Federation of Teachers (AFT), was one of the original backers of the charter school concept, publicizing the name and idea in his weekly "Where We Stand" column of July 10, 1988? Charter schools, unions, and public schooling were not always enemies. But, more than two decades later, the teams have changed, and the debate over charter schools has become so polarized as not to be productive. Critics on the left tend to lump charter schools together and include them with the voucher movement as a threat to public schools (even though charter schools are public schools—albeit ones that function with considerable autonomy from districts). The right, for its part, uses charter schools to beat up unions and demonize teachers.

As one who works at a charter school despite complicated feelings about them, I'd like to take you inside the Wissahickon Charter School in Philadelphia, where I work as Lower School Director, and show you a way I believe charter schools can use their structure to succeed.

What makes our charter school different from other non-charter urban public schools where I have worked is a shared sense of purpose—a common set of commitments about what school should be and the kind of world we are trying to create. Without those shared commitments, the priority of many schools in the era of the No Child Left Behind Act (NCLB) often gets narrowed down to high test scores, creating a race to the bottom in which only reading and math skills count; the rush to meet too many objectives then interferes with deep learning and a meaningful connection to the outside world. The autonomy given to charter schools has, in our case, fostered a unique and unifying mission that has allowed us to resist the prevailing mechanistic and reductive view of learning while still staying part of the public system.

Charter schools are the focus of endless debate. Even the term is complicated, meaning anything from "start-up charters," created when sufficiently likeminded people write an application to their state Department of Education to receive funding to start a school; to "conversion charters," created when a public school in a district petitions to become a charter and have increased autonomy; to charters affiliated with for-profit or nonprofit charter management organizations (CMOs), often in chains of similarly run schools.

The data on student achievement in charter schools are similarly complicated. One recent review of the literature in the *Journal of Educational Change* (2009) by Lea Hubbard and Rucheeta Kulkarni, of the University of San Diego and Arizona State University respectively, summed up whether charter schools are raising achievement in a frank, four-word statement: "We still don't know."

Wissahickon is a "start-up charter." In 1999, in a living room in Northwestern Philadelphia, a group of twenty or so parents and educators fashioned a statement about what our school would be and applied to the State of Pennsylvania for a charter. "To start a school is to make a claim about the purpose of life," I read somewhere long ago. In writing the mission statement for our school, that living room group made such a claim. They felt so strongly about it that a number of them put liens on their homes to secure additional funding, and the legacy of this commitment pervades the room whenever someone suggests that the only thing that really matters is the test scores.

The school that grew out of their vision opened its doors in 2001 and is located in what once was the world's largest radio factory. It sits at the border of a residential neighborhood of row houses and a deindustrialized wasteland, with enormous empty factories and weedy lots, but also some recent signs of revitalization, such as a new super-modern Salvation Army athletics center. Being in a converted factory, our classrooms have walls made of those multi-pane factory windows that downtown designers covet for their lofts. The sun shines into the rooms onto rugs and reading areas, and then into the hallways through the picture windows in the interior walls. There, kids read on old sofas or gather for small-group work around a table. Across the street is a sixty-acre park. Of our student body of four hundred students in grades K-8, 94 percent are African American and 70 percent meet the lower income requirement for free and reduced price lunch. Average class size is twenty-two students. Although it is not a collectively run operation, teachers have a great deal of input: details of curriculum are written by teams of teachers hired to produce material during the summer. The faculty determines curriculum emphases during the preceding school year.

Like most charter schools, the mission of our school tends to get abbreviated into a single phrase. For us it's usually "an environmentally focused charter school." The phrase "environmentally focused" comes from the part of our mission statement promising "a curriculum that teaches children about the interconnectedness of the physical and human environments."

*   *   *

In 2010 a strange thing happened regarding our environmental mission. While schools all over the country narrowed their curricula due to pressure to perform well on high-stakes tests, Wissahickon missed the mark for making Adequate Yearly Progress (AYP)—the NCLB seal of approval—but still significantly increased its commitment to its environmental curriculum and made AYP as well.

Two years of failure to make AYP triggers a mandatory School Improvement Planning process, and failure to make it in successive years results in continually decreasing autonomy over school programs, until a school is "reconstituted." The heat is turned up farther when fifth-grade test scores (an arbitrary choice) and AYP status are published each spring in the *Philadelphia Inquirer*. The only subject test scores that matter for AYP are reading and math, so if a school misses AYP once, it doesn't take long for even an idealistic fight-the-system faculty to concentrate its resources (instructional time, staffing, materials, and professional development) in these areas. Our school wasn't immune to these pressures, but we found ways to focus on skills needed for the tests and to dedicate resources to environmental studies.

In practice, our environmental focus plays a role in both the explicit and implicit curricula of our school. Our academic curriculum is organized around inquiry into central topics. In the youngest grades—to fit with children's development—these topics are concrete, close to home, and close to the present time (that is, not historical). Example topics include a farm, a neighborhood, a comparison of a supermarket and a food co-op, and so on. In the middle grades, in keeping with students' expanding ability to think abstractly, the central topics include more historical topics and the concentric circles widen: the biomes of the United States, ancient civilizations, studies of different regions of the world, and so on.

These central topics are studied as "wholes"—ecologies in which the role of human beings is understood as part of, rather than separate from, nature. When second graders compare the supermarket and the food co-op, they buy lunch at both places and trace the ingredients back to their sources, learning about geography, carbon outputs, food processing, nutrition, the mathematics of money, and so on. When fifth graders study desert biomes, they do a simulation of the politics of land development, with students taking the roles of land developers, environmentalists, local residents, and so on. When eighth graders study Asia—including the challenges in its rapid population growth—they work in teams to create their own miniature models of sustainable cities that they enter into a national competition, and are later challenged to reduce their own carbon footprints to offset that of their field trips to sites such as a water treatment plant. One eighth grader, Thandiwe, wrote in a self-evaluation for her report card, "I learned a lot doing the carbon footprint project. I became a vegetarian, and although it was hard, I kept going. When we did the research portion of the project, I found a great article that taught me about how being a vegetarian can keep carbon dioxide and nitrous oxide emissions out of the atmosphere." (Names of all students and teachers have been changed.)

In connection with the environmental curriculum, students go on a series of outdoor experiences that become progressively longer and more remote: from cabin camping in fifth grade to backpacking in sixth to Outward Bound trips in seventh and eighth. All these activities are collaborations between the classroom teacher and the Discovery teacher—a full-time, publicly funded teacher certified in environmental science.

Extracurricular activities include the bio-diesel conversion team—an after-school club of middle-school students working with our middle-school science teacher to convert vegetable oil from the kitchens of students' families into fuel that runs the Outward Bound vans used for our trips. Another—the junior Solar Sprint Competition—is a regional competition for middle-school students who make solar-powered cars from recycled materials. We do these things because we believe they are important educational experiences for kids, even if it's not clear whether or not they raise test scores.

Along with the content we teach through the explicit or academic curriculum, we also teach, of course, through the ways we live—the implicit or hidden curriculum. Our school lunches use locally prepared food, fresh fruit, and biodegradable trays. We recycle throughout the school and use green cleaning materials. Our school building itself is retrofitted in accordance with our mission statement calling for "a physical space harmonious with the natural environment": large, interior windows in the walls of each classroom designed to allow natural light into the hallways and common spaces; solar panels with a computer kiosk with data on the panels' performance, a water catchment basin that allows rainwater to be absorbed into the soil rather than flooding the sewer system and causing sewage run-off into the Schuylkill River. And finally, our community events often center on fun in nature: scavenger hunts by the creek, sledding, Park Day, the Earth Day Celebration, the Solstice Celebration, and Screen-Free Week (formerly TV Turn-off Week).

*   *   *

But, as I said, a funny thing happened this past year. We had not met AYP; yet, after much discussion about how we could improve our AYP status without sacrificing our mission, we were able to restructure our program to more successfully integrate the academic curriculum with our environmental studies program. The environmental curriculum committee began by proposing we move from an environmental program to a sustainability/environmental program—the difference being that environmental programs tend to focus on science and often end up focusing on natural environments, such as parks or preserves. Sustainability, as the term is used in the field, includes environmental science but also social and economic issues and consideration of constructed environments. In keeping with this move toward education for sustainability, the committee proposed a series of questions that would be posed to each grade related to each grade's central topics and calling students to make our own school community more sustainable. The school-wide motto became the statement, "We take care of the earth that takes care of us." The problems we would pose to the students were versions of the question of how we could make that statement more true.

For their part, first-grade teachers Marisol Poe and Juliana Wei, during their unit on trash, asked their students, "How do we take care of the earth by taking care of waste?" Before long "Ms. Juliana" was up to her elbows in the large plastic trash can from the lunchroom, pulling out one item after another, her class gathered around the kidney shaped table, while her assistant, Abrianna Bynum, tallied the contents on an easel.

Another day, when the first graders brainstormed what they could do to decrease the school's amount of waste, ideas flew like sparks—"Songs!" they said. "Speeches! Signs! A march!" A march? "ComPOST! ComPOST! ComPOST!" they began chanting, like some tree-hugger remake of *Lord of the Flies*.

So the first graders went to work creating a school-wide composting system for our lunchroom. They experimented to see what would decompose in the worm bins and what would not. Here were the classes' notes after just two weeks of waiting:

Pudding: GONE
Straw
Spork
Potatoes: GONE
Banana peel: GONE
Lunchmeat: GONE
Aluminum foil
Hoagie wrapper: GONE

After their research (lunchmeat, it turned out, although compostable, attracted rodents and smelled bad), the first-grade students wrote presentations and then broke into teams that visited every classroom in the school, teaching—even to the towering middle schoolers—what to compost and what not to. They created posters with the same. Do you put paper in the bins? Brown paper, yes, ripped into small pieces. Other paper, no.

Once each first-grade class had its own worm bin and the lunchroom got red plastic compost buckets to pass down the tables, students began their advertising campaign to win participation by their peers, and first-grade attendants took turns missing recess to shepherd the composting process. Different students signed up for different tasks. Some first graders wrote speeches that they gave over the public address system during morning announcements exhorting students to compost; another group wrote a song about composting that they performed a capella at each lunch.

* * *

It worked. Six weeks later, I saw the first graders coming out of the lunch-room late in the day looking like the Phillies after they won the World Series. I stopped them to ask what was going on. Seven-year-old Dwayne explained, "We wanted to see if there was the same stuff that was in there last time. There wasn't. There wasn't a lot of food in there. There was a lot of plastic. It's good, 'cause food is not going to waste. It's going to the compost bucket and that helps the worms and they poop it out and that helps the soil and that helps the plants and that helps us!" In that last, wonderful, run-on sentence, Dwayne is doing what management gurus call systems thinking, that is, "thinking in circles." Given the complex feedback loops affecting our world today, systems thinking is a good thing, and a skill that is hard to get if one proceeds lockstep through a series of separate and de-contextualized tested objectives.

After Dwayne, six-year-old Xavia was ready to take it to the next level: "We didn't see any fruits or vegetables but we still saw the trays, the sporks, and the milk cartons. . . . Maybe we can re-use things! Last time, Galen asked to rinse out her milk carton and she used it as a jewelry box!" Thinking creatively and taking initiative? Also hard to get in a curriculum that lacks au-thentic problems.

Every day, we also see the power of a curriculum to motivate and assist students in doing the kinds of work that they couldn't—or wouldn't—other-wise do. After a session of speech writing about their compost program, Ju-liana Wei waved a student paper and said, "I haven't been able to get him to write anything all year long and he just wrote an entire page!" Indeed later, that same struggling first grader wanted so much to be in the group that gave speeches about composting to the middle school that he was paired with a higher level student to come up with a solution: they highlighted certain words in the speech, and he would read those when they got to them.

This was the first grade's project. Each grade had its own guiding ques-tions related to the central topics it studied, each addressing a different aspect of our school community's relationship to sustainable practices: our conflict-resolution practices, our gardening, pest management, water use, electrical

use, local animal habitats, and so on. Eighth graders each did individual projects. What was new was the seamless integration of the implicit curriculum
of how we live with the explicit curriculum of what we study. With the prevailing logic of many schools that had missed AYP the previous year, this
might not have happened. In ours, because of our unique mission, it did.

*   *   *

Implementing a new environmentally focused service learning program in
our school didn't happen without tension, specifically in connection to our
AYP status. Interestingly, this tension came not from among the parents, but
from the faculty. Our commitment to the new sustainability program was
first put to the test in August 2010 when the teacher-led team working on
curriculum laid out its proposal for focusing professional development sessions on environmental/sustainability throughout the year. The team's re-
quest seemed to ignore the problems created by not making AYP and the
statement in the school strategic plan that "at least 50 percent of the year's
professional development would be devoted to reading instruction." Strategic
plans, the guiding force in the school, made every three years, are drawn up
with input from parents, faculty, staff, and administrators. Reading had to be
a priority, but it wasn't the only priority. The environmental program ended
up with nearly 50 percent of professional development time (with connections to reading instruction happening whenever possible).

In spring 2011 we again faced questions about how to use precious professional development time and money. This time the ad hoc reading committee
came to the administrative team with a proposal for dedicating all next year's
professional development time and more money than we had to reading instruction alone. The administrative team had to ask how we could do that,
given the need to continue development of the sustainability/environmental
curriculum. One administrator said, "We have to be both—we have to be the
environmental charter school with the great reading program."

Ultimately, for us, that's the answer: "*We have to be both.*" We have to
improve our students' reading and math ability, including, but not limited to,
our standardized test scores—*and* we need to keep our commitment to sus-
tainability/environmental education. In practice, that means teaching about
tenths and hundredths by using a rainfall map, as our third-grade teacher
Robert Davis does, and drawing circles around puddles to learn about

evaporation as part of the water cycle, as first-grade teacher Marisol Poe does, and working on units of measurement in relation to a study of desert biomes, as fifth-grade teachers and Discovery instructors Helen Harney-Jones and Ellen Beck do. In the end, we *did* do both—expanding and deepening our environmental curriculum and *still* making AYP that year.

The "shared sense of purpose" around our mission could not be sustained without buy-in from a broad base of our school's community. It's not as if our parent body comes with a predisposition to environmental concerns—according to our 2011 Parent Survey, only 37 percent of parents who responded said our environmental mission reinforces a focus of their home, and only 15 percent said it was their most important reason for initially choosing our school. But when parents come to our informational sessions to decide whether to apply, we discuss all aspects of our mission—including integrated, project-based learning around environmental themes—and say, "If you're looking for a more traditional approach, we're probably not for you." We reinforce school learning related to sustainability with articles in the weekly newsletter, articles on the website, homework that involves the parents, and community events. In the end, that same survey revealed that a bit more than 98 percent of the sixty-six parents who responded said, "Wissahickon's environmental focus changes how my child views the earth," and 95 percent said that they were "very satisfied" or "satisfied" with the education their child was receiving at Wissahickon.

We build broader support in the community by hosting monthly "Discover Wissahickon" sessions during which elected officials, businesspeople, academics, and other community members attend morning meeting in classrooms before coming together with school administrators for an information session.

Just as we're clear about who we are when we're "selling" the school to prospective parents and the community, we're similarly so in hiring our staff. We start by looking for résumés that reflect experience in education for sustainability and then tell the applicants about our focus in the interviews. We ask them what they would bring to this mission. We need great teachers, but we especially need great teachers who are a good fit with our approach. Pre-selecting faculty for values, experience, and skills that fit our mission is not something that was possible in the days when I was hired in the School District of Philadelphia Central Office. In that instance, I was given a list of schools and their addresses and told to pick one (the principal would decide later on what grade I would be assigned to).

Our mission is one reason we are able to get the faculty we have. Charter schools in Pennsylvania receive 80 percent of the per-pupil expenditure of the non-charter schools in the School District of Philadelphia, already near the bottom among districts in the state. Not surprisingly, our teachers are paid less than they would be if teaching in a non-charter public school. We administrators take an even larger hit than the teachers compared to our non-charter peers. So why do we—teachers and administrators—who could be working for more money in other schools, choose to work for less pay? Ultimately, we would rather get up in the morning and come to a school where we are co-creators of a project that we believe in than implementers of someone else's program in a unionized, higher-paying school. If you ask me or the rest of the faculty if we are pro-union, I suspect nearly all of us would say yes. If you ask if we would rather be back at the unionized schools where we used to work, we would say no. Quality of life for educators depends on much more than the pay scale and work hours. Mission matters here, too.

Nonetheless, we still live with the tension that arises from trying to balance test-driven pressures with our broader mission. Even though there is wide support for our mission, there were times during the year when, one could argue, test-driven pressures did lead us to narrow the curriculum. For example, our Martin Luther King Day celebration became less ambitious because of teachers' concerns about being able to get to all the content they had to teach. Professional development regarding teaching across racial and socioeconomic differences got edged out by the need for professional development in reading instruction. And shared summer reading on teaching across difference got squeezed out by reading about reading instruction. But note here that these were all decisions about curricula that were not explicitly part of our mission or part of how we sell ourselves to the outside world. If our emphasis were on multiculturalism, we undoubtedly would have done more in those areas while doing less, for instance, for Earth Day. Having an explicit mission can help fight against, if not completely stop, the erosion of the curriculum and the dumbing down of pedagogy due to the test-driven pressures of NCLB.

There is evidence that our charter school isn't the only one that sees values in teaching things besides what is on the tests. A study by the RAND Corporation of 357 charter schools and the same number of non-charter comparison schools found that the two kinds of schools reported similar hours on core subjects, but that elementary charters reported spending more time on foreign languages and fine or performing arts. Charles Payne and Tim Knowles of the University of Chicago make a similar claim in the *Harvard Educational Review* (2009) about successful charters in relation to teacher quality: "Our observations tell us that truly high performing charters ... have not fallen prey to the nation's obsession with results on single standardized tests as the primary determinant of teacher quality."

*   *   *

If the requirement of charter schools to spell out a shared sense of purpose can lessen the tendency to narrow the curriculum to isolated skills of reading and math that count for AYP, are there ways non-charter schools can do this, too? The answer is yes, but districts and unions have to be willing to allow enough autonomy for schools to make different claims about what schools should look like.

In 1994, the Boston Public Schools in partnership with the Boston Teachers Union began creating "Pilot Schools," schools that have control over budget, staffing, curriculum, governance, and time. Pilot schools were created to be models of educational innovation and to serve as research and development sites for effective urban public schools. Today, Boston has twenty-three pilot schools, and the comparison to the district averages more than ten years out are impressive: test scores are higher, students show better rates of attendance, and more students go on to attend university or technical college. As of fall 2011, there also were thirty-two pilot schools in Los Angeles and a smattering of others across the company. These schools build from their predecessors of public school choice programs such as that in Cambridge, Massachusetts, and the now-famous successes in New York City's East Harlem led by then-district superintendent Anthony Alvarado, in which the percentage of students reading on grade level rose from 25 percent in 1979 to 48 percent in 1982.

If pilot schools are successful, why aren't there more? Dan French, executive director of the Center for Collaborative Education, which studies and helps set up pilot schools, wrote in an e-mail to me, "They haven't spread more because the model requires both the school district and teachers union to step outside of their traditional roles in governing schools and work conditions. . . . Granting that freedom to principals, teachers, and parents is still difficult for many institutions to do." Creating schools with a shared sense of purpose requires a change in the assumption that there is one best way to educate children and that once a district finds that way then all schools should look alike. It means accepting that it's okay for some schools to be more "traditional" and some schools to be something else, and allowing parents to make choices that fit their child and their values.

In Philadelphia, our union has taken a step in the direction of school autonomy, agreeing in its current contract to allow 90 percent of teachers to be hired at the school level by local teams composed of parents, teachers, and the principal, rather than through the centralized seniority-based system.

The stakes couldn't be higher. It's no secret what directions most schools are moving in, and that these directions are in most ways wrong: toward a narrower curriculum, a narrower pedagogy, less experience with the natural world, less emphasis on the arts, less physical activity, fewer kids sitting next to kids of a different race or social class, and less critical analysis of our society or place in the world. Even multinational CEOs and global warming activists would agree that schools have to do a better job at helping students understand complex systems and do nonroutine, multistage problem solving. Yet we've created a riptide pulling in the opposite direction—toward the teaching of decontextualized reading and math skills to the exclusion of other subjects and complex problem solving. In the age of the narrowing curriculum and the separation of learning objectives from any meaningful connection to the world, charter schools—and non-charter public schools with clear commitments to a different mission—remind us that school can be something more.

Chapter 18

The Achievement Gap and the Schools We Need: Creating the Conditions Where Race and Class No Longer Predict Student Achievement

Pedro Noguera

The term "achievement gap" is commonly used to describe disparities in academic outcomes and variations on measures of academic performance that tend to correspond to the race and class backgrounds of students. Though such disparities are by no means new, in recent years the effort to "close the achievement gap" has become something of a national crusade. Politicians and private foundations have exhorted educators to take urgent steps to close the gap and put an end to this social scourge. Former president George W. Bush went so far as to accuse those who thought the gap couldn't be closed of practicing "the soft bigotry of low expectations." While it's not clear what he meant by this (or that he even understood what he was saying), it is clear he strongly believed it could be done.

With the enactment of the No Child Left Behind Act (NCLB) in 2001 and its requirement for states to collect data on student achievement and disaggregate test scores by race and other demographic and educational characteristics, awareness about pervasive academic disparities has grown. As a consequence, achievement data in schools and districts throughout the nation have been publicly revealed and discussed. Thus far, public discussions about racial disparities in achievement have done little to actually close the gap or prompt widespread improvement in the nation's schools. Dropout rates remain high, particularly among black and Latino males in urban areas, as noted in 2010 by Jennifer Gonzalez in the *Chronicle of Higher Education* ("High School Dropout Rate Is Cited as Key Obstacle to Obama Education Goals"), and thousands of schools have been labeled "failing." U.S. Secretary of Education Arne Duncan has announced that he does not believe schools in the United States will achieve the NCLB mandate of bringing all children to academic proficiency by 2014, and has agreed to grant states waivers from some of the NCLB mandates. Though there has been no formal surrender declared, there now appears to be a growing realization that the achievement gap will not be eliminated any time soon.

For those who've been following the policy charade closely, it was obvious long ago that it would take more than a clever slogan or public pressure to close the achievement gap. Unfortunately, under NCLB, slogans and pressure are about all schools have received. Over the last eleven years, federal and state governments have mandated the use of standardized tests to hold students and schools accountable. More recently, policy makers have called for higher national standards to prevent states from gaming the system (by adopting lower standards for passing standardized exams), and forty-three states have adopted a federally approved "common core" curriculum. However, neither the states nor the federal government has provided schools with guidance on what they should actually do to reduce disparities in student achievement. Moreover, in a retreat from previous commitments when Title I (now called No Child Left Behind) was regarded as a civil rights statute to provide supplemental aid to economically disadvantaged children (see Richard Rothstein, *Class and Schools*, 2004), there is almost no mention of the fact that racial segregation has grown in America's schools and failure rates are most pronounced in the areas where poverty is concentrated.

Close examination of the persistent and widespread disparities in academic outcomes that correspond to the race and class backgrounds of students reveals that they are actually a multidimensional phenomenon related first and foremost to larger patterns of inequality in society. Family income and to a lesser degree parental education continue to be the strongest predictors of academic performance; see, for instance, Paul Barton and Richard Coley's 2010 *The Black-White Achievement Gap: When Progress Stopped*. Additionally, gaps in academic performance are closely tied to unequal access to quality early childhood education (the preparation gap), inequities in school funding (the allocation gap), and differences in the amount of support well-educated, affluent parents can provide to their children versus poorer, less-educated parents (the parent gap).

Research also suggests that gaps in academic outcomes are sometimes related to strained relations between students and their teachers and may be influenced by lower expectations, particularly for poor and minority students (the teacher-student gap). This is often the case in affluent school districts with relatively small numbers of minority students. In such communities, ability grouping or tracking often re-segregates students within schools and has the effect of denying minority students access to college preparatory courses and the most effective teachers (see the essays in Pedro Noguera and Jean Wing's *Unfinished Business: Closing the Achievement Gap in Our Nation's Schools*, 2006). Finally, as many parents know, there are often gaps between how well students do in school (as measured by grades or test scores) and how well they might have actually done if they were motivated to work to their ability (the performance gap). All these dimensions are important to understanding student performance but none are considered in most of the discourse about the achievement gap. Moreover, there is little evidence that our policy makers even consider how these dimensions interact and influence student learning.

As one who has studied these issues for several years, written extensively on the topic, and worked closely with schools and districts across the country on efforts to address them, it is clear to me that our nation's lack of progress is not merely due to a lack of effort. As a result of the pressure applied by NCLB and the strict accountability that has led districts to fire superintendents and principals when test scores don't improve, educators across the country have been scrambling, and in some cases even cheating, to find ways to raise scores and show that gaps in performance can be closed. By now it is clear that neither pressure nor a narrowed focus on test preparation has worked in eliminating the achievement gap or substantially raising achievement levels for all students. The National Assessment of Educational Progress (NAEP) scores, also referred to as the nation's report card, have been flat and in some cases declined over the last several years; graduation rates have barely improved; and on most international measures of academic performance, American children have fallen farther behind children in other wealthy nations. Actually, a 1999 look by the National Center on Education Statistics at the Program in International Student Assessment (PISA), used to compare the performance of students in various nations on a variety of academic measures, reveals that when the performance of U.S. students is disaggregated by income, school districts with poverty rates lower than 25 percent score as high as the top performing nations in the world. Again, the international comparisons reveal that inequality is America's greatest educational challenge, but the policy approach we have taken for the last twelve years refuses to acknowledge this issue at all.

Instead of addressing poverty and inequality, a growing number of "reformers" have argued that our lack of educational progress can be attributed to the fact that educators are not working hard enough. Former Washington, D.C., chancellor Michelle Rhee has argued that we could substantially improve schools simply by firing bad teachers, and New York mayor Michael Bloomberg has gone so far as to suggest that if we simply shut down the failing schools and replaced them with charter schools, our educational problems would be solved. Of course, there is no empirical evidence supporting either argument, and neither Rhee nor Bloomberg can explain why the schools they have been responsible for have failed to experience substantial improvement under their leadership. This includes many of the new schools they created. Like so many new reformers, they prefer to espouse catchy slogans like "education is the civil rights issue of the twenty-first century" without ever spelling out what this means for the communities whose educational rights continue to be denied.

In my work with schools throughout the country, I am often struck by the frenetic pace at which teachers and school administrators are working. However, I am also struck by the fact that many educators are working hard without fully understanding the nature of the problem they are trying to solve. Without clarity and support, and without some willingness to look closely at the schools where progress is actually being made and a willingness to learn from them, I am certain we will not succeed in making much of a dent in closing the achievement gap. More important, to the degree that a school or district is mired in debates over who is to blame for the existence of the gap—lazy and culturally deficient students, uncaring parents, inept teachers, etc.—combined with a reluctance to share responsibility for finding solutions, there is little chance at all that we will make much progress in addressing the factors that perpetuate the achievement gap in the first place.

*　*　*

In the research literature, much of the attention on the role and significance of race in disparities in academic outcomes can be traced to a seminal book by Christopher Jencks and Meredith Phillips entitled *The Black-White Test Score Gap* (1998). The authors documented what had been well known for some time: African American children, even from middle-class families, consistently perform less well than white children. Yet, while the book presented numerous studies—most based on statistical analyses of large databases, it actually did relatively little to clarify the phenomena other than to document their existence. Since the book's release, several other studies on the subject have been written, but in most cases, aside from reminding readers of the existence of the gap, relatively little has been offered with respect to what might be done to address it.

With so little guidance from researchers, it is hardly surprising that there is so much confusion among educators across the country about what should be done to improve the academic performance of students, or how race is related to the challenges they face. As is true on other matters pertaining to race, such as crime, voting behavior, or immigration, inserting race into a policy discussion often has the effect of distorting how an issue is perceived and understood. Consider the fact that not all white students are high achievers. Indeed, in the Appalachian regions of Pennsylvania and southern Ohio, African American students often achieve at higher levels than white students. In states like Maine, Vermont, and West Virginia, where there are relatively few minority students, large numbers of white students drop out of school, perform poorly on standardized tests, and do not enroll in college. Yet, because the policy discourse about the achievement gap has framed the issue largely in racial terms, policy makers and many educators have overlooked the fact that many white students across the country are not receiving an education that will adequately prepare them for college or adulthood.

A closer look at the evidence reveals that children from impoverished families from all ethnic backgrounds (with the notable exception of some immigrants) typically perform less well than affluent children. So too do children whose first language is something other than English, unless they are literate in their native language and were well educated in their home country prior to coming to the United States. Likewise, children with learning disabilities, in foster care, or with incarcerated parents all tend to do less well in school than children without these disadvantages. Again, this is because gaps in achievement are a reflection of disparities in other opportunities (income, parental education, health care, etc.). There are of course exceptions—poor black children who excel, wealthy white children who don't, Asian students who are not good at math, and so on. The exceptions are important because they remind us that race is an imprecise and misleading indicator of academic performance. Rather than framing the educational challenges in racial terms, we must be more attentive to the ways concentrated poverty, race and gender stereotypes, and educational opportunities generally, influence academic outcomes. The existence of a significant number of racially segregated, high performing, high poverty schools throughout the country serves as the most important proof that there is nothing inherently deficient about students who happen to be low achievers, regardless of their backgrounds, as reported in 2010 by Karin Chenoweth, *It's Being Done: Academic Success in Unexpected Schools.*

Once we acknowledge the ways that other inequities—in income, health, housing, etc.—interact with learning outcomes, then it will become clear that the real work that must be done is to find ways to ameliorate these obstacles. In a small but growing number of schools across the country, educators are working closely with community-based nonprofits, churches, universities, and local businesses to expand learning opportunities for students and address the non-academic issues—nutrition, safety, health, etc.—that affect learning and child development. When carried out with attention to quality in implementation, such an effort makes it possible for educators to focus exclusively on the academic needs of children because other service providers are responding to their other needs. Organizations such as the Children's Aid Society in New York, Communities in Schools, and the widely heralded Harlem Children's Zone are showing that when there is a consistent effort to address both the academic and non-academic needs of children, academic performance can significantly improve.

One of the most troubling aspects of the achievement gap is that gaps in academic outcomes between white and minority students generally grow wider over time, even among children attending the same school. See, for instance, Ronald Ferguson's 2007 *Toward Excellence with Equity* (2007) and his *How High Schools Become Exemplary* (for the Harvard Kennedy School of Government, 2010). Whereas measured differences between white and minority children are generally small in kindergarten, by the third grade the disparities are often pronounced. This is particularly evident in higher-order

skill domains such as deriving meaning from text, drawing inferences beyond the literal text, and understanding rate and measurement in mathematics, as noted by C. M. Ellison et al. for the National Center for Research
Teacher Learning (*Classroom Cultural Ecology*, 2000). This pattern suggests
that two things may be occurring: the supports white middle-class children
frequently receive outside school in the form of parental help, tutors, enriched summer camps, and so on contribute to a widening in academic performance over time; and rather than reducing differences in performance,
schools may actually be contributing to them. Research from several studies
(e.g., A. W. Boykin's 1986 "The Triple Quandary and the Schooling of Afro-
American Children"; Oscar Barbarin's 2002 "The Black-White Achievement
Gap in Early Reading Skills"; James Griffith's 2002 "A Multilevel Analysis of
the Relation of School Learning and Social Environments to the Minority
Achievement in Public Elementary Schools") suggests that both processes
are occurring and contributing to widening of academic disparities. For this
reason, in order for greater progress to be made in in closing achievement
gaps it will be necessary to address contributing factors both within and outside schools.

Achievement and attainment gaps are revealed through a host of schooling indexes, including grade point averages; performance on district, state,
and national achievement tests; rates of enrollment in rigorous courses such
as advanced placement and honors classes; and differential placements in
special education and gifted-and-talented programs. Significantly, gaps that
correspond to race and class backgrounds of students are also manifest across
behavioral indicators such as school dropout, suspension, and discipline re-
ferral rates. Typically, minority students from families that have the least in
the way of financial resources receive most of the punishment in school; see
Anne Gregory et al. "Closing the Discipline Gap" (2010). A study on Texas
by the Council of State Governments, entitled *Breaking School Rules* (2011),
followed every incoming seventh grader in Texas over a three-year period,
and in some cases beyond high school graduation. Its most striking finding
is that nearly 60 percent of the students in the study were suspended at least
once (this includes in-school suspension), and an alarming 31 percent were
suspended at least four times. African American students were over-repre-
sented among those who had been suspended and subjected to the harshest
forms of discipline, including placement in alternative classrooms. A shocking 83 percent of African American males and 74 percent of Latino males

were suspended at least once, and one in seven students at least *eleven times*. Obviously, students who are excluded from school for punishment tend to do less well academically, but the connection between the discipline gap and the achievement gap has drawn little if any attention from policy makers. This is one more example of the way policy makers ignore the many dimensions of the achievement gap.

* * *

Throughout the history of the United States, there have been striking, persistent, and often predictable gaps in achievement between African American, Native American, and Latino students (both boys and girls) and their white counterparts. This is hardly surprising given America's history of racial exclusion, oppression, and discrimination. For the greater part of American history, white privilege and supremacy was rooted in the belief in the inherent superiority of whites over non-whites (see Noel Ignatiev's 1991 *How the Irish Became White*). The view of intelligence that prevailed throughout most of the nineteenth and twentieth centuries held that non-whites, particularly blacks, Native Americans, Hispanics, and even some Eastern Europeans, were genetically inferior and had lower levels of intellectual capacity than Caucasians, particularly those who originated in northwestern Europe (see Stephen Jay Gould's 1981 *The Mismeasure of Man*). Such views about the relationship between race, ethnicity, and intelligence had considerable influence on social science research, psychology, and the theories that guided the development of the IQ test and, more generally, the development of the comprehensive high school.

Given this history, one could argue that the very notion that the achievement gap can and should be closed represents a step forward because it is in effect a repudiation of the notion that innate differences in intelligence would make equality in academic outcomes impossible. Yet the history of beliefs about the relationship between race and intelligence in the United States continues to be highly relevant to current efforts at closing the achievement gap, because racist thinking about the intellectual capacity of different ethnic groups has contributed to the development of racist educational policies and practices. For example, maintaining racially segregated schools by law or social convention was widespread throughout the United States, premised on the notion that racially inferior children should be educated separately. This was true in most cases not only for African American children (in both north and south), but also for Mexican children throughout the Southwest and Asian children in California (see Ronald Takaki, *Strangers from a Different Shore*, 1990.) Japanese Americans were required to attend racially segregated schools in San Francisco until 1947, and Native American children were educated on reservations or involuntarily taken from their families to be educated far away in boarding schools by missionaries (Michael Omi and Howard Winant, *Racial Formation in the United States*, 1986). Even after such practices were effectively outlawed with the *Brown* decision in 1954, schools throughout the United States continue to this day to be characterized by a high degree of separation on the basis of race and class.

What is especially important about this history is that even though there are no public officials who openly call for the maintenance of racially separate schools, there is almost no objection, much less outrage, raised over the continuation of de facto segregation. Today, schools throughout the country serving poor children are not only *racially separate but also profoundly unequal*. This suggests an implicit acceptance of the racial hierarchy that has prevailed for centuries. As is true with other forms of racial inequality (e.g., in health care or the criminal justice system) in the post-Civil Rights period, it is important to understand how inequities are maintained even after laws banning discriminatory practices have been enacted. For example, in most parts of the country, local property taxes are used to generate revenue for public schools. This uniquely American approach to school funding makes it permissible for wealthy communities to spend considerably more money on their children than poor communities. Revenues from local property taxes are used to pay for teacher salaries, fund school facilities, and purchase learning materials and other educational resources. As a result of this practice, inequities in funding reinforce inequities in educational opportunities. Throughout the United States, we generally spend the most on the children from families that have the most resources, and the least on those with the greatest needs. It is indeed noteworthy that in all the talk about closing the achievement gap over the last eleven years, not one major policy figure has suggested that equalizing school funding should be included as part of the strategy.

*   *   *

Advocates of NCLB, and this includes many national civil rights organizations, have aggressively called for common national standards and defended using high stakes testing to ensure accountability. They fear that if we remove NCLB's accountability requirements states will invariably lower standards and we will effectively condemn low-income children of color to an inferior education. Their concern is understandable given that prior to NCLB it was not uncommon for large numbers of students to graduate from high school with minimal skills, unprepared for college or work. Moreover, they fear that if test scores are not disaggregated by race, affluent suburban school districts will disguise the lower achievement levels of minority students as many have done in the past. However, while NCLB has drawn attention to racial disparities in achievement, it hasn't solved the problem. In fact, there is growing evidence that it may have made the problem worse. In schools serving poor children there is a growing tendency for the curriculum to be narrowed to little more than test preparation, and throughout the country, large numbers of students who have passed state exams are being required to take remedial courses in college because they lack basic writing and math skills.

NCLB defenders fail to see that there is an alternative to the narrow use of standards and accountability. Rather than lowering standards for some students to compensate for their inadequate learning opportunities, we could do far more to level the educational playing field by focusing policy on the need to create optimal learning conditions for all children.

This is the approach a handful of schools and districts have taken, and in several cases it's working. For example, at Brockton High School in Massachusetts, a school where over 70 percent of students are from low-income, minority families—many of whom do not speak English as the first language at home—over 80 percent of students score at proficiency on the state exam, and in spring 2011 over 90 percent passed the exam. In 2012, one-third of the senior class received the Massachusetts prestigious Adams scholarship, providing a four-year scholarship at a state university. The accomplishments of Brockton High School are particularly noteworthy given that the Massachusetts exam is widely regarded as the most rigorous in the nation. What makes Brockton High even more impressive is the fact that with over 4,100 students it is the largest school in the state. The school has obtained these impressive results by methodically providing targeted help to students who enter high school struggling in reading and writing, and training teachers in all subjects, including science, math, and physical education, to develop the literacy skills of students in their classes.

Similar results have been obtained at Ossining High School in New York. Like Brockton, Ossining is very diverse, but it has been ranked as one of the country's top 100 high schools for three years in a row. The superintendent, Dr. Phyllis Glassman, attributes the school's success to a relentless focus on meeting the academic needs of students. Unlike some schools that make it difficult for students from low-income backgrounds to enroll in challenging honors and advanced placement courses, Ossining High School actively encourages all students to take such courses, and it provides afterschool tutorial support to students who struggle and lack support at home. In a controversial move, the school set up a special mentoring program for African American male students when it found these students consistently lagging behind their peers. Called Project Earthquake, the program provides mentoring, visits to local colleges and universities, and positive peer support to create a climate where, Dr. Glassman believes, "they no longer accept the negative stereotypes that have been projected onto them."

Schools like Brockton and Ossining may be the exceptions, but they are by no means alone. Emerson Elementary School in Berkeley, Long Beach Unified School District in California, Montgomery County Public Schools in Maryland, and several others are showing that significant progress can be achieved when educators focus on expanding learning opportunities for students. This requires them to recognize that students who receive less support at home will need more in school, that students who don't come from middle-class families will need to be pushed and encouraged to take challenging courses and need greater support when applying to college, and that teachers will need to work collaboratively to share instructional strategies and discuss ways to overcome the learning obstacles their students face.

What these schools have accomplished is noteworthy; they have created learning environments where a child's race or class doesn't automatically predict how well he or she will do. Not all poor and minority students are excelling in these schools, but many of them are, and when patterns of achievement become less predictable, the expectations of students and their teachers also begin to change. However, it is important to acknowledge that the success of these schools does not mean that the achievement gap has been eliminated, or that disadvantages related to income and parental support are not still in play. The 2009 results of the international student assessment test administered by the Organization for Economic Cooperation and Development (OECD), hardly a left-leaning think tank, demonstrate convincingly the relationship between achievement in math, science, and reading; the quality of education; and socioeconomic factors like education, income level of parents, a country's distribution of income, and its social safety net for children. The United States does not fare so well on these measures. Good schools can help reduce the effects of poverty, but more is needed.

* * *

In 2008, a coalition of scholars, policy makers, and educational leaders issued a policy statement that called for three major revisions in federal education policy: expanded access to learning time through quality after-school and summer school programs; universal access to pre-school; and universal health care for children. Called the Broader, Bolder Approach to Education (BBA), this ambitious reform project was launched as an attempt to develop a comprehensive school reform strategy that could address issues and challenges arising out of the distressed social contexts within which poor families and public schools are situated. The goal of the BBA was to shift educational policy away from a narrow focus on standards and accountability, and toward a recognition that social services, child development, and civic engagement were essential to ensure that all children received the educational opportunities they deserved. (For a detailed discussion of the BBA plan, go to www. boldapproach.com.)

The BBA reform agenda is part of a larger national effort to change the focus and direction of educational policy to address the social and economic factors that often undermine schools and children. In cities like Newark, New Jersey, and Syracuse, New York, where this strategy is presently being implemented, systems are being put in place to address the effects of concentrated poverty and the social conditions often associated with it: poor health, high crime rates, and substance abuse. The BBA approach calls for schools to be provided with the resources and support to mitigate the risks that might otherwise undermine their efforts to meet the learning needs of students. It is based on the premise that *fixing schools* in high poverty neighborhoods must include strategies that make it possible to respond to the wide range of challenges that affect child development and learning. Breaking with precedent, proponents of the BBA in cities such as Orlando, Boston, and New York City, have embraced a strategy that should make it possible to address what we have known for years: children's lives are situated in ecological systems that invariably shape their development.

Such an approach is the only way we could realistically begin on a broad scale to reduce gaps in student achievement. In a society as inequitable as the United States, where disparities in income and wealth are growing and typically reproduced across generations, schools cannot be expected to serve as the only force for equity. Still, if we hope to use education as a vehicle to counter social inequities and create a more equitable society—and as long as we remain unwilling or unable to adopt more far-reaching measures such as redistributing wealth through a more progressive tax system—then strategies like BBA may be our best bet for now.

Not surprisingly, such an approach has critics and opponents. Shortly after BBA was announced, another national group of educational leaders and policy makers launched what they called the Coalition for Civil Rights and Education (CCE). Led by an unusual combination of prominent public figures including Joel Klein, chancellor of New York City schools, Newt Gingrich, former House Republican leader, and Reverend Al Sharpton, a prominent civil rights activist, the CCE described education as the most important civil rights issue of the twenty-first century and called for affirming the principles of NCLB: standards-based reform and accountability through high stakes testing. The CCE also suggested that any effort to shift the focus of school reform to an effort aimed at reducing poverty or improving the health and welfare of children would be nothing more than an attempt to use poverty as an excuse for not educating all children at high standards.

Despite its critics, the BBA strategy is moving forward and gaining momentum as a broad array of stakeholders across the country agree to support it. Still, getting such a strategy to be adopted as federal policy will not be easy. With a broad array of lobbyists including major foundations such as Gates, text book companies that produce standardized tests such as Pearson, and major civil rights organizations such as the NAACP and the National Council of La Raza, working to defend NCLB, revamping the law even under a Democratic administration will be hard to pull off. Nonetheless, slow but steady progress is being made in a growing number of communities that have been willing to embrace a more holistic and integrated strategy to school reform, largely because they realize that it is the only approach that makes sense.

For the last thirty years or more the schools-alone strategy has been pursued by educational policy makers. Billions of dollars have been spent on plans to revamp school curriculum, retrain teachers, introduce new technology, and make schools smaller, but none of these costly measures have had the impact on academic and developmental outcomes of the most disadvantaged children that was expected or hoped for. The history of failure in past school reform efforts has made it clear that a strategy based on a more holistic framework that explicitly tackles inequality is the only way sustainable progress in public education will be achieved.

Chapter 19

¡*Ya Basta!* Challenging Restrictions on English-Language Learners

Eugene E. Garcia

During the last decade, the population of children entering American schools unable to speak English grew by 40 percent. One in ten pre-K-12 students, a total of 5.3 million, are categorized as English-language learners (ELLs). This number is a direct result of the large wave of immigration over the last fifteen years. Those new immigrants gave birth to "new Americans," children born in the United States with full citizenship rights but whose families are non-English-speaking. Therefore, the number of ELLs is projected to increase by some 20 percent in the next decade. The achievement gap between them and their English-speaking peers has not diminished, with ELL students underperforming by 30–50 percent compared to English-speaking white peers at almost all grades across national and state assessments. In almost all instances, this is the case even if you control for median family income and other indicators of social class. The education of ELL students in the United States need not remain a story of underachievement. Research points to effective methods for turning around their educational trajectory. Unfortunately, however, ELL policy remains mired in political ideology that restricts its potential and blocks its supposed intentions.

ELL education policy, which evolved from the nativism of earlier periods, once again reflects the politics of xenophobia. We see these politics played out in aggressive state-level anti-immigration measures such as the "birther" bill, restrictions on ethnic studies, administrative actions to exclude teachers with Spanish accents, and laws requiring English-only instruction. Although the increase in the number of children who do not speak English reflects immigration from Asia and Eastern Europe among other countries, it is the fear of the "other" along the southern border that has made language policy a battleground. Especially in states in the Southwest, where Latinos promise to become both the numeric and voting majority, immigration and language policy respond to anxieties about demographic change and the impact of the economic meltdown that has devastated many American communities. In this sense, Latinos have become the latest scapegoats in the displacement of cultural and economic worries onto immigrants. Where once citizens worried about the Irish, Chinese, and southern and eastern Europeans, now it is the "Mexicans."

Although other Latino populations on the East Coast, particularly Puerto Ricans and Dominicans, have added to ELL population growth, the wave of Mexican immigration to all regions of the country has generated increased policy attention to ELL and immigrant issues. In Arizona, my home state, immigrants have been blamed for the state budget crisis, crime, forest fires, and almost all "problems" in the state. Directing blame onto immigrants is a time-honored way to deflect the public from the real source of problems, which in this state as in many others can be traced to the role of massive tax cuts over the last several years.

My approach to the education of ELLs recognizes that we walk in varied and diverse cultures with the varied languages associated with those cultures. In the United States, over 150 languages are spoken by over 100 identified ethnic groups. We all live with diversity, some of us more than others. No one escapes this challenge or its advantages and disadvantages. ELL children and their families are no different in that they are in many ways similar and in many ways similarly diverse. But at the heart of my approach is the belief that diversity is a cultural and linguistic resource, not a problem. With this approach, successful education interventions for ELLs include respecting the cultural and linguistic roots of this population and sustaining and using those roots in their education. Therefore, for ELL students, bilingual education values the heritage language while at the same time addressing English development in the school setting.

There are other ideas about what it means to educate ELLs in the United States. Linda Chavez, an adviser in the Reagan White House, journalist commentator, and author of *Out of the Barrio: Toward a New Politics of Hispanic Assimilation* (1985), argues the following: "Every previous group—Germans, Irish, Italians, Greeks, Jews, Poles—struggled to be accepted fully into the

social, political and economic mainstream, sometimes against the opposition of a hostile majority. They learned the language, acquired education
and skills, and adapted their own customs and traditions to fit an American context" (17). The key for success in America, Chavez believes, is to promote assimilation and decrease public/government recognition of language
and cultural differences. She chides the federal government for its federal
bilingual education programs. She similarly criticizes Hispanic leaders for
promoting permanent victim status and vying with black Americans for the
distinction of being the poorest, most segregated, and least educated minority, thereby entitling them to government handouts. There are gradations
in between, and feelings run strong along the continuum.

Starting in 1974, major court cases established the rights of non-English-
speaking students to special instruction, often in their own languages, until
they were proficient in English. No longer were they expected to sink or swim
in the sea of foreign words, in immersion-only programs. There was a great
deal of controversy about which methods worked best. By the end of the twentieth century, though, education experts had reached consensus on key points.
Although this chapter deals primarily with children in the lower grades, when
new language learning is easiest, enough research exists to tell us what works
at all levels. We know that the following are necessary for children to learn
language: literacy-rich environments in the native language, early childhood
experiences to develop pre-literacy skills, qualified staff at every level, and
quality professional development. Various instructional programs attempt to
meet these requirements, although the settings that serve ELLs may be distinct
and call for adaptations of instruction. In a setting with many ELL students
with the same heritage language, use of that language is recommended. When
there are various heritage-language students in a school or classroom, English-
as-a-second-language strategies that recognize the significance of the students'
heritage language and culture are recommended. Even the presence of one ELL
student in a classroom requires adjusting the curriculum to meet the needs of
that student. Unfortunately, national policy has moved in the opposite direction, toward a one-size-fits-all approach.

                              *   *   *

In 2001, federal language policy for ELL students reversed direction. The
No Child Left Behind Act (NCLB)—the name for the 2001 reauthorization

of the 1965 Elementary and Secondary Education Act—abandoned almost thirty years of practice and made a U-turn from the 1994 version of the Bilingual Education Act, which still included among its goals "developing the English skills and, to the extent possible, the native-language skills" of Limited English Proficiency (LEP) students. At a time when globalization means workers and goods flow across borders, NCLB focuses only on "English proficiency." In fact, "bilingual" has been eliminated completely from the law and all government offices affiliated with it. The Office of English Language Acquisition, Language Enhancement, and Academic Achievement for Limited English Proficient Students (OELA) has replaced the Office of Bilingual Education and Minority Affairs. The National Clearinghouse for Bilingual Education has become the National Clearinghouse for English Language Acquisition and Language Instruction Educational Programs.

The federal government cannot require states to follow its lead in educational change. But it can threaten to withhold funds if they do not. Federal legislation now mandates an annual assessment of English proficiency for any student who has attended school in the United States (excluding Puerto Rico) for three or more consecutive years and requires states to hold schools accountable for adequate yearly progress (AYP) toward "measurable achievement objectives." States that fail to make AYP standards can lose federal funds.

NCLB is up for reauthorization in 2013, and the federal government has shifted again and called for a return to ELL programs based on research and experience—comprehensive literacy programs at federal, state, and local levels that link learning from birth to the pre-kindergarten years through grade 12 with emphasis on the need to develop a bilingual workforce. This is a welcome change, one that is pedagogically sound, but it confronts political roadblocks. The "English only" ideology, with its powerful political support, lurks as a substantive barrier to the policies needed to support the nation's English learners.

*   *   *

State referendums in California, Arizona, and Massachusetts have mandated restrictive instructional models for ELL education, with the Arizona referendum and subsequent legislation the most restrictive. Proposition 203, passed in 2000, requires a Structured English Immersion Model (SEI).

Local flexibility in the choice of program models for ELLs ended as Arizona required SEI to be used in all school districts and charter schools. The Arizona English Language Learners Task Force made the regulations even more restrictive by requiring implementation of what is called the four-hour block model. This model requires students during their first year classified as ELLs to be taught English in an English-only immersion setting for a minimum of four hours in a six-hour instructional day.

The four-hour English-language development period assumes that ELLs can reach proficiency in English quickly (usually within a year) in an English-only instructional environment. However, to leave these segregated classes, students must show "mastery" of English at grade level as measured by the state English language test, the Arizona English Language and Literacy Assessment. The SEI also requires grouping ELLs based on English language proficiency and specifies the number of minutes for each component of language instruction. According to Arizona law, English-language development consists of improving phonology, morphology, syntax, lexicon, and semantics. Unfortunately, no one learns a living language this way.

The Arizona model contradicts research on both second-language acquisition and cognitive infrastructure theories of bilingual development. To progress in language learning, ELLs need ample opportunities to interact with more proficient students and to hear and participate in language and cognitive activities. By denying these opportunities to ELLs, Arizona's current language regulations restrict academic achievement and dilute the quality of educational experiences. In fact, achievement gaps are usually larger in states with restrictive language policies. Data from the National Assessment of Educational Progress (NAEP) confirm that English-only instruction has not benefited ELL reading and math achievement in Arizona. This puts Arizona in violation of the U.S. Supreme Court decisions that require states to give proof of the success of their ELL programs. Since the implementation of Arizona's English-only policy, moreover, schools have placed increased numbers of ELLs in special education programs, possibly to compensate for the inadequate language instruction those students have received. The instructional model that separates ELLs from mainstream students and classrooms for 80 percent of the school day only reduces their social and cultural well-being, silencing and marginalizing them in the greater school context and diminishing their sense of belonging. Even more, the policy gives students no opportunity to develop their heritage languages and cultural knowledge, both of which build self-esteem, social skills, personal identity, and linguistic and academic achievement.

The mandated four-hour block is a major problem for older students, who must pass standardized writing and content-based exams to graduate from high school. While they are learning "about" English for four hours a day, they are not learning math, science, and social studies. At a key point in their education, their motivation and interest in academic progress are dampened, reducing their chances for higher education.

Arizona policy discriminates against ELL students by denying them access to core academic content in a rich, cognitively demanding educational setting. By blocking them from receiving the same education as students fully proficient in English, the state violates their access to an education that respects their linguistic rights. State policy, moreover, prevents teachers and school districts from implementing the practices most likely to enhance the linguistic and academic achievement of ELL students.

*   *   *

Is Arizona the bellwether? The state's approach to the equal education of bilingual students is the most extreme of the highly restrictive language education policies across the nation. Like Arizona, a number of other states have recently passed referendums calling for restrictive instructional models that do not reflect widely accepted best practices for the education of ELLs. This mandated "one-size-fits all" approach has harmed students. The results are clear: these policies have generated no substantive decrease in achievement gaps. Nonetheless, still more states are considering similar policies, which could even find their way into federal legislation through the reauthorization of NCLB.

*   *   *

¡Ya Basta!—enough is enough. Despite Supreme Court decisions in the 1970s, the civil rights of ELL students have been disregarded. Nationally, the achievement gaps between them and other students remain wide while they have increased in states with restrictive language policies. Even in states with less restrictive language education policies for ELLs, most are programs similar to the ELLs in Arizona. They are in those programs because school of-

ficials have chosen these restrictive language-education environments, not because restrictive policies dictated that choice. We will not get the education of these students right until we jettison the "English-only" ideology and implement policies and practices that respect their linguistic and cultural diversity and guarantee their civil rights and educational opportunities. This is not really much to ask of a country that has always embraced the idea that "all children can learn to the highest levels" and that "no child should be left behind." In an era that has been consumed again with nativism and anti-immigrant sentiments, this large and growing population of ELL students is being discarded both as members of a needed work force and as intellectually engaged citizens of the future. This reality is never articulated in the debates regarding ELL education or immigration policy.

Chapter 20

Sharing Responsibility: A Case for Real Parent-School Partnerships

Rema Reynolds and Tyrone C. Howard

Parent involvement is all the rage. From the president to local superintendents to foundation directors, all agree parents need to be involved in their children's education. One policy mechanism pushing this call to action is a provision within the federal No Child Left Behind Act (NCLB) that states that parents are to be included in decision-making practices as full partners with school officials. But as legislators grapple with revisions of the policy, parents have been eclipsed from the reform conversation—twice.

As NCLB is being revised for reauthorization, the provision has been omitted, but its power remains. Unfortunately, the original provision about parent involvement offered little or no guidance regarding implementation. Perhaps the authors of NCLB's parent involvement clauses thought it best to leave translation of the provision to local districts. That seems plausible. Each community is unique and has particular characteristics to consider when forming partnerships; no two communities are the same. But to provide schools with a mandate and no direction seems disingenuous or inept. It is unlikely that schools will instinctively know what steps to take to invite parents in as partners, particularly when we consider the low priority this mandate has in a typical district.

Yet parent participation *should* be a focal point in school reform. We know from research that when parents are involved, math and reading scores increase, truancy rates and disciplinary issues decrease, and college success is more likely.

One way involvement is characterized in schools is "send me parents, but, not *all* parents." This stance is punitive toward many parents except for those who fit the middle-class ideal. Parents are an afterthought—until there is a problem. Then parents are ushered into the conversation as a centerpiece for blame. In 2011 New York City mayor Michael Bloomberg lamented the disappearance of what he termed the "Norman Rockwell family" who value education. Given the racial and ethnic composition of the students in New York City's public schools, the mayor conjures an interesting image of the ideal American family.

Preceding the mayor, President Obama was one of the more vocal critics of parents. Almost immediately after assuming office, the president issued public announcements urging parents to get involved in the schooling of their children, offering a glimpse of a day in the life of the Obama daughters structured by him and his wife Michelle. Two months into his tenure, the president told a joint session of Congress, "There is no program or policy that can substitute for a mother or father who will attend those parent-teacher conferences or help with the homework or turn off the TV, put away the video games, read to their child. Responsibility for our children's education must begin at home."

Recently we have lauded the Tiger Mom and positioned the strategies of Yale professor Amy Chua as ideal for mothers to adopt when rearing their children. Absent from the pats on the back, Professor Chua received an acknowledgment of her privilege. She was able to speak as a peer with teachers about her daughters' progress in the classroom and supplement their education with activities outside school. These enrichment opportunities—piano lessons and private tutoring—were pricey. While dialogue about school reform is often centered in struggling communities—schools with concentrated populations of poor and minority students—it seems that the models for parent participation are often patterned on the privileged. Most families in the United States lack the material and social capital of the Obamas and the Chuas. Hiring people to augment the free education received at neighborhood schools is not an option for the average family, much less families in communities we acknowledge as needing reform. For some families, taking time from work to attend a conference scheduled during the day, a duty President Obama never neglects, can mean a loss of wages. So what about the neediest schools located in the poorest communities with the most vulnerable student populations? What does parent participation look like in these places?

Consider the following ethnographic snapshot of a parent advocacy group meeting held during the 2011–2012 school year to illustrate a second way involvement plays out in schools. A group of about sixty parents meet at a community center at the beginning of the school year. Balloons and signs mark the entrance, and the smell of grilled chicken wafts down the block. Inside, an unassuming woman welcomes everyone from a podium near the stage. Some folks sitting at tables munching salad have headphones on for interpretation. These are the few English speakers in the group since the meeting will be conducted in Spanish. The superintendent and two board members are introduced and given an opportunity to speak—briefly. Then the organizers light up the LCD projector with professional visuals that illustrate the school district's performance in terms of discipline, college-going rates, test scores, and attendance at the secondary level. The bar graphs tell a story of failure to prepare children to be "viable twenty-first century competitors." The meeting ends with suggestions to collectively address the issues illustrated in the presentation. The organizers bid farewell and give the date of the next meeting, where an action plan will be formulated.

The scene appears ideal at first glance. Situated in a space within the community for easy access, parents are informing parents, partnering with high-level school officials, and providing solutions to problems plaguing their children's schools. It would seem that this kind of engagement is just what NCLB envisioned. Yet NCLB in fact does not specify this level of engagement at all. It is true that the parent advocacy group can exist and this kind of presentation can be made for a community because of the high-stakes testing and varied accountability measures demanded in NCLB. The data presented by the parents at this meeting are accessible to all, thanks to the reporting edicts handed down by the Department of Education.

If only the parents were involved in gathering the data themselves in a way that taught them how to do it on their own. These parents were brought together by an outside agency, Parent Revolution. This agency has been active for over a year, staking its claim to fame initially in Compton, California, where it successfully closed a relatively high-performing elementary school and turned it over to a charter. The fancy graphs? Their work. The organizing? Their strategies. The grilled chicken? Their budget.

In early 2010, when Arnold Schwarzenegger was governor of California, the state legislature passed the Parent Empowerment Act, commonly known as the Parent Trigger. Parents with children attending low-performing schools are better able to organize and levy various sanctions: fire staff, create charter management, or close schools altogether. So far, two districts in the state have launched parent trigger campaigns—Compton and Adelanto. Such options are similar to the Department of Education School Improvement Grant (SIG) Program, a provision that gives funding for schools with low test scores. In concert with recent reform efforts, the Parent Trigger offers a punitive manifestation of parent participation. Instead of working alongside school officials to change the school for the better, parents are positioned as adversaries to be feared. Neither the Parent Trigger nor the federal SIG program offers constructive models of parent engagement.

Supporters of the Parent Trigger contend that this legislation empowers parents, particularly underrepresented parents, educates them about school operations, and equips them with tools to engage with and improve their schools. Without knowing the backdrop, parents would leave the community meeting thinking of the wealth of information presented, impressed with the caliber of knowledge the parents possessed and provided, and never questioning the underlying intent of the "organizers."

Consider the source. Who created the Parent Trigger? The main driver of the legislation was Parent Revolution, the organizers of that community meeting. It is funded by charter school operators like Green Dot and a host of pro-charter philanthropists that include the Broad Foundation, Gates Foundation, Hewlett Foundation, Walton Family Foundation, and the Wasserman Foundation.

It seems that parents are positioned as either scapegoats, bearing the blame for poor educational outcomes for the neediest students, or opponents who should be feared, not necessarily respected or welcomed as full partners with educators.

But there is a third way to envision parent participation: parents as partners. Without much fanfare, a few schools in "at-risk" neighborhoods serving "at-risk" students have connected with their communities to form effective partnerships. These partnerships go beyond what current NCLB legislation mandates but do not exact punitive measures for low test scores as the Parent Trigger promotes.

The partnerships are dedicated to breaking age-old barriers that exclude particular communities from accessing essential information for social, economic, and political mobility. In California, for example, the Parent Project at the University of California, Los Angeles, provides research-based programs that focus on developing and sustaining parent leadership in the Los Angeles Unified School District (LAUSD). Given the varied challenges families can encounter in LAUSD schools, including inexperienced teachers, lack of technology, and inadequate transportation, the project looks to engage parents as advocates by providing them information regarding their rights. The project brings parents and educators together through open forums facilitated by UCLA faculty and staff. Dialogue between the two is essential to improve student performance.

The Urban League also recognizes the connection between safe, healthy, thriving neighborhoods and education, and like the Parent Project, it has been actively engaging parents in community transformation. Its Neighborhoods@Work Initiative centered in South Los Angeles partners with community members to tackle problems related to education, employment, health, housing, and safety in a 70-block area in the city's center. Modeled after the Harlem Children's Zone in New York, the Neighborhoods@Work Initiative effectively collaborates with community members, social service entities, elected officials, law enforcement agencies, health practitioners, and educators. Their efforts have decreased violent crime, increased student achievement at certain schools, and made affordable housing more accessible.

Initiatives such as the UCLA Parent Project and Neighborhoods@Work choreograph collaboration through relationship building, hearing the concerns of community members, and empowering them to be problem-solving partners. Often, legislators and educators seek to change schools in isolation, attempting to "protect" the school from its own community, instead of recognizing that the two are the same and that to change one means paying close attention to changing the other.

One of the explanations for the breakdown in community and parent partnership has been the strong reliance on schools or other educational institutions to initiate, structure, and sustain the relationship. Developing shared responsibility between community and parent organizations, individual families, and educational institutions requires work. In some ways it is easier to make parents scapegoats or even adversaries rather than partner with them and pursuing the dialogue and shared decision-making partnership requires.

Modern day parent involvement has much to learn from historical models of community engagement. In addition to churches that have long served as a central meeting place for parents to convene, a number of community service organizations—Big Brothers and Big Sisters of America, 100 Black Men, and Boys and Girls Clubs—have developed initiatives designed to engage youth and parents around discussions of educational outcomes. Much of the social and intellectual capital in these organizations can be leveraged to assist parents in better understanding how to navigate complex school systems. Schools can be intimidating and seemingly inaccessible to parents who lack the knowhow to garner information and services for the benefit of their children. There is, after all, only one Amy Chua. Bridges between those who have been excluded from the landscape of reform, achievement, resources, and the knowledge to effect change can be erected and maintained in vulnerable communities.

There is one more thing to say about parent participation that is rarely discussed when talking about the topic—some parents have difficult lives. The failure to critically analyze race and class dynamics assumes that to move from disengaged to engaged, all families need to do is work harder, make better choices—in short, the proverbial "pull yourself up by your bootstraps" message. It goes without saying that hard work and better choices influence life chances, but these attributes alone cannot facilitate the type of social and economic transformation that has eluded families for generations. A continued critique of parent involvement practices without acknowledging the social conditions parents experience leaves our conversation about the power of the parent in furthering school reform disjointed, if not deceptive.

Parents, politicians, and practitioners will agree that monitoring activities at home, such as limiting media intake and checking homework, is an effective way for parents to work alongside educators. However, this kind of involvement still falls short of the fuller kind of involvement. While allowing autonomy from community to community, lawmakers can also offer prescriptions and accountability measures to ensure the construction of parent partnerships. We can all recognize the value of parent participation, after all, authentic partnerships between educators and parents—*all* parents—have the power to transform our schools. Perhaps the next legislation will be No Parent Left Behind.

Chapter 21

Calling the Shots in Public Education: Parents, Politicians, and Educators Clash

Eva Gold, Jeffrey R. Henig, and Elaine Simon

The gap between calls for parental engagement in education and institutional realities is wide. Educators say they value parent participation, but by that they often mean a junior partner role in which parents monitor homework, make sure kids get to school on time, show up at school-sponsored events, and generally act as an extension of the teacher and school. Many parents and community advocates, however, see themselves as more than just the supporting cast. When a neighborhood school fails to perform well on standardized tests, should it be closed, turned over to private management, or reinforced with more resources and stronger leadership? When budgets are tight, is it music and art instruction that should be scaled back, or social studies, or are there other options to explore? Those who favor strong democracy over simple representative democracy argue that parents and community groups should play an active role in setting public priorities, debating public options, and negotiating policy solutions.

In muscling aside teachers' unions and traditional school bureaucracies, the contemporary education reform movement echoes earlier ideas of parental engagement, but the results are similar. Contemporary school governance reforms may have streamlined command structures and increased choice, activating some forms of parental participation and some new actors, but these reforms often diminish avenues for parents to act collectively and to shape policies rather than simply help to implement them. Proponents of these reforms often discredit forms of school governance that include avenues for strong democracy, charging they are inefficient, rife with corruption and patronage, and marked by low student performance. Our research on the political battles over extending mayoral control in New York City shows the tactical dilemmas of pursuing a vision of strong democracy in a changing political landscape.

*   *   *

Mayoral control of schools is one of a series of institutional shifts that are reconfiguring relationships among the branches of government; levels of government; and government, markets, and the nonprofit sectors. Typically, mayoral control consists of giving mayors power to appoint some or all of the school board members who were previously elected, but in its more extreme versions, it involves broadly incorporating separate school districts into general purpose municipal government.

Contemporary reformers began to focus on mayoral control during the 1990s as a way to bypass the iron triangle of school boards, school bureaucracies, and teachers' unions that they argued were buttressing a dysfunctional status quo. During the 1990s, four major cities opted for mayoral control instead of separately elected school boards: Boston (1992), Chicago (1995), Cleveland (1998), and Detroit (1999). Momentum built slowly but accelerated after the turn of the century, with Harrisburg, Pennsylvania; Oakland, California; Providence, Rhode Island; Philadelphia, Pennsylvania; Washington, D.C.; and, most prominently, New York City, among those that have recently moved to mayoral control to at least some degree.

Prior to the 2001 election of Michael Bloomberg, the New York City school system was known for both its massive bureaucracy and its controversial experimentation with decentralized community control. The former was meticulously described in by David Rogers in his widely read 1968 book *110 Livingston Street*, named for the address and popularly used nickname of the micro-managing central offices. The latter was launched by the New York City school board in 1967 in response to protests from minority communities that the system was insufficiently responsive to their children's needs. The board sought to forge a "limited partnership" with the community, granting locally elected school boards relatively cautious guidelines for teacher recruitment and revisions in school curriculum. However, in the Ocean Hill-Brownsville section of Brooklyn, the majority-black local school board claimed sweeping authority and proceeded to fire nineteen white Ocean Hill-Brownsville teachers. The resulting tensions sparked three teachers' strikes, becoming one of New York City's most racially divisive moments and making elite observers in other major cities much more skittish about decentralization proposals circulating in their communities.

The experiment was terminated in 1969, and the state legislature put in place a more attenuated version of decentralization in which thirty-two Community School Districts (CSDs) administered elementary and junior high schools and managed the district budgets of tens of millions of dollars. Some CSDs, especially those in the more affluent areas of the city, were able to mobilize and use decentralization as an avenue for educational innovation, but many had reputations for malfeasance and patronage. Dismissing earlier rounds of reform that addressed these problems, Bloomberg broadly labeled the system a gross failure and convinced the state legislature to put in place a new governance arrangement, with him controlling the key levers.

Over a similar time span, power over education policy has been moving up the ladder of federalism, with states and the national government playing increasingly prominent roles. The growing state role was led in part by governors who came to see public education as a critical component in their economic development strategies. It was given additional momentum by state court decisions regarding school finance that expanded reliance on state sources rather than local property tax revenues. The 1989 Charlottesville Summit, called by President George H. W. Bush and attended by the nation's governors, acknowledged the expanding role of the state in education and was an early sign of growing nationalization of education politics. It helped set the stage for the No Child Left Behind Act and President Obama's Race to the Top Fund, two dramatic expansions of national government intervention into what has been historically regarded as a reserved power for states and localities.

While mayors, governors, and presidents increased their roles, the private sector in education expanded by leaps and bounds. School-choice proposals designed to make education providers more responsive to families qua consumers have been the most visible face of the privatization phenomenon, but, as detailed in Patricia Burch's *Hidden Markets: The New Education Privatization* (2009), the past two decades have also seen a substantial expansion of for-profit and nonprofit providers of direct school management, teacher and principal training, supplemental services, test preparation, test publication, and test analysis.

*   *   *

The proliferation of players not directly accountable to residents challenges conventional forms of organizing for community engagement. Traditional grassroots organizing strategies emerged during a period of localism, when school boards and superintendents called the shots, and parents were organized within spatially defined school attendance zones, in which the demarcation between the public and private sectors were much more sharply defined. In New York, the rapid recentralization that accompanied mayoral control drastically diminished places for parent and community collective action. Parents and groups representing them had to reorganize to meet the challenges of the new environment, and identify new mechanisms through which to exercise parental voice.

The battle around mayoral control in New York City provides a window into what this change might mean for a vision of strong democracy in the education sphere. Parent and community groups want political voice and policy influence in education. Now, though, educational advocates must compete in general purpose, multi-issue arenas where the levers of power are more distant; where blurring boundaries between public and private make the rules of the game less transparent; and where traditional constituency-based politics competes with national networks comprising foundations, private investors, and social venture capitalists.

*   *   *

In 2002, at the urging of newly elected mayor, Michael Bloomberg, the New York State Legislature dramatically altered New York City school governance, shifting from a decentralized system to mayoral control, with the idea of creating a system with clear lines of accountability. The legislature set a five-year sunset date for the law, in June 2009. This ensured an opportunity to evaluate whether the new governance system should be continued, amended, or ended.

Bloomberg and Klein defined parent engagement in narrow terms. In place of *involvement* in setting goals and priorities, the Bloomberg-Klein approach focused on *implementation* of their policies. In place of community voice, their approach put a strong emphasis on individual exit—giving families the option to go elsewhere if they were unhappy with their assigned school. Democratic participation in setting policy was relegated to the four-year mayoral election cycle, channeled into an arena where other issues compete for priority and where most groups do not have a direct stake in public education.

By early 2008, as the sunset date approached, Bloomberg had a strong wind at his back. He and Chancellor Joel Klein were boasting of test score improvements and had the broad approval of the business community as well as mainstream media for their education policies. Bloomberg had extensive resources at his disposal, including a powerful public relations machine in the Department of Education and billions of dollars of his own money. Many nonprofits that might have voiced dissent were receiving funding either from the city or from Bloomberg personally, leading some journalists to observe that most of those that might constitute a critical voice were in Bloomberg's pocket. And as of 2008, Bloomberg had a fresh ally in the Obama administration. Newly appointed education secretary Arne Duncan unabashedly supported Bloomberg and his brand of mayoral control. The Obama administration's support presented mayoral control as a cause that had high level bipartisan support.

*   *   *

Despite Bloomberg's immense power, the changes brought substantial push-back: grassroots groups did not accept the parameters Bloomberg-Klein had set for parent participation. By fall 2008, two groups emerged that gained attention in calling for greater public voice in education matters. Both represented a broader and more diverse opposition to mayoral control than the administration was willing to acknowledge. The Parent Commission, an all-volunteer group of parent leaders and activists, called for an end to mayoral control and reinvigorated decision-making bodies at both the school and the community level.

The other group, the Campaign for Better Schools (the Campaign), was a diverse coalition of twenty-six groups that took the stance that mayoral control could be improved substantially through real checks and balances, greater transparency, and authentic public participation. A subset of groups that had received past support from the Donors' Education Collaborative (DEC), a group of New York City funders that had worked together for more than a dozen years to promote broad public engagement in education reform, initially got a planning grant, and later funding for implementation from DEC. In order to understand whether its support for the coalition had made any difference in the mayoral control debate and legislation, DEC funded the authors to follow the activity of the Campaign from May 2008 to May 2010.

The Campaign did not win all the changes to the law that it proposed, but it did win some legislative provisions that created levers for public engagement in education decision making. These wins show that even in this new political grid, there is room to maneuver. Specifically, four of the Campaign's defining characteristics were crucial to winning some checks on the authority of the mayor: its structure as a loose coalition of diverse groups, its ability to balance the tensions between political pragmatism and grassroots constituency building, its combination of experience at both the local and state levels, and its focus on the creation of institutionalized levers for collective action.

*　　*　　*

The sunset of the mayoral control law offered a window of opportunity for groups that wanted to expand public participation in school governance. To succeed, however, they needed an organization that could mobilize parents across the city and have credibility in the state capital of Albany, where, ultimately, the decision about the parameters of mayoral control would be made.

DEC funding provided modest support for a set of core groups to play a facilitator role; as the Campaign expanded, it drew in a broader set of well-established, mostly multi-issue organizations. Some had wide reach across the city, while others were embedded in local communities. The diversity of the Campaign membership had advantages for mobilization and gaining clout. First, because it represented a range of constituencies across the city, the Campaign could not be pegged as a narrow interest group. It included immigrants, English-language learners, youth, and low-income African Americans and Latinos as well as middle-class activists. The Campaign was also diverse in the types of groups that were members. In addition to constituency-based groups, the Campaign included public school advocacy groups, policy and research organizations, and a statewide education advocacy group with considerable experience working in Albany. The combination of citywide issue advocacy, localized and constituency-based grassroots organizing, and knowledge of state politics proved invaluable. The issue-advocacy groups brought important connections and broad policy perspective. The constituency-based groups were able to tap into their bases to turn out large numbers at rallies, hearings, and events, demonstrating the extent and depth of dissatisfaction with mayoral control. Finally, the groups with experience in city and state level politics brought the skill necessary to operate in a complex and shifting political environment.

*   *   *

While diversity among groups in the Campaign's coalition was a significant asset, differences in the groups' experiences, structures, and approaches to mobilization also brought tensions. The coalition members had to reconcile competing priorities and instincts. Some, accustomed to ongoing battles to shape policy, anticipated the need to compromise and were prepared to adjust demands to fit the parameters of what was winnable. Grassroots organizations, expressing the passion of their members, were more willing to take a strong stand and go down fighting.

Gauging that elite preferences supported mayoral control and that broad public sentiment was wary about going back to the pre-Bloomberg arrangements, the group concluded early on that it would not be taken seriously if it came out against mayoral control. By taking a "mayoral control with changes" stance, the Campaign gained a reputation as a reasonable critic of the mayor. Getting everyone on the same wavelength and willing to agree on a particular position and platform details, however, entailed many months of give-and-take among the coalition groups. Drawing on the experience of their members—parents, students, and community residents who were frustrated with the quality of the schools and their lack of voice—the constituency-based groups saw the platform as an opportunity to make a principled argument. For example, they wanted the platform to be explicit about which groups should be represented in decision making at different levels. On the other side, those who believed losing battles would hurt their long-term credibility with elected officials recommended platform wording that would carry the spirit if not all the details of the principles the constituency-based groups believed in so passionately.

With these tensions, decision making was not a simple matter of coming to consensus among the group representatives in the room. The constituency-based groups were committed to taking every platform decision back to their own members before they could agree to proposed platform provisions. Although this back and forth slowed down the platform process, it had the advantage of building a strong base among the coalition's constituents, who gained sophistication with the issues surrounding mayoral control, became sensitive to the nuances of state politics and lawmaking, and were able to deliver a consistent message.

The painstaking process of arriving at a platform had several benefits in the end. It assured informed, strong showings at Campaign rallies, city and state hearings, and press events, which brought the Campaign visibility and recognition as a credible parent and community voice. The platform also provided the team wrangling with Albany legislators a clear set of priorities. Ultimately, the platform resonated with the Campaign's base and provided some cover for legislators who saw a need to rein in some of the mayor's powers.

*   *   *

Campaign members experienced the frustrations of concentrated power brought by mayoral control locally, but, in the new political grid, the solution to the problem meant gaining modifications to the law at the state level, giving the Campaign a dual task. Not only did the Campaign have to get traction for greater public voice in the conversation about school governance in New York City, it also needed access to and influence with the state and local elected officials who would hash out the new provisions of the law. The Alliance for Quality Education leadership, with its in-depth knowledge of the state legislature, along with several Campaign groups with previous experience working together in Albany, were important in this arena. Knowledge of both local and state political arenas allowed the Campaign to be at the table in the final negotiations and illustrates how critical it is for a group operating in the new political grid to be able to work at different levels of government for mobilization around school reform issues.

Political savvy and flexibility are particularly important because the political terrain can shift, and what can be won constantly has to be reassessed. Two events in the Campaign's experience were particularly important during the last stage. When New York City teachers' union president Randi Weingarten and New York State house speaker Sheldon Silver came out in favor of mayoral control without changes to Bloomberg's authority, a little more than a month before the sunset date, the Campaign's Albany-based leaders concluded there would have to be substantial compromise if they were to win anything. But in mid-June, just weeks from the end-of-month deadline for renewing the law, there was a surprise challenge to the Democratic leadership of the Senate; the Senate effectively closed down for two weeks and postponed the vote on the mayoral control legislation. The Campaign used the time to regroup and reevaluate possibilities. Without state-level access and experience, the Campaign would not have been as successful in gaining some last-minute, but key provisions in the law, which have proved critical for opening up the possibility for public voice and public action.

*   *   *

The relentless efforts of the Campaign, the Parent Commission, and others created a wedge, with sympathetic legislators receptive to changes that would give parents a greater opportunity to have input to priority setting and policy making. On the law's most visible terms, the mayor was able to resist alteration to his authority. But concessions won by groups that championed stronger forms of community engagement, which appeared in summer 2009 to be largely symbolic victories, turned out to have more substantial impact. Probably the most important win was the requirement that school closures require an education impact statement, a public hearing, and six months' notice.

School closings are a particularly sore spot for parents and represent a significant chasm between the school district administration and many public school constituents. Many parents believe that schools are low performing because the district has allowed them to fail. Rather than closing schools and forcing their children to go elsewhere, perhaps out of their neighborhood and farther from home, these parents want the district to invest in their schools, providing the resources and quality teachers that would make them successful. The provisions for impact statements and public hearings seem to have set the stage for massive protest and for ongoing legal challenges to the administration's closure and turnaround policies. By negotiating for advance public notice and an education impact statement, the Campaign created levers for collective action that are codified in the law. These provisions created room for public challenge and may develop into a vision of and organizational foundation for an alternative view of public education reform.

*   *   *

The shifts toward centralization of education policy don't necessarily mean a lack of possibilities for expanded democratic engagement. The old structure of localized and often bureaucratized school governance reinforced funding disparities based on inequities in property wealth and was often parochial, pinched in its aspirations, elite-dominated, and unable to leverage complementary changes in non-school agencies with the potential to promote better learning outcomes. States and the national government are in a better position to redistribute funding to better target needs, but such redistribution cannot be taken for granted. The infusion of new participants in education debates and provision has added energy, ideas, and both human and investment capital.

The intensity of the battle over mayoral control in New York City is a reminder, though, that many parent and community groups want to influence policies, not simply play a supportive role in their implementation. The baseline power to "vote the rascals out" every four years does not suffice, and that's the case whether the rascals are old-style school boards, new-style mayors, so-called education governors, or an education-oriented president. With the policy levers to change education lifted from the hands of traditional, localized education decision makers, parents who bang on the schoolhouse door have little influence. Education advocates have no choice but to seek new coalitional partners if they want to have a serious place at the table in a more complicated environment; forging alliances with progressive organizations operating outside the education arena is a strategy that may be as much an opportunity for greater reach as a necessity to maximize impact in an increasingly complex political landscape.

New York City's Campaign for Better Schools shows that it is possible to make an impact on education decision making and provides some hints of what a model for more effective engagement might entail. First, it created a loose-jointed, flexible coalition of diverse groups capable of joining forces as opportunity afforded action around a shared interest in public engagement. Second, through hard work the Campaign managed to find a balance between principles and pragmatic compromise, which positioned it as a reasonable and savvy group reinforced by the clout of constituency-based groups representing members from across the city. Third, it incorporated groups with experience and established access at both the local and state level, so it was able to play in multiple venues. And finally, it aimed to create change through institutionalized levers for collective action, which gave it teeth and contributed to sustainability.

That does not mean the authors are sanguine about the prospects overall. The challenges presented by the new political grid are real, and the Campaign's model is not a sure-fire solution. The Campaign lost on most of the big-ticket items on its wish list. Groups like the Parent Commission are critical of the Campaign's brand of tactical pragmatism, believing that a stronger, sharper challenge to mayoral control was both the right thing to do and could have leveraged more substantial reforms, at least in the long run. And the unique conditions that gave rise to and supported the Campaign suggest that this type of coalition may not be replicable or sustainable, particularly without the kind of philanthropic community that exists in New York City, which was ready to allocate funding to support such efforts.

*   *   *

But community and grassroots organizing is not obsolete. Much of the passion and animating drive in the mayoral control battle came from the constituency-based organizations. The challenge is to maintain those elements while scaffolding them onto loosely linked, ad hoc, contingent and yet reliable frameworks of collaboration across issues and across decision making venues. The contemporary reform movement's shift toward a more top-down corporate style of governance and the accompanying narrowed focus on test scores makes attention to the relationship between schools and democracy seem fusty and out-of-date. But education is too important to leave to technocrats; we cannot have public schools without a real public voice.

PART IV

Conclusions

Chapter 22

What Is Education Reform?

Michael B. Katz and Mike Rose

No reform movement in any domain—the law, agricultural development, education—can do everything, and it is an unreasonable demand that it try. Reform movements need to be selective, and need to be clear and focused. In some ways the current mainstream education reforms are just that: standardized test scores are used as a measure of achievement; a teacher's effectiveness is determined by improvement in those scores; funds are awarded by competition, and so on. Yet, although it is unreasonable to demand everything, it is legitimate to scrutinize what is left out—for something left out might be crucial to the success of what is left in—and it is legitimate to question whether the reforms themselves contain within them elements that could unintentionally subvert the very goals of reform.

One of the concerns raised in this book is that there does not seem to be an elaborated philosophy of education or theory of learning underlying the current reform movement. There is an implied philosophy, and it is a basic economic/human capital one: education is necessary for individual economic advantage and for national economic stability. This focus is troubling, as we have seen, for it distorts and narrows the purpose and meaning of education in a democracy. The theory of learning embedded in an accountability system based on standardized testing is a simplified behaviorist one. Learning is pretty much the acquisition of discrete bits of information measured quantitatively by a standardized test. Teaching is likewise reduced to a knowledge delivery system based on the mastery of a set of teaching techniques.

This characterization of the reformers' theories of learning and teaching might not be true to their beliefs, but it's hard to know what they believe since learning and teaching are rarely discussed in more robust terms. What they advocate suggests the behaviorist theory sketched above—a theory long since discredited in fields from anthropology to cognitive science.

Perhaps the greatest strength of the current reform movement is its focus on inequality, on the poor performance of low-income and minority students. This is definitely a point of agreement for people along the ideological spectrum. Because reformers want to keep focus with "no excuses" on the unacceptable performance of poor children, they insist on addressing outcomes (in the form of test scores) rather than on inequality of resources and social conditions. This is an understandable strategy, but its narrow focus has a potent liability. Poverty itself tends to be pushed out of the picture.

Poverty is mentioned, but in a variety of ways it is downplayed. So all the damage poverty does to communities and to households, to schools and to other local institutions is rarely addressed. And it's hard to find discussion of the economic, political, and social history of poverty, leading to an oddly antiseptic and ahistorical treatment of community, schools, and achievement. Low achievement then, by default, has to be attributed to teachers and administrators, whose work seems pretty straightforward, given the aforementioned theory of learning that underlies reform. If kids aren't learning, it's because teachers de facto lack the techniques or motivation to deliver information to them.

Although the reformers rightly focus on low-performing children, there is not much treatment of subpopulations within the overall group of low-performers. There is little mention of special needs children, English-language learners, immigrant students, migrant students, or undocumented students. In some schools, these subpopulations form a significant percentage of the student body. This thin treatment in part results from a lack of a rich theory of learning that takes account of social and cultural context and from a reluctance to address a school's local history and sociology.

Finally, current reformers display no knowledge of—or apparent interest in—the history of school reform, or, for that matter, the history of education in the United States. As well, they show little interest in local reforms, the grassroots efforts of parents and other actors to improve their schools. The result is an ahistorical hubris that, at the least, prevents one from learning from past mistakes and, worse, alienates (and sometimes quashes) local groups who also have an interest in gaining a better education for their children.

Without a rich conceptualization of teaching and learning, without an understanding of the origins and maintenance of inequality, without an appreciation of cultural and linguistic diversity, and without a knowledge of history, school reform limits itself to technology and management systems—necessary but hardly sufficient to achieve its grand aims, and certainly insufficient to address the educational inequality that is at the center of its efforts.

If the current school reform movement comes up short on a theory of teaching and learning, an appreciation of context, and a strategy for addressing inequalities, then who are the real reformers and what, exactly, is education reform? Everyone claims the mantle of reformer. No one wants to be tarred with the defense of the status quo. As the authors in this book show, a rough consensus which crosses political lines blames poor teaching, ineffective teacher preparation programs, teachers' unions, the lack of accountability for results, and monopolistic public systems for the failures of student achievement measured, primarily, by test scores. In mainstream reform discourse, teachers and their unions emerge as the major villains, the primary stumbling blocks to assuring every child an adequate education. Powerful foundations, the national government, and the media—as in the film *Waiting for Superman*—reinforce and disseminate these views. The reform agenda includes two primary components: first, hold teachers accountable for student achievement, primarily through tests that track individual student growth; and second, break up public monopolies by introducing choice, mainly in the form of charter schools, and dismantle anti-competitive practices such as teacher tenure and seniority, all of which undermine the power of teachers' unions. The corrosive impact of the reform agenda on teacher morale came to a head in fall 2012 in the Chicago teacher strike. Whether Chicago was a harbinger remains to be seen, but the strike tapped deeply felt teacher anger and demoralization throughout the country.

Anyone who challenges the core elements of the mainstream consensus risks branding as a self-interested or naïve guardian of the existing state of affairs. But the matter is not so simple, as the authors in this volume point out. Along with mainstream reformers, dissenters from the dominant template for reform share a belief that all children are capable of learning and a strong dissatisfaction with the way things stand in education. They worry, however, about the directions in which mainstream reform wants to push public education. They show that most of the testing regimes advocated by mainstream reformers are unreliable. They point out that tests, by themselves, do not measure teacher quality. They value teaching experience far more than mainstream reformers, and they summon examples of good teaching and exciting classrooms where students learn unencumbered by worries over high stakes tests. They believe, too, in the limits of markets as models for educational policy and practice and believe that market models will result in new forms of educational inequality. Although they agree that the poverty of students should not provide an excuse for poor educational outcomes, they consider it disingenuous and misleading to evaluate teachers without taking into account the obstacles they face and the factors that inhibit the performance of their students, and they particularly object to the exclusion of reforms such as job creation, housing, and health care from the mainstream reform agenda.

The fact of the matter is that the "problem" of American education is to a large extent a problem of poverty. By international standards, American students who attend schools where only a small percentage of students come from families with incomes below the poverty line measure up well against the best in the world. As Joanne Barkan and Pedro Noguera point out in their chapters, the Program for International Student Achievement (PISA) found that in schools with fewer than ten percent of students from poor families the American students' tests scores ranked them high on international comparisons, more or less matching the Nordic countries often held up as examples of high achievement. This comparison is relevant because in these countries overall child poverty generally is below ten percent in contrast to about twenty-one percent in the United States.

Most of all, perhaps, critics of mainstream education reform, like the authors in this book, object to "reform" imposed from the top down by foundation-funded projects or federal government mandates that take no account of the situation on the ground. They know that the history of education shows there are no silver bullets, that real educational reform is rooted in local contexts and built from the bottom up, or from collaboration between the troops on the ground and outside "reformers." That is why critics of mainstream education reform remain uneasy about the imposition of a reform agenda resting on wealth and power.

The current moment in educational reform raises profound questions about who controls public education. There is, on one hand, tension between the federal agenda and localities. Although the federal government cannot impose educational changes on states, the possibility of federal funding is a powerful incentive to bring practice in line with the federal agenda. The escalation of the federal role in education has upended the historic pattern of community control in education. The active involvement of foundations with immense wealth further tilts the control of the reform agenda away from local communities; mayoral control which marginalizes the role of elected school boards and community members serves the same purpose. As never before in American history, the locus of authority and power in public education has shifted upward, away from its historic grounding in states and localities.

But just what is public education in the twenty-first century? Do the spread of charter schools and proposals for vouchers threaten the existence of public education? Certainly, in some instances they are the Trojan horses of privatization. But for many educators, as Paul Skilton-Sylvester writes about in this book, charter schools represent the chance to realize an alternative vision of education. Neither mainstream reformers nor their critics have grappled with the plastic definition of public. A complex term, public has meant different things over the course of American history and, indeed, has multiple referents in our own time. (For instance, a parade takes place in public; Wikileaks made government secrets public; my children go to public schools.) In Colonial times, with reference to education, public meant education conducted outside the home; in the late eighteenth and early nineteenth centuries it referred to education broadly accessible to children from poor families even though the schools were owned and operated by voluntary associations; in these years public education was equated with pauper education. Breaking the equation between public and pauper constituted one of the most difficult tasks faced by antebellum education reformers like Horace Mann and Henry Barnard—and perhaps their greatest achievement. As a result of their success, in the middle of the nineteenth century, public, as in public schools, acquired its contemporary meaning which unites ownership and control. Public schools became schools owned and administered by local governments. There were reasons why this definition emerged in the mid-nineteenth century. Do the same reasons remain in place today? Do we need to think about a new definition of public appropriate for the twenty-first century? Do we have trouble moving forward with reform partly because we are locked into nineteenth-century definitions? Today, in big cities, as affluent parents either leave for the suburbs or choose private schools, public once again is becoming a synonym for pauper. Can this trend be reversed?

Mainstream reform echoes one of the oldest tropes in discourse about public education. In this view, articulated by reformers from Horace Mann to Barack Obama, education reform constitutes the most effective war on poverty, accelerator of social mobility, and direct route to greater equality. It is the nation's primary engine of human capital development and national prosperity. (More than contemporary reformers, Mann stressed the civic purposes of education, too.) Since the origins of public school systems in the days of Mann, public school promoters have turned to education to soften the rough edges of capitalism, improve race relations, boost economic growth, and promote social harmony. In the years when European nations introduced social protections, such as unemployment, health, and old age insurance, Americans built high schools; they defined equality as opportunity, while in Europe nations focused more on condition. The problem was that in America school promoters oversold education. By themselves, schools proved unable to abolish poverty and racism, reduce crime, assure economic growth, or reach any of the myriad other goals dumped on them. Schools proved convenient, safe repositories for laudable goals whose realization, in fact, required hard political choices and, often, the redistribution of power and wealth. Schools were, and remain, necessary to reach these goals, but, as education promoters too often forget, they are not sufficient.

The situation is even worse, as these chapters show. Schools reflect and perpetuate key inequalities. The distribution of resources for education and the quality of schools for the most part follow the distribution of population into municipalities stratified by wealth. Accidents of geography remain powerful determinants of school quality and undermine the common school ideal at the core of American public education by effectively segregating by income and race. Within larger, more heterogeneous districts, various forms of testing and tracking have served the same purpose. Today, schools are re-segregating by race, while in old cities gentrification results in new patterns of inequality and post-secondary education floats increasingly beyond the reach of low-income students.

The point is this: mainstream education reform elides the paradox of inequality in public education—the expectation that public education will lessen key inequalities in American life when, as it was institutionalized, public education was the product of those inequalities, which it still reflects and reinforces. The authors of these chapters, it is fair to say, call for recognizing the sources and forms of educational inequalities and attacking them directly, both inside and outside schools.

Mainstream education reform replicates a pattern common elsewhere in America's welfare state. "Reformers" identify a problem, for instance, the rising cost of workers' compensation, and trace its origin to individuals—malingering workers trying to avoid work. In education, this individualization of the problem leads straight to blaming teachers for educational failure. Individualizing problems proves a useful strategy because it defines a reform agenda that ignores existing distributions of power and resources and, in the case of education, avoids dealing with systemic inequalities. Blaming teachers extends quite easily to blaming their unions that are seen to aggregate inadequate, self-protective teachers into powerful self-protective unions that block fundamental change and, not incidentally, jack up the cost of public education. This attack on teachers' unions forms one strand in the larger politically right-wing assault on the public sector, its employees, and its unions. Together, these are misrepresented as a bloated, inefficient, costly monopoly blocking more effective and economical delivery of services by private contractors.

Attacks on the public sector, including education, rest on a particular narrative of recent American history. The story goes something like this. In the 1960s, well-meaning but misguided liberals mobilized massive amounts of federal funds for new social programs aimed at eliminating poverty, fixing cities, restoring the environment, extending income support for the nonworking poor, and injecting resources into schools that served poor children—to name the most obvious. Unfortunately, none of these programs worked as intended. Welfare use expanded; poverty refused to disappear; urban renewal replaced existing housing with high-rise public housing that quickly turned into violent and dangerous slums; urban decay intensified; instead of improving, the educational achievement of students declined. Public education became a stultifying bureaucracy with students and parents held hostage to teachers' unions focused on their own economic security and advancement rather than on the education of their students. The implication is obvious: replace the public sector with private enterprise; substitute markets for bureaucracy; stop throwing hard-earned dollars at counterproductive social programs. Government, to cite President Ronald Reagan, is the problem, not the solution.

It is remarkable how widely this narrative of public failure is shared.

Opinion polls show low public levels of trust in government, even among citizens supported in whole or in part by Social Security and provided with health care by Medicare; who drive on interstate highways largely funded with federal dollars; rely on an Internet developed in the Department of Defense; breathe air significantly cleaner than thirty or forty years ago; depend on federal authorities to certify the safety of the airplanes they fly and the food they eat; and, whatever their criticisms, for the most part still send their children to public schools. This is why mainstream reform straddles conventional political divides. To be sure, motivations differ—some "reformers" want to dismantle public education; others are more focused on the education and well-being of children ill-served by the current system. But a shared story helps keep them focused on a similar agenda.

A progressive twenty-first-century politics demands a new narrative of recent American history, including the history of education. The authors of these chapters provide some of the elements for a different story. Without denying the dismal state of many urban schools, the stultifying influence of bureaucracy, and the inadequate preparation of a number of teachers, they offer a more nuanced account rooted in economic, geographic, and racial inequality. They highlight the vulnerability of teachers that underlies the formation of teachers' unions and the factors which make teaching a unique and difficult occupation. They give examples of excellent schools and successful teachers. And they use a metric that rests on a philosophy of education that embraces the civic, democratic purposes of education as well as the economic. This new narrative is not complete yet, or wholly coherent. It is a work in progress, but one that will find much material in this book.

A new narrative need not be entirely positive; it need not cast a false glow over the past or rehash outworn myths. There was no golden age of public schooling to which we can or should want to return. That said, the focus of a new narrative's dark side will differ from that of the mainstream. At the same time, it will include more hopeful, positive elements, and it will suggest alternative directions for reform.

Inequality is the spine of the new narrative—in two senses. Throughout American history, inequality—refracted most notably through poverty and race—has impinged on the ability of children to learn and of teachers to do their jobs. More to the point, as the chapters of this book, as well as an extensive body of literature, make clear, the history of education is studded with "reforms" that ended up increasing inequality. Think, for instance, of testing, tracking, vocational guidance, or school improvement aimed at promoting gentrification. None of these were introduced with the blunt intent of increasing inequality, but that was one result. Here is a suggestion that flows from this history: educational policy makers should consider a process analogous to the one involving environmental impact statements. Just as a project affecting the natural and built environment must undergo review, a proposed educational reform would be subject to a review to assess its possible positive or negative consequences for educational inequality.

The new narrative should also trace the changing balance between civic and economic purposes in public education. Early school promoters, like Horace Mann, held the two in balance, giving preference, arguably, to the civic broadly defined. The chapters in this book make clear that today the civic role of education—notably its role in promoting an informed citizenry and the practice of democracy—has virtually dropped out of the conversation about educational reform. That is not to deny that many teachers successfully incorporate the practice of democracy into their teaching. Thus, another suggestion: require proposed reforms/changes to serve civic as well as economic goals. To facilitate this reorientation of practice, the federal government could build a multi-media database of exemplary teachers in action. Both philosophers of education and effective civic-minded teachers could be key members of teams designing and proposing education reforms. In the current market-driven climate, these suggestions may well seem fanciful. But they serve to highlight the task: restoring civic purpose to public education. It is commonplace to complain of apathy and ignorance among potential voters. Why not do something about it? Why not help children realize that there is more to the good life than market success?

The new narrative must remind readers why teachers' unions came into existence. It needs to bring out the terrible pay, insecurity, and gender inequity that marked teaching as an occupation in the long era prior to unionization. It needs to remind readers of the abuse and lack of academic freedom to which teachers were subjected, and not just in the McCarthy era. The narrative needs to underline how unionization emerged as a key component of a professionalization project designed in part to attract and retain talented individuals. It has to ask, as do chapters in this book, why teachers and their unions became targets of attack, the villains preventing educational progress. In the end, the narrative needs to provide the elements for a fair assessment of the unions' strengths and weaknesses and suggestions for how to break the current impasse between union supporters and critics.

What is hugely important to include in the new narrative is that there is variability in the nature and goals of local union chapters and even wider variability among union members on all the issues currently on the reform agenda—from evaluation to seniority—and this has been the case for some time. Claire Robertson-Kraft's proposal for a professional union model provides one way to move through the current union battles, and in a number of chapters across the country there are internal debates and political maneuvers in play that hold the potential to redefine teacher unionism. The unions are simply not a monolithic and negative force on the reform landscape, though some reformers' intention of dismantling the unions forces a strong protective response from union leadership. Again, we have an example of the way a reform strategy sabotages positive change in American education.

Central to the new narrative will be the story of accountability measured largely by high stakes tests, and how and why this version of accountability came to constitute the core of mainstream education reform. The narrative will also provide ways to think about accountability that are truer to teaching and learning, that are based on the best of current thinking in education, cognitive science, sociology, and philosophy. This new system could well include a statistical measure, but one that is used in a way that fits its psychometric design and purpose. The system would draw on multiple measures from expert observation and peer review to student and parental evaluations. A number of reformers are advocating multiple measures, though problematic statistical measures tend to dominate in their model. It is important to note that more comprehensive models of assessment have been around for some time and some teachers' unions are advocating them.

The new narrative also must be about power. It needs to trace the shifting sources and balance of power in public education over time, differentiating among rural, suburban, and city settings. Topics will include the supersession of parental and community control by professionals in the late nineteenth and early twentieth centuries; the massive increase in federal involvement with desegregation, the War on Poverty and Great Society, and No Child Left Behind; the recent assertion of power by national foundations; and the new mayoral control of public schools in some cities. Balanced against this account should be a counter-story of attempts to shift the balance of power back to parents and communities through decentralization and community organizing around schools. One example is the story of New York told here by Eva Gold, Jeffrey Henig, and Elaine Simon; another is provided by Rema Reynolds and Tyrone Howard in their chapter on partnerships between educators and parents. The narrative will show the imbalance between the power of authorities and the power of parents and communities and how that has worked against the interests of children and teachers. One suggestion that flows from this history (supported by the early years of the Chicago School Reform which started in 1989) is to place a community organizer in each school with the goal of mobilizing parent participation and support and exercising a type of accountability other than testing. (Unfortunately, local foundations only supported hiring community organizers for schools for a few years.)

The career of "public" in the idea of public education, sketched earlier in this chapter, has to frame any narrative of public education over time. The reversion of "public" to its early nineteenth-century equation with "pauper" requires emphasis both to define the situation confronting education reform and to put the question of how to break the equation high on an alternative education reform agenda. The problem is difficult because the denigration of "public" applies far more widely than to public schools. "Public" has lost whatever luster it once had; it connotes inadequate outcomes, inefficiency, and dominance by an impoverished clientele. The denigration of "public" forms an important strand in the popular denigration of government. Like other "public" institutions, public education has lost much of its legitimacy. Thus a new narrative should highlight the positive and essential role of government, and its achievements as well as failures. Without a reorientation of thinking about government, however, it will be difficult to restore legitimacy to public schools.

But there is more to the issue. The new narrative will offer no support to champions of public education who want to deny the shifting, contextual meaning of public by reifying a historically contingent definition into a fixed, inviolable template. The implication of public's historicity is, perhaps, the most sensitive and difficult issue to arise from the new narrative. What definition of public in education is appropriate for this moment in the twenty-first century? Reformers in policy areas outside education are asking the same question. In his 2009 book, *The Housing Policy Revolution*, David J. Erickson, for one, describes the changed meaning of public housing and its provision by loose networks of governments, banks, community development agencies, and others not usefully described by conventional definitions of public and private. Where does a similar analysis in education lead? Is there a definition for our times that fosters learning and innovative teaching while avoiding capture by market templates and the structures of inequality which have reshaped the good intentions of so many education reformers?

The new narrative needs also to be a story of hope and possibility. To be sure, the No Child Left Behind Act and Obama's Race to the Top Fund affirm the right of all children to a quality education and affirm their ability to achieve academically. These are powerful egalitarian principles. As the authors in this book point out, however, the principles might be compromised by an accountability mechanism that results in a narrowing of curriculum. Furthermore, the exclusively economic focus of educational policy—which predates current reform—combined with the technological-managerial nature of current reform leads to a high-energy but strangely bloodless rhetoric of achievement.

In an earlier book, one of us asks the reader: When was the last time you were moved by a high-level policy or political speech about education? Probably not in a while. The way we talk about school matters. It affects the way we think about education, what we want from it, and how we define what it means to be an educated person. Educational discourse affects what gets taught and how it's taught. We hear so much about test scores and proficiency levels, but hardly anything about intellectual engagement, curiosity, creativity, or aesthetics—or about taking a chance, pursuing an idea, being reflective. There's pitifully little about ethical deliberation or thinking things through with others. For that fact, we don't hear much about public education as the core of a free society.

In the midst of all the heat of school reform, it would be good to step back and remind ourselves what we are ultimately trying to achieve. What is the end goal of school reform? We think most would agree that the goal is to create vital classrooms and schools, better than we have now in scope and equitable distribution.

Here are the basic questions that should be our touchstone for reform. What is the purpose of education in a democracy? What kind of person do we want to emerge from American schools? What is the experience of education when it is done well?

Let us bring these questions to life with a vignette from a first-grade classroom in inner-city Baltimore. There are thirty children in the class, all from modest to low-income households—the kind of children at the center of school reform.

As we enter the classroom, teacher Stephanie Terry is reading to her students from a book called *A House for Hermit Crab*. Hermit crabs inhabit empty mollusk shells, and as they grow, they leave old shells to find bigger ones; in this story, a cheery hermit crab is searching for a more spacious home. The class has a glass case with five hermit crabs, supplied by Stephanie. As Stephanie reads the book, she pauses and raises broader questions about where the creatures live, and this leads to an eager query from Kenneth about where in nature you'd find hermit crabs. "Well," says Stephanie, "let's see if we can figure that out."

She gets up and brings the case with the hermit crabs to the center of the room, takes them out, and places them on the rug. Then she takes two plastic tubs from the cupboard above the sink and fills one with cold water from the tap. "Watch the hermit crabs closely," she says, "while I go to the kitchen. Be ready to tell me what you see." She runs down the hall to get warm water from the women who prepare the children's lunches. Then she places the tubs side by side and asks five students, one by one, to put each of the crabs in the cold water. "What happens?" she asks. "They don't move," says Kenneth. "They stay inside," adds Miko.

Stephanie then asks five other students to transfer the crabs to the second tub. They do, and within seconds the crabs start to stir. Before long, the crabs are moving like crazy. "Okay," says Stephanie. "What happens in the water?" An excited chorus: "They're moving." "They're walking all over." "They like it." "They're happy like the crab in the book." "Well," Stephanie says, "What does this suggest about where they like to live?"

That night the students write about the experiment. Many are just learning to write, but Stephanie told them to write their observations as best as they could and she would help them develop what they write. The next day they take turns standing before the class and reading their reports.

Miko goes first: "I saw the hermit crab walking when it was in the warm water, but when it was in the cold water it was not walking. It likes to live in warm water." Then Romarise takes the floor, holding his paper way out in his right hand, his left hand in the pocket of his overalls: "One, I observed two legs in the back of the shell. Two, I observed that some of the crabs changes its shell. Three, when the hermit crabs went into the cold water, they walked slow. Four, when the hermit crabs went into the warm water, they walked faster." One by one, the rest of the students read their observations, halting at times as they try to figure out what they wrote, sometimes losing track and repeating themselves. But, in soft voice or loud, with a quiet sense of assurance or an unsteady eagerness, these young people read their reports on the behavior of hermit crabs.

There's a lot to say about Stephanie's modest but richly stocked classroom and the skillful way she interacts with the children in it. We want to focus on two things: what Stephanie demonstrates about the craft and art of teaching and the experience of learning that she generates for her class.

Everyone in the current reform environment acknowledges the importance of good teaching. But most characterizations of teaching miss the richness and complexity of the work. When you watch Stephanie you see that she is knowledgeable and resourceful across multiple subject areas—and is skillful at integrating them. She is spontaneous, alert for the teachable moment, and able to play out the fruits of that spontaneity, incrementally planning her next steps as the activity unfolds. She apparently believes that her students can handle a sophisticated assignment, and she asks questions and gives directions to guide them. It also seems that her students feel comfortable in taking up the intellectual challenge.

What is interesting is that none of the current high-profile reform ideas would explain or significantly enhance her expertise. It is not merit pay that inspires her inventiveness: it didn't exist in her district (though she would be happy to have the extra money, given that some of her classroom was furnished from her own pocket). And it is not a standardized test that motivates her. In fact, some of the intellectual display we witness would not be captured by the typical test. What motivates her is a complex mix of personal values and a drive for competence. These lead her to treat her students in certain ways and to continue to improve her skill. Several years before this event, she participated in a National Science Foundation workshop aimed at integrating science into the elementary school classroom.

As we think about this teacher we begin to wonder what would happen if the considerable financial and human resources spent on the vast machinery of high-stakes testing were channeled instead into a robust, widely distributed program of professional development. We don't mean the quick-hit, half-day events that so often pass for professional development, but serious, extended engagement of the kind offered by the National Science Foundation and the National Writing Project—the sort of program that helped Stephanie conjure her rich lesson with the hermit crabs.

These programs typically take place in the summer (the National Writing Project runs for four weeks), though there are other options, including ones that extend through part of the school year. Teachers work with subject matter experts; read, write, and think together; learn new material, hear from others who have successfully integrated it into their classrooms, and try it out themselves. Electronic media would be hugely helpful here, creating a variety of ways for teachers to participate, bringing in people from remote areas, and further enabling everyone to regularly check when trying new things. Such ongoing participation would be crucial in building on the intellectual community created during the program. All this already exists, but could be expanded significantly if policy makers had a different orientation to reform, one that embodied a richer understanding of teaching and the teaching profession.

Although pragmatic lifestyle issues certainly come into play in choosing any profession, the majority of people who enter teaching do so for fairly altruistic reasons. They like working with kids. They like science or literature or history, and want to spark that appreciation in others. They see inequality and want to make a difference in young people's lives. The kind of professional development we're describing would appeal to those motives, revitalize them, and further realize them as one's career progresses. Enriched, widely-available professional development would substitute a human development model of school reform for the current test-based technocratic one. And because such professional development would positively affect what teachers teach and how they teach it, there would be a more direct effect on student achievement.

The bottom-line question is whether a particular reform will enable or restrict the kind of thing happening in Stephanie's classroom. The hermit crab episode is, of course, drawn from a few days in one classroom, but it represents some qualities that you'll find in good schools, K-12, urban or rural, affluent or poor. We'll list these qualities, and as you read them, ask yourself to what degree the reforms currently being proposed—from value-added assessment to plans to turn around failing schools—would advance or impede their realization.

Good classrooms create a sense of safety. There is physical safety, which for some children in some environments is a real consideration. But there is also safety from insult and diminishment. And there is safety to take risks, to push beyond what you can comfortably do at present.

Intimately related to safety is respect. The word means many things, operates on many levels: fair treatment, decency, an absence of intimidation, and, beyond the realm of individual civility, a respect for history, the language and culture of the people represented in the classroom. Respect also has an intellectual dimension. As one New York principal put it in a conversation with one of us, "It's not just about being polite—even the curriculum has to convey respect. [It] has to be challenging enough that it's respectful."

Talking about safety and respect leads to a consideration of students' opportunities to partake in intellectual work, to think through, to make knowledge, to demonstrate ability. Even in classrooms that are run in a relatively traditional manner, students contribute to the flow of events, shape the direction of discussion, and become authorities on their own experience and on the work they are doing. Think of Stephanie's students observing closely, recording what they see, forming hypotheses, and reporting publically on their thinking.

The good classroom, then, is a place of expectation and responsibility. Teachers take students seriously as intellectual and social beings. Young people have to work hard, think things through, come to terms with each other—and there will be times when such effort takes a student to his or her limits. "They looked at us in disbelief," said another New York principal, "when we told them they were intellectuals." It is important to note that such assumptions are realized through a range of supports, guides, and structures: from the way teachers organize curriculum and invite and answer questions, to the means of assistance they and their aides provide (tutoring, conferences, written and oral feedback), to the various ways they encourage peer support and assistance, to the atmosphere they create in the room—which takes us back to considerations of safety and respect.

How directly do current reforms contribute to this assistance through reducing student-teacher ratio, or providing material or paraprofessional aid, or helping teachers experiment with ways to better organize their classrooms?

The foregoing characteristics combine to create vital public space. In an important postrevolutionary essay on education, eighteenth-century journalist Samuel Harrison Smith wrote that the free play of intelligence was central to a democracy, and that individual intellectual growth was intimately connected to broad-scale intellectual development, to the "general diffusion of knowledge" across the republic. As we consider what the reform initiatives might achieve, we should also ask the old, defining question: what is the purpose of education in a democracy? The formation of intellectually safe and respectful space, the distribution of authority and responsibility, the maintenance of high expectations, and the means to attain them—all this is fundamentally democratic and is preparation for civic life. Students are regarded as capable and participatory beings, rich in both individual and social potential. The realization of that vision of the student is what finally should drive school reform in the United States.

Chapter 23

A Letter to Young Teachers: The Graduation Speech You Won't Hear, But Should

Mike Rose

Let me begin by celebrating your calling to join one of our society's grand professions. What is more important than to play a central role in the development of young people's lives? Cherish this calling, for it will be tested.

You are entering teaching at a troubled time. For all the political talk about the importance of education, a number of cities and states are trying to balance their budgets through cuts to schools. You will also hear conflicting messages in the national conversation about education. Teachers are universally praised as the solution to our educational problems and simultaneously condemned as the root cause of all that's wrong with our schools.

What underlies this bipolar craziness is an ideological battle to define what teaching is. And if there's not much you can do to affect the economy, you can be tough-minded and vocal about what it means to teach.

As is the case in so many spheres of modern life, there is a strong push to define teaching in technical and managerial terms. Education policy is increasingly being shaped by economists who have little knowledge of classroom life. Curricula are "scripted," directing the teacher what to do when. Student learning is reduced to a few scores on a standardized test. The teacher becomes a knowledge-delivery mechanism whose effectiveness will be determined primarily by the scores on those tests.

You hear little from either the federal Department of Education or the local school board about engaging young people's minds or about teaching as an intellectual journey. You don't hear about the values that brought you into teaching. So let's talk about these things now, for they are the mind and heart of the work.

Teaching is a profoundly intellectual activity, and this applies to kindergarten as much as to Advanced Placement Physics. Most people will grant the brain work in physics, but it takes intellectual chops to teach any subject to any age. The good primary school teacher knows about child development and how to engage young people across a range of subjects. She takes in a room full of kids at a glance to see who needs help, she thinks on her feet, and she knows how to respond to a wrong answer, providing the apt example or comparison to guide a child toward clearer thinking.

You might not fancy yourself an intellectual. New teachers sometimes say that they're going into teaching because they "like kids." But remember, this is a special kind of caring, a relationship focused on children's cognitive, emotional, and social development. This is way more than affection; you are using your mind in the service of others.

Teaching, then, is a special kind of relationship. You'll need to learn about the young people in front of you, where they come from, and what matters to them. This will call for special effort if you—like many teachers—are a foreigner to the communities in which you teach. Listen to your students. Try to understand the world as they see it. You will be both troubled and inspired by what you hear. And you'll be smarter for it.

Don't expect things to be reciprocal. Kids will not always respond, will even shun you. But stick with it. Show them that you're serious and available even when they're not. This will register. Young people are hyper-alert to betrayal and consistency. A veteran teacher I know tells her beginning teachers, "Don't think that because a kid can't read, he can't read you."

Get ready to fail. A lesson you slaved over will flop, or your understanding of a child's problem will be way off base. This will happen during your first year or two, but, believe me, it happens to all of us through the years. Education, wrote W. E. B. Du Bois, is "a matter of infinite experiment and frequent mistakes."

For some of you, this will be the first time you've failed in a classroom. It will be painful and disorienting. So it is essential you know how to handle failure, for at those moments you will be vulnerable to your own insecurities and to those who are cynical about young people, some as close as the Teachers' Lounge.

It is imperative, then, that the minute you walk through the schoolhouse door, you start looking for the good teachers. Buy them coffee. Get to know them, for when you fail you'll need them to help you make sense of things, to convert those failures into knowledge rather than doubt and bitterness. The same holds for some of the parents you'll meet. Learning to teach well is a long journey, full of deliberation and self-assessment. You don't want to make that journey alone.

You've surely noticed by now that I haven't given you any advice about what to do on Monday morning. This takes us back to the issue of what teaching is. Knowing the nuts and bolts of running a classroom is hugely important, and if your training was any good, you'll have some plans in place. Furthermore, you soon will be swarmed with advertisements for products that promise to make your classroom hum.

I'm more interested in the way you *think* about what to do on Monday morning. Every good teacher I've known, regardless of grade level, subject, or style, has the equivalent of what musicians call "big ears"; they are curious, open, on the lookout for anything they can use in the service of some larger goal. They possess a mindfulness about materials and techniques and have their fingers on the pulse of their students, figuring out if and how something will work with them. That is what it means to think like a teacher, and that thinking defines the work you are about to begin.

CONTRIBUTORS

Joanne Barkan is a writer who lives in Manhattan and on Cape Cod. Her articles cover a wide array of topics, most recently the education reform movement in the United States. She is author of *Visions of Emancipation: The Italian Workers Movement Since 1945* and a member of the editorial board of *Dissent* magazine. She also writes fiction and verse and has authored over 120 books for young readers. She has a B.A. and M.A. in French literature.

Maia Cucchiara teaches in the Urban Education program at Temple University. She is author of *Marketing Schools, Marketing Cities: Who Wins and Who Loses When Schools Become Urban Amenities*.

Ansley T. Erickson teaches history and education at Teachers College, Columbia University. She is writing a history of metropolitan educational inequality.

Eugene E. Garcia is Professor of Education and Transborder Studies at Arizona State University. He has published extensively in bilingual development and English-language learner education.

Eva Gold is a Senior Research Fellow and founder of Research for Action (www.researchforaction.org) and Adjunct Professor of Education at the University of Pennsylvania. Her research focuses on family and community school dynamics; she has published widely in the area of civic and community engagement in school reform.

Jeffrey R. Henig is Chair of the Department of Education Policy and Social Analysis, Teachers College, Columbia University. His most recent books are *Between Public and Private: Politics, Governance, and the New Portfolio Models for School Reform* (co-edited with Katrina E. Bulkley and Henry M. Levin) and *Spin Cycle: How Research Is Used in Policy Debates: The Case of Charter Schools*.

Tyrone C. Howard teaches in the Division of Urban Schooling in the Graduate School of Education and Information Studies at UCLA. Best known for his scholarship on race, culture, and education, he is one of the most renowned scholars on educational equity, the African American educational experience, black males, and urban schools.

Richard D. Kahlenberg, a senior fellow at The Century Foundation, is author of several books, including *Tough Liberal: Albert Shanker and the Battles over Schools, Unions, Race and Democracy*, and *All Together Now: Creating Middle Class Schools Through Public School Choice*. His chapter draws from his previous articles in *New Republic, Slate, Washington Post, Education Next*, and *American Educator*.

Harvey Kantor is Chair of the Department of Education, Culture, and Society at the University of Utah. He is author of numerous publications on the politics of educational reform in the United States in the twentieth century.

Michael B. Katz is Walter H. Annenberg Professor of History at the University of Pennsylvania and Research Associate of the Population Studies Center. His books have focused on the history of public education, history of social structure and family organization, and history of poverty and welfare. In the last few years, his research has concentrated on immigration as well as on the welfare state. His most recent book is *Why Don't American Cities Burn?* (published by University of Pennsylvania Press).

David F. Labaree is Professor of Education at Stanford University. His latest book is *Someone Has to Fail: The Zero-Sum Game of Public Schooling*.

Julia C. Lamber is in the Maurer School of Law of Indiana University in Bloomington. A leading scholar in employment discrimination law, she previously served as Dean for Women's Affairs at Indiana University.

Robert Lowe is Professor of Education at Marquette University. He has published numerous articles on race, class, and school in historical perspective.

Deborah Meier has spent more than four decades in public education as a teacher, writer, and public advocate. She is currently at New York University's Steinhardt School of Education and a board member and Director of New Ventures at Mission Hill, director and advisor to Forum for Democracy and Education, and on the board of the Coalition of Essential Schools. She is on the editorial board of *Dissent*, *The Nation*, and *Harvard Education Letter*. Her most recent book, with Brenda S. Engel and Beth Taylor, is *Playing for Keeps: Life and Learning on a Public School Playground*.

Pedro Noguera is Peter L. Agnew Professor of Education at New York University. He is an urban sociologist whose scholarship and research focuses on the ways schools are influenced by social and economic conditions in the urban environment. His most recent book, with A. Wade Boykin, is *Creating the Opportunity to Learn*.

Rema Reynolds is a postdoctoral fellow at UCLA and teaches Education at Azusa Pacific University. A former teacher, counselor, and administrator, she currently organizes black parents for the improvement of student achievement in various schools. Her research interests center on equity and access for underrepresented students and families in American public schools.

Claire Robertson-Kraft is a doctoral student in education policy at the University of Pennsylvania. Her research focuses on the effects of new teacher evaluation, compensation, and support systems. She is co-editor of *A Grand Bargain for Education Reform: New Rewards and Supports for New Accountability*.

Jean C. Robinson is Executive Associate Dean of the College of Arts and Sciences and Professor in the Department of Political Science at Indiana University in Bloomington. Her most recent book, co-edited with Janet E. Johnson, is *Living Gender After Communism*.

Mike Rose teaches at the UCLA Graduate School of Education and Information Studies. He is author of *Lives on the Boundary: The Struggles and Achievements of America's Underprepared*; *The Mind at Work: Valuing the Intelligence of the American Worker*; *Possible Lives: The Promise of Public Education in*

America; Why School? Reclaiming Education for All of Us; and *Back to School: Why Everyone Deserves a Second Chance at Education.*

Janelle Scott teaches in the Graduate School of Education and African American Studies Department at the University of California at Berkeley. Her research on philanthropy and charter schools was supported by a National Academy of Education/Spencer Foundation Postdoctoral Fellowship. She is the editor of *School Choice and Diversity: What the Evidence Says.*

Elaine Simon is Co-Director of the Urban Studies Program and Adjunct Associate Professor of Education and of Anthropology at the University of Pennsylvania. Her research and publications focus on the intersection of communities and schools through the study of education policy and community organizing.

Paul Skilton-Sylvester is an independent educational consultant interested in curriculum development, new school initiatives, and school-level systemic change. Most recently he has been working in a community in Costa Rica with the staff of a rain forest preserve to design educational programs to combat poaching, logging, and trapping on its borders.

Joi A. Spencer is Associate Professor of Mathematics Education at the University of San Diego. She is the founder of King's Academies: Schools for Non-Violence and Social Justice.

Heather Ann Thompson is Associate Professor of History in the Department of African American Studies and the Department of History at Temple University. She is completing a major history of the Attica Prison uprising of 1971.

Tina Trujillo teaches in the Graduate School of Education at the University of California at Berkeley. She uses mixed methods to study trends in educational leadership, the unintended consequences of policies and reforms for students of color and English learners, and the political dynamics of urban district reform.

Pamela Barnhouse Walters is James H. Rudy Professor of Sociology at Indiana University-Bloomington. Her recent research, supported with fellowships from the Guggenheim Foundation, Spencer Foundation, and Center for Advanced Study in the Behavioral Sciences, examines the politics of unequal educational opportunity in the United States. She is editor (with Annette Lareau and Sheri H. Ranis) of *Education Research on Trial: Policy Reform and the Call for Scientific Rigor.*

Kevin G. Welner is Professor of Education and Director of the National Education Policy Center (NEPC) at the School of Education of the University of Colorado Boulder. His research examines the use of research in policy-making, the intersection between education rights litigation and educational opportunity scholarship, and the school change process associated with equity-focused reform efforts. He is co-editor of *Exploring the School Choice Universe: Evidence and Recommendations.*

Sarah Woulfin teaches in the Neag School of Education at the University of Connecticut. She uses organizational sociology and qualitative methods to study the relationship between education policy, leadership activities, and classroom practice. Her commitment to raising the quality of instruction motivates her research on how policy influences—and is influenced by—administrators and teachers.

ACKNOWLEDGMENTS

This book originated in an invitation by *Dissent* magazine to edit a series of articles on education reform. The majority of the articles in the book first appeared in the magazine. We want to thank the editors for the invitation and especially to acknowledge the support and editorial assistance as well as sustaining enthusiasm for the project of the magazine's remarkable executive editor, Maxine Phillips. A grant from the Spencer Foundation supported the series. We also want to thank Peter Agree of the University of Pennsylvania Press for his faith in this project and his skill in arranging for its publication by the Press. The comments of the anonymous outside reviewer provided a brilliant set of suggests for the necessary reorganization of the book's structure. We are grateful beyond words to Audra Wolfe of The Outside Reader who served as project editor, first preparing the manuscript for external review and, with the help of her colleague Adi Hovav, dealing with the final editing of the manuscript and all the details necessary for its submission to the Press—all with amazing skill and efficiency. Finally, our deep thanks to, and admiration for, the contributors to this volume who bore with the project over a long period of time.

Mike Rose would like to thank the following people for their help with "The Mismeasure of Teaching and Learning": Megan Franke, Judy Johnson, Felipe Martinez, John Rogers, Shirin Vossoughi, Noreen Webb, and Kyo Yamashiro. A section of the Conclusion is adopted from his article "Reform: To What End?" in the April 2010 issue of *Educational Leadership*, and the vignette about Stephanie Terry's classroom is drawn from his *Possible Lives: The Promise of Public Education in America*. "A Letter to New Teachers" first appeared in the *Los Angeles Times*, June 4, 2010.

Michael Katz would like to thank Daniel Amsterdam and Viviana Zelizer for helpful comments on "Public Education as Welfare."